Multimedia
and Virtual Reality

Designing Multisensory
User Interfaces

Multimedia
and Virtual Reality

Designing Multisensory
User Interfaces

Alistair Sutcliffe

University of Manchester Institute of Science and Technology

Routledge
Taylor & Francis Group

NEW YORK AND LONDON

First published by Lawrence Erlbaum Associates, Inc., Publishers
10 Industrial Avenue
Mahwah, NJ 07430

This edition published 2012 by Routledge
711 Third Avenue, New York, NY 10017
2 Park Square, Milton Park, Abingdon, Oxfordshire OX14 4RN

Routledge is an imprint of the Taylor & Francis Group, an informa business

First issued in paperback 2012

Cover design by Kathryn Houghtaling Lacey

Library of Congress Cataloging-in-Publication Data

Sutcliffe, Alistair, 1951–
Multimedia and virtual reality : designing multisensory user inter-
    faces / by Alistair Sutcliffe.
        p.   cm.
        Includes bibliographical references and index.
    ISBN 0-8058-3950-X (hc : alk. paper)
    1. Interactive multimedia.   2. Virtual reality.   3. User interfaces
        (Computer systems)   I. Title.

QA76.76.I59 S88   2002
006.7 —dc21   2002069623
                                                        CIP

ISBN 978-0-415-65031-1 (pbk)
10 9 8 7 6 5 4 3 2 1

Contents

Preface

The title of this book owes more than it should to marketing. Multimedia and virtual reality (VR) are media-friendly terms that may have caught your eye, so if you are browsing the preface before deciding whether to buy this book, here is my explanation of its motivation and contents. It is primarily a summary of the research I have done over 10 years in multimedia and VR, which fits within my wider interest of exploiting psychological theory to improve the process of designing interactive systems. I have tried to make the text accessible to designers, students, and researchers, with as few assumptions about prerequisite knowledge as possible; however, in curriculum terms, student readers would benefit from an introductory course in human–computer interaction (HCI) before progressing on to this book.

The subject matter lies firmly within the field of HCI, with some cross-referencing to software engineering (SE) because I believe that HCI and SE should be integrated components in the development process. Indeed, the terms *user interface* and *human–computer interface* are probably responsible for this false separation; I prefer *designing interactive systems*, which does not differentiate the user interface as a special entity. Although I am taking a system-wide view, there is only minimal treatment of the technology, system architecture, or history of either multimedia or VR in the following chapters. History can be finessed for interactive technology, which, apart from Ivan Sutherland's pioneering work (Sutherland, 1963), is less than 10 years old. Sutherland invented many of the elements of what we now call virtual reality, including 3D immersive graphics projected from head-mounted displays. There are plenty of books that cover these topics, and I do not intend to duplicate their coverage. Furthermore, the pace of technical change is accelerating so I don't think there is much point in describing the merits of devices that may have become obsolete by the time you read this book.

Multimedia and VR pose considerable challenges to HCI. VR has been driven by technology and very little usability research has been undertaken, although the work of Debbie Hix (Hix et al., 1999) stands out as an exception. Multimedia, in contrast, has been driven by forces of technology and more recently by artistic design, so HCI finds itself as a potential arbiter between the technologists who are concerned with bandwidth, graphics, compression algorithms, and so forth, and creative designers who want software tools to empower their abilities to create new forms of digital media. I do not address the design of tools for designers' issues in this book; instead, I hope to explain how usability should be reflected in design with technology and how artistic design can be employed to make interfaces more attractive and usable.

The book's subtitle indicates my agenda a little more clearly. Design of human–computer interfaces was covered in my earlier book (Sutcliffe, 1995a), so the current work extends my views on the design process to more complex interfaces that have evolved in recent years. However, multimedia and VR are to an extent just technology. The fundamentals of good design for people haven't changed, and that forms my main purpose: to explain a process for usability engineering, or design of usable and useful interactive systems. In doing so I hope to illuminate one of the debates that has been ongoing in HCI for at least 15 years: how to transfer the insights from psychology into sound design. After all, human–computer interaction is about design for people, so one would assume that the sciences of people, that is, psychology and sociology, should have a direct bearing on design. This quest has proven illusive. Although the design of human–computer interfaces has improved, there are still too many examples of poor design. Two of the products I have used in writing this book are cases in point. Many illustrations were created in Microsoft PowerPoint and transferred into Microsoft Word. The unpredictable effects of the Paste Special command leave me annoyed and dumbfounded that such bad software still exists. For those who haven't suffered from Microsoft Word's Paste Special, the command enables you to insert graphics and other objects into a text document. Unfortunately, it has a myriad of unpredictable effects instead of doing what you really want it to do: insert a diagram while moving the text up to create the necessary space. Moreover, there is the question why I should even have to bother about a Paste Special command. A well-designed system would shield me from the complexities of embedded objects, which should know their own provenance and act accordingly.

Returning to the theme of bringing psychology into the design process, there has been a long history of trying to bridge this gap, most notably in the AMODEUS research project (Barnard, 1991) that tried to integrate cognitive models from psychology with modeling languages familiar to computer scientists, such as modal action logic. Closely coupled integration didn't work, leading to a fallback position of synthesizing the contributions that cognitive science and computer science models make within an informal framework of design rationale (Bellotti, 1993). However, the quest for more powerful coupling is still ongoing. One of the prime movers in this search, Phil Barnard, has proposed that a framework of theories may be necessary to deal with different aspects of the design problem (Barnard & May, 1999). I will use Barnard's cognitive model (Interacting Cognitive Subsystems; Teasdale & Barnard, 1993) to motivate design principles and guidance in this book.

Interactive system design is not short of cognitive models from which to draw inspiration and advice. The most elaborate model is the ACT–R family (Anderson & Lebiere, 1998); EPIC (Kieras & Meyer, 1997) and LICAI (Kitajima & Polson, 1997) also provide theory-based accounts of human cognition. The problem with all of these models is that they can only account for a small fragment of interaction, such as menu selection. When faced with the complexities of multimedia and VR, the modeling effort becomes daunting and has yet to be addressed. Cognitive models give detailed accounts of human information processing but at a price of painstaking modeling to predict a small segment of interaction. At the other end of the modeling spectrum lies Norman's (1988) simpler model of action, which has been widely adopted in HCI. Its merit lies in providing a general framework for human action that can be readily applied to designing interactive systems, although the downside of Norman's model is that it provides little psychological content for informing design. In my research I have been interested in using Norman's model as a means of bridging between the design process and detailed models of psychology. This interest started in Mark Springett's doctoral dissertation (Springett, 1995) that extended Norman's model to cover GUIs and more cognitive phenomena (Sutcliffe & Springett, 1992), and developed further in Kulwinder Kaur's dissertation (Kaur, 1998) on VR modeling. Developments of this work appear in chapter 3. For more detail on the cognitive modeling and design debate, see articles in the special 2000 issue of ACM *Transactions on CHI: HCI in the new millennium* (Barnard, May, Duke, & Duce, 2000; Sutcliffe, 2000; and Vicente, 2000). To summarize, the subtext in my agenda is to propose a method via Norman's inspired bridging models by which knowledge from cognitive psychology can be transferred into the design process.

To give you a reading guide to the chapters which follow, some items are tutorial in nature, some provide background survey knowledge, and all relate to the design process. In spite of my attempts in chapter 1 to convince you that multimedia and VR are a continuous design problem separated only by convention and technology, I have bowed to that convention and created separate chapters for multimedia and VR design, although both aspects of multisensory user interfaces do appear in a common chapter on evaluation. I toyed with the idea of merging the material but eventually decided on separation on the grounds that my users (yourself) will probably come from either a multimedia or a VR design background; to integrate would only confuse. The other reason is historical. The multimedia research was mainly conducted in collaboration with one of my graduate students, Peter Faraday (Faraday, 1998), who is now battling to improve the usability of Microsoft PowerPoint. This work led to a series of publications in CHI conferences (Faraday & Sutcliffe, 1996, 1997a, 1998b, 1999) and produced a design method that was tested with Philips Research (Sutcliffe, 1999b) and subsequently incorporated in the International Standards Organization (ISO) 14915 standard for multimedia user interface design, part 3: "Media combination and integration" (ISO, 2000). The ISO guidelines for media selection and combination are listed in Appendix A. Other contributions to the multimedia research were made in the EU-funded Multimedia Broker project (Sutcliffe, Ryan, Doubleday, & Springett, 2000), and Sandra Caincross' dissertation on educational multimedia (Cairncross, 2001). Kulwinder Kaur's thesis (1998) produced the VR models and design guidance that was tested with designers from Intelligent Systems Solutions and revised since in the EPSRC ISRE (Immersive Scenario-Based Requirements Engineering) project.

Chapter 1 introduces the background to multisensory user interfaces, and surveys the design issues and previous HCI research in these areas. Chapter 2 is tutorial in nature and explains the basic psychology for design of multisensory user interfaces, including the Interacting Cognitive Subsystems (ICS) cognitive model. A set of design principles summarizes the psychological knowledge that can be applied to design. Chapter 3 is a theory chapter that describes elaborations of Norman's models of action for multimedia and VR, relates these models to the ICS cognitive model and explains how the models can be applied to predict the design features necessary for successful interaction. These features, called Generalized Design Properties (GDPs), are listed in Appendix B, together with the rules that specify when each GDP should be applied.

Chapter 4 is a self-contained design method for multimedia, and VR is treated in a similar manner in chapter 5. Multimedia design focuses on design issues of media selection and design for attention, so the user can follow a theme within an integrated presentation. VR covers design of interactive agents and presentation of the user's presence, as well as 3D virtual worlds. Both chapters provide a design process from requirements, user, and domain analysis to design of representation in media or virtual worlds and facilities for user interaction therein. I had expected that writing the two chapters as design processes would result in considerable redundancy, but surprisingly, there is not a great deal of overlap in content. The design process in both chapters starts with requirements and task analysis and progresses to detailed design and guidelines.

Chapter 6 covers usability evaluation for multisensory interfaces by extending existing well-known HCI approaches of heuristic evaluation and observational usability testing. *Inter alia*, this chapter reports work on another of my concerns, improving the diagnostic guidance for evaluation methods, so there are more general lessons on bridging the gap between observing a user's problem and prescribing a design fix. This chapter also deals with evaluating web-based multimedia, including issues of attractiveness and aesthetic design, not normally covered in usability evaluation methods. The interaction models reappear in this chapter as a walkthrough method for evaluation. Chapter 7 is, I admit, something of a ragbag. It covers two special application areas for multisensory interfaces: educational applications and virtual prototyping for design refinement. It concludes with a brief review of ubiquitous interfaces as another facet of multisensory UIs. So in conclusion, the book is methodological and tutorial in nature, but summarizes a research story that was evolved over a number of years, and will continue to change as I and others continue with the quest for sound theories of interaction and design processes built thereon.

Many people have contributed to developing this research over a number of years, some in active collaboration and others in conferences and workshops. The theses of Peter Faraday and Kulwinder Kaur provided the foundation for this research. Development took place in several research projects. In particular Ashok Gupta and Dave Bell of Philips Research played an important role in critiquing and improving the multimedia design method reported in chapter 4; Leo Poll, also of Philips Research, contributed to this work and introduced me to the tension of the creative design versus software engineering approaches to multimedia. Colleagues in the ISO standardization community, working group 5 in SC4/TC159, helped me refine several ideas during the process of editing ISO 14915 part 3, "Media Selection and Integration"; in particular, Juergen Zielger, Richard Hodgkinson, Jim Williams, and Scott Isensee, along with comments from national committees, helped to shape part 3. The work of Debbie Hix in VR has had an important influence of the VR GDPs in chapter 3, whereas Rex Hartson's work on evaluation methods and his debate on affordances have influenced the methods in chapters 5 and 6. The CHI '99 workshop on Multimedia Usability Engineering contributed many ideas, especially from Mary Hegarty, Rick Meyer, and Hari Narayanan. On the Esprit projects INTUITIVE and Multimedia Broker, where many of the multimedia design ideas were developed and deployed, the help of Michelle Ryan, Mark Ennis, Mat Hare, and Jacqui Griffiths was vital, whereas conversations with Peter Rosengren and Neil Sandford gave many insights into commercial applications. In my VR work, Bob Stone provided the applications and validation for work with Kulwinder Kaur; David Corrall and John Martin of BAE systems have refined ideas on virtual prototyping in chapter 7. Also, many thanks to Andy Dearden and Anthony Hornof who commented on draft chapters in detail, and to colleagues Leon Watts and Sri Kurniwan who made other helpful suggestions. Finally, I owe a considerable debt to Gillian Martin without whose patient preparation and checking this book could not have been completed.

—Alistair Sutcliffe
UMIST, July 2002

1

Background
and Usability Concepts

This chapter introduces usability problems in multimedia and virtual reality (VR), motivates the need for Human–Computer Interface design advice, and then introduces some knowledge of psychology that will be used in the design process. Multimedia and VR are treated as separate topics, but this is a false distinction. They are really technologies that extend the earlier generation of graphical user interfaces with a richer set of media, 3D graphics to portray interactive worlds, and more complex interactive devices that advance interaction beyond the limitations of keyboards and the mouse. A better description is to refer to these technologies as multisensory user interfaces, that is, advanced user interfaces that enable us to communicate with computers with all of our senses. One of the first multisensory interfaces was an interactive room for information management created in the "put that there project" in MIT. A 3D graphical world was projected in a room similar to a CAVE-like (Collaborative Automated Virtual Environment) environment. The user sat in a chair and could interact by voice, pointing by hand gesture and eye gaze. Eye gaze was the least effective mode of interaction, partly because of the poor reliability of tracking technology (which has since improved), but also because gaze is inherently difficult to control. Gazing at an object can be casual scanning or an act of selection. To signal the difference between the two, a button control had to be used.

Design of VR and multimedia interfaces currently leaves a lot to be desired. As with many emerging technologies, it is the fascination with new devices, functions, and forms of interaction that has motivated design rather than ease of use, or even utility of practical applications. Poor usability limits the effectiveness of multimedia products which might look good but do not deliver effective education (Scaife, Rogers, Aldrich, & Davies, 1997; Parlangeli, Marchigiani, & Bognara, 1999); and VR products have a catalogue of usability problems ranging from motion sickness to difficult navigation (Wann & Mon-Williams, 1996). Both multimedia and VR applications are currently designed with little, if any, notice of usability (Dimitrova & Sutcliffe, 1999; Kaur, Sutcliffe, & Maiden, 1998). However, usability is a vital component of product quality and it becomes increasingly important once the initial excitement of a new technology dies down and customers look for effective use rather than technological novelty (Norman, 1999). Better quality products have a substantial competitive advantage in any market, and usability becomes a key factor as markets mature. The multimedia and VR market has progressed beyond the initial hype and customers are looking for well-designed, effective, and mature products.

The International Organization for Standardization standard definitions for usability (ISO, 1997, Part 11), encompass operational usability and utility, that is, the value of a product for a customer in helping him or her achieve their goal, be that work or pleasure. However, usability only contributes part of the overall picture. For multisensory UIs, quality and effectiveness have five viewpoints:

- *Operational usability*—How easy is a product to operate? This is the conventional sense of usability and can be assessed by standard evaluation methods such as cooperative evaluation (Monk & Wright, 1993). Operational usability concerns design of graphical user interface features such as menus, icons, metaphors, movement in virtual worlds, and navigation in hypermedia.
- *Information delivery*—How well does the product deliver the message to the user? This is a prime concern for multimedia Web sites or any information-intensive application. Getting the message, or content, across is the *raison d'être* of multimedia. This concerns integration of multimedia and design for attention.
- *Learning*—How well does someone learn the content delivered by the product? Training and education are both important markets for VR and multimedia and hence are key quality attributes. However, design of educational technology is a complex subject in its own right, and multimedia and VR are only one part of the design problem.
- *Utility*—This is value of the application perceived by the user. In some applications this will be the functionality that supports the user's task; in others, information delivery and learning will represent the value perceived by the user.
- *Aesthetic appeal*—With the advent of more complex means of presenting information and interaction, the design space of UIs has ex-

panded. The appeal of a UI is now a key factor, especially for Web sites. Multisensory interfaces have to attract users and stimulate them, as well as being easy to use and learn.

Usability of current multimedia and VR products is awful. Most are never tested thoroughly, if at all. Those that have been are ineffective in information delivery and promoting learning (Rogers & Scaife, 1998). There are three approaches for improving design. First, psychological models of the user can be employed, so that designers can reason more effectively about how people might perceive and comprehend complex media. Secondly, design methods and guidelines that build on the basic psychology can provide an agenda of design issues and more targeted design advice, that is, design guidelines. Design for utility is a key aspect of the design process. This involves sound requirements and task analysis (Sutcliffe, 2002c), followed by design to support the user's application task, issues that are addressed in general HCI design methods (Sutcliffe, 1995a). The third approach is to embed soundly-based usability advice in methods supported by design advisor tools; however, development of multimedia and VR design support tools is still in its infancy, although some promising prototypes have been created (Faraday & Sutcliffe, 1998b; Kaur, Sutcliffe, & Maiden, 1999).

DESIGN PROBLEMS

Multisensory user interfaces open up new possibilities in designing more exciting and usable interfaces, but they also make the design space more complex. The potential for bad design is increased. Poorly designed multimedia can bombard users with excessive stimuli to cause headaches and stress, and bad VR can literally make you sick. Multimedia provides designers with the potential to deliver large quantities of information in a more attractive manner. Although this offers many interesting possibilities in design, it does come with some penalties. Poorly designed multimedia can, at best, fail to satisfy the user's requirements, and at worst may be annoying, unpleasant, and unusable. Evidence for the effectiveness of multimedia tutorial products is not plentiful; however, some studies have demonstrated that whereas children may like multimedia applications, they do not actually learn much (Rogers & Scaife, 1998). VR expands the visual aspect of multimedia to develop 3D worlds, which we should experience with all our senses, but in reality design of virtual systems is more limited. Evaluations of VR have pointed to many usability problems ranging from motion sickness to spatial disorientation and inability to operate controls (Darken & Sibert, 1996; Hix et al., 1999; Kaur, Sutcliffe et al., 1999). Multisensory interfaces may be more exciting than the familiar graphical UI, but as with many innovative technologies, functionality comes first and effective use takes a back seat.

Multisensory UIs imply three design issues:

- Enhancing interaction by different techniques for presenting stimuli and communicating our intentions. The media provide a "virtual world" or metaphor through which we interact via a variety of devices.
- Building interfaces which converge with our perception of the real world, so that our experience with computer technology is richer.
- Delivering information and experiences in novel ways, and empowering new areas of human–computer communication, from games to computer-mediated virtual worlds.

Human–computer communication is a two-way process. From computer to human, information is presented by rendering devices that turn digital signals into analogue stimuli, which match our senses. These "output" devices have been dominated by vision and the VDU, but audio has now become a common feature of PCs; devices for other senses (smell, taste, touch) may become part of the technology furniture in the near future. From human to computer the design space is more varied: joysticks, graphics tablets, data gloves, and whole body immersion suits just give a sample of the range. The diversity and sophistication of communication devices, together with the importance of speech and natural language interaction, will increase in the future. However, the concept of input and output itself becomes blurred with multisensory interfaces. In language, the notion of turn-taking in conversation preserves the idea of separate (machine–human) phases in interaction, but when we act with the world, many actions are continuous (e.g., driving a vehicle) and we do not naturally consider interacting in terms of turn-taking. As we become immersed in our technology, or the technology merges into a ubiquitous environment, interacting itself should become just part of our everyday experience.

To realize the promise of multisensory interaction, design will have to support psychological properties of human information processing:

- *Effective perception*—This is making sure that information can be seen and heard, and the environment has been perceived as naturally as possible with the appropriate range of senses.
- *Appropriate comprehension*—This is making sure that the interactive environment and information is displayed in a manner appropriate to the task, so the user can predict how to interact with the system. This also involves making sure users pick out important parts of the message and follow the "story" thread across multiple media streams.
- *Integration*—Information received on different senses from separate media or parts of the virtual world should make sense when synthesized.

- *Effective action*—Action should be intuitive and predictable. The system should "afford" interaction by suggesting how it should be used and by fitting in with our intentions in a cognitive and physical sense.

Understanding these issues requires knowledge of the psychology of perception and cognition, which will be dealt with in more depth in chapter 2. Knowledge of user psychology can help to address design problems, some of which are present in traditional GUIs; others are raised by the possibilities of multisensory interaction, such as the following:

- Helping users to navigate and orient themselves in complex interactive worlds.
- Making interfaces that appeal to users, and engage them in pleasurable interaction.
- Suggesting how to design natural virtual worlds and intuitive interaction within the demands of complex tasks and diverse abilities in user populations.
- Demonstrating how to deliver appropriate information so that users are not overloaded with too much data at any one time.
- Suggesting how to help the user to extract the important facts from different media and virtual worlds.

An important design problem is to make the interface predictable so that users can guess what to do next. A useful metaphor that has been used for thinking about interaction with traditional UIs is Norman's (1986) two gulfs model:

- The *gulf of execution* from human to computer: predictability and user guidance are the major design concerns.
- The *gulf of evaluation* from computer to human: understanding the output and feedback are the main design concerns.

In multisensory UIs, the gulf of execution involves the communication devices, for example, speech understanding, gesture devices, and the predictability of action in virtual worlds, as well as standard input using menus, message boxes, windows, and so forth. In VR, affordances are a key means of bridging the gulf of execution by providing intuitive cues in the appearance of tools and objects that allow users to guess how to act. Designers have a choice of communication modalities (audio, visual or haptic), and the particular hardware or software device for realizing the modality, for example, pen and graphics tablet for gesture, keyboard for alphanumeric text, speech for language, mouse for pointing, and so forth. For the gulf of evaluation, that is, computer to user communication, the designer also has a choice of modality, device, and representation. Choosing communication devices is becoming more complex as interaction becomes less standardized. As we move away from the VDU, keyboard, and WIMP (Windows, Icons, Mice, Pointers) technology to natural language interaction and complex visual worlds, haptic (pressure, texture, touch sensations), olfactory (smell), and even gustatory (taste) interaction may become common features. However, devices are only part of the problem. Usability will be even more critical in the design of dialogues. In multisensory environments, we will interact with multiple agents, and have computer-mediated communication between the virtual presences of real people and realistic presences of virtual agents. Dialogues will be multiparty and interleaved, converging with our experience in the real world. Furthermore, we will operate complex representations of machinery as virtual tools, control virtual machines, as well as operating real machines in virtual environments (telepresence and telerobotics). Dialogue is going to be much more complex than picking options from a menu.

ARCHITECTURES AND DEVICES

The design space of multisensory interfaces consists of several interactive devices; furthermore, interfaces are often distributed on networks. Although the software and hardware architecture is not the direct responsibility of the user interface designers, system architectures do have user interface implications. The more obvious of these are network delays for high bandwidth media such as video. In many cases the user interface designers will also be responsible for software development of the whole system, so a brief review of architectural issues is included here.

Multimedia Architectures

The basic configuration for multimedia variants of multisensory systems is depicted in Fig. 1.1. A set of media-rendering devices produces output in visual and audio modalities. Moving image, text, and graphics are displayed on high resolution VDUs; speakers produce speech, sound, and music output. Underlying the hardware rendering devices are software drivers. These depend on the storage format of the media as well as the device, so print drivers in Microsoft Word are specific to the type of printer, for example, laser, inkjet, and so forth. For VDU output, graphics and text are embedded in the application package or programming environment being used; so for Microsoft, video output drivers display .avi files, whereas for Macintosh, video output is in QuickTime format.

On the input side, devices capture media from the external world, in either analogue or digital form. Analogue media encode images and sound as continuous patterns that closely follow the physical quality of image or sound; for instance, film captures images by a photochemical process. Ana-

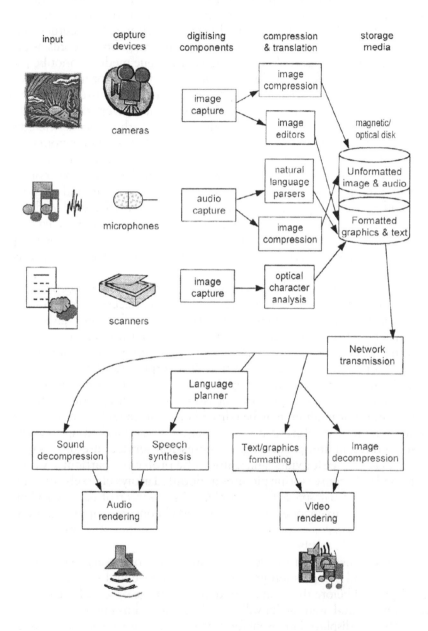

FIG. 1.1 Software architecture for handling multiple media.

logue devices such as video recorders may be electronic but not digital, be-cause they store the images as patterns etched onto magnetized tape; similarly, microphones capture sound waves which may be recorded onto magnetic audio tape or cut into the rapidly vanishing vinyl records as pat-terns of grooves corresponding to sounds. Analogue media cannot be pro-cessed directly by software technology; however, digital capture and storage devices are rapidly replacing them. Digital cameras capture images by a fine-grained matrix of light sensitive sensors that convert the image into thousands to millions of microscopic dots or pixels that encode the color and light intensity. Using 24 bits (24 zeros or ones) of computer storage per pixel enables a wide range of 256 color shades to be encoded. Pictures are composed of a mosaic of pixels to make shapes, shades, and image compo-nents. Sound is captured digitally by sampling sound waves and encoding the frequency and amplitude components. Once captured, digital media are amenable to the software processing that has empowered multimedia tech-nology. Although analogue media can be displayed by computers with ap-propriate rendering devices, increasingly, most media will be captured, stored, and rendered in a digital form.

Compression and translation components form a layer between capture devices and storage media. Translation devices are necessary to extract in-formation from input in linguistic media. For speech, these devices are recognizers, parsers, and semantic analyzers of natural language under-standing systems; however, text may also be captured from printed media by OCR (optical character recognition or interpretation) software, or by handwriting recognition from graphics tablet or stylus input as used on Palm Pilot™. Translation is not necessary for nonlinguistic media, al-though an input medium may be edited before storage; for instance, seg-ments of a video or objects in a still image may be marked up to enable subsequent computer processing. Compression services are necessary to reduce disk storage for video and sound. The problem is particularly press-ing for video because storing pictures as detailed arrays of pixels consumes vast amounts of disk space; for example, a single screen of 1096 × 784 pix-els using 24 bits to encode color for each pixel consumes approximately 1 megabyte of storage. As normal speed video consumes 30 frames per sec, storage demands can be astronomic.

When the media are retrieved, components are necessary to reverse the translation and compression process. Moving image and sound media are decompressed before they can be rendered by image or sound-creating de-vices. Linguistic-based media will have been stored as encoded text. Text may either be displayed in visual form by word processor software or docu-ment processors (e.g., Acrobat and PDF files), but to create speech, addi-tional architectural components are needed. Speech synthesis requires a planner to compose utterances and sentences and then a speech synthesizer to generate the spoken voice. The last step is complex, as subtle properties of the human voice have to be created to drive the rendering device (a loud-speaker). As current speech synthesis software cannot match the complex tones of human voice, artificial speech still sounds mechanical.

As well as the architectural components for capturing, storing, and rendering multimedia, there are services for network transport and synchronization between media streams. Network transport services are a complex area in their own right; see Crowcroft (1997) for an overview. The UI requirements are to deliver a continuous stream of media to a network client so that presentation is coherent. This need is critical for streamed multimedia (video and sound). If the network services cannot deliver video or sound at the constant required rate, then the presentation will either have to be disrupted or the presentation quality degraded (Watson & Sasse, 1998). Managing bandwidth and transmission quality is the responsibility of network services. Bandwidth is the quantity of data that can be transmitted through a communication channel. This is ultimately limited by the physical capacity of the transport channel (e.g., fiber optical cable or radio band allocated); in reality, it is also an economic trade-off concerning how much bandwidth a service can buy or grab on a channel in competition with other users. The consequence is that there is a limit to the quantity of information that can be transmitted across a network connection; furthermore, this limit might vary over time. The Internet tries to be democratic in allocating bandwidth on demand and sharing the available resources fairly. As a result, when traffic becomes heavy the network becomes congested and heavy users of bandwidth, such as video conferencing, suffer.

Virtual Reality Architectures

The first virtual reality system was created by Sutherland (1963); however, it was not described as such, although it did contain the basic idea of an immersive head-mounted display to surround the user in a virtual 3D world. VR uses the same architectural components as multimedia but it adds components to handle more complex interaction. VR comes in two principal variants:

- *Desktop* VR, in which the 3D graphical virtual world is displayed on a standard VDU. Desktop VR is similar to multimedia apart from adding a more complex control device such as a space (3D) mouse or data glove.
- *Immersive* VR, in which the user wears head-mounted binocular displays and has the sense of being immersed or surrounded by the 3D virtual world. Immersive VR may also be achieved by placing the user in CAVEs. These are rooms that display the virtual environ-

ment on all walls to surround the user or on wide-angle IMAX screens that also give the impression of immersion (i.e., being there in the virtual world).

An overview of a generic VR architecture is given in Fig. 1.2.

Immersive VR rendering devices are either head-mounted mini-VDUs, one for each eye, with images that are created from slightly different viewpoints to preserve stereopsis or the sensation of visual depth. CAVEs or wide angle screens provide the sense of depth by projecting alternate right and left eye images at a high frame rate while the user wears special shutter-filter or polarizing glasses that direct the appropriate images into right and left eyes. Audio output uses stereophonic and quadraphonic sound more extensively than in multimedia to provide the sensation of being immersed in an audio as well as a visual virtual world. Other components may be present for kinesthetic and haptic (sense of touch) interaction. These devices are truly interactive because they combine force feedback with input from the user. Devices range from thimbles that provide proprioceptive feedback as pressure against which the user can push (e.g., Phantom™), to devices that fit

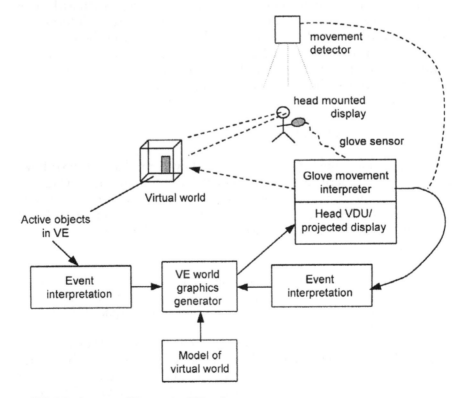

FIG. 1.2   Immersive VR generalized UI architecture.

the whole arm and detect or render force feedback in fingers, wrists, and arms by electrical, hydraulic, or pneumatic transducers. These devices are still at the prototype stage and are very intrusive to wear, but no doubt the technology will improve. Haptic feedback can also be delivered by pizo-electric transducers in gloves that vibrate to give an approximate sense of the roughness or smoothness of a surface. Olfactory feedback is synthesized by burners that evaporate or combust chemicals to generate an odor from a specification of its chemical composition. Such feedback is limited by the range of chemicals available and their volatility, but remarkably sophisticated odors can be generated. Taste feedback still presents a problem because the stimulus has to be delivered to the user's mouth, although the necessary technology will arise to satisfy a complete computer-generated sensory experience.

As well as providing multisensory feedback, VR systems have to track the user's body (or presence). The sophistication of architectural components for user-tracking depends on the degree with which the user is represented in the virtual world. There are two aspects that need to be detected.

- One aspect is the user's location and motion in the real world, subsequently translated into the virtual environment. This entails tracking user motion in the world and changes effected by movement.
- The other aspect is the position of the user's head and limbs, from hand and finger positions in gloves to posture in whole body immersion.

Tracking devices have to interpret user commands for movement that may be communicated via simple joystick or space mouse devices that allow six degrees of freedom for movement (lateral, forward and back, up and down, and rotations on these axes), or gestures for controlling motion. Gestures interpreted from a dataglove allow the user to fly through the virtual world by shifting the hand forward to initiate motion and changing the position of the palm for turns, climbing, or descent. Controlling the pace of motion is a problem for gesture interpretation, which some systems solve by relative speed of displacement of the hand. In immersive VR, users can really move around and this movement has to be reflected in change in the virtual world, so monitoring the user's absolute position is necessary. This is handled by sensors for tracking the user's head position. Trackers can be implemented by a variety of technologies, such as infrared beams, ultrasonics, or wireless transmission of movements. If motion in VR does not match the perceived change in the virtual world very accurately, it can lead to some users experiencing motion sickness. One attempt to alleviate this is by providing a treadmill to detect motion (Barfield, Zeltzer, Sheridan, & Slater, 1995). Besides interactive devices for communicating via gesture and action, VR applications may also employ standard UI components such as pop-up menus and dialogue boxes. Finally, VR, as with multimedia, can be networked in collaborative applications to multiple user presences. This and the complexity of rendering 3D graphical worlds make heavy demands on network bandwidth, so for effective distributed VR interaction, dedicated communication channels are necessary.

Augmented Reality

As the name suggests, augmented reality is a halfway house between virtual and real reality. The concept is to simulate part of the world in a computer VR while preserving some aspects as tangible devices (Barfield & Caudell, 2001). Augmented reality has been present for many years in specialized applications such as games and flight simulators. The computer projects a graphical 3D world that the user interacts with via controls that are similar to their real-world counterparts. A familiar example is a flight simulator in which the controls and environment faithfully represent details of an aircraft cockpit, with computers providing the simulated virtual world viewed through the cockpit window. Computer games provide 3D worlds for flying jet fighters or spacecraft and zapping aliens. Augmented reality comes in several forms. In projected overlays, the computer simulation of the world is projected on top of a horizontal board that contains tangible objects (Fig. 1.3). The computer can detect movement of objects and interprets users' actions by updating the simulated world; for example, in a simulation of street layout for architectural planning (Fischer et al., 1995; Fjeld, Lauche, Dierssen, Nichel, & Rauterberg, 1998), the computer projects simulations of the world of urban planning which the user can interact with by moving houses, street lights, police cars, and so forth. Augmented reality adds sensors for detecting and interpreting users' actions on tangible objects.

Augmented reality was also motivated by providing information overlays on the real world. The user sees information on head-up displays or glasses that are placed by appropriate objects. Thus, in an aircraft maintenance application, the engineer can see the identity of an electrical component aligned with the real-world object while viewing fault-finding instructions.

Tangible User Interfaces

A further development of augmented reality is design of computerized artifacts where the real is more prominent than the virtual. Tangible User Interfaces (TUIs) have computer software on microprocessors embedded in real-world pick-up-and-use things. The main applications to date have been entertainment, education, and psychological therapy. A good example of the former is Musicbottles (Ishii, Mazalek, & Lee, 2001). This system consists of a set of colored bottles with a touch-sensitive surface. Taking

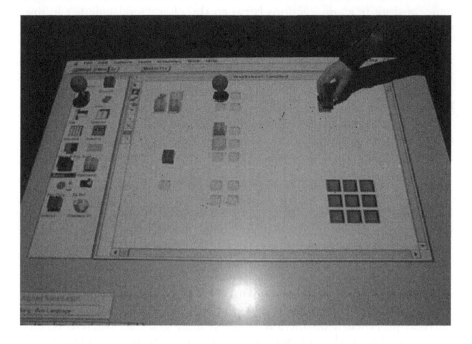

FIG. 1.3   This is an augmented reality system from the Collaboratory, Center for Life-Long Learning, University of Colorado. The system projects the display from above on to a touch-sensitive board. The user can build a model world with tangible model house, roads, trees, and so forth, then run simulations to study traffic flow. Reprinted with permission by Gerhard Fischer.

stoppers out of bottles causes music to play; moving the bottles results in changes in color. More general TUI architectures have a set of building blocks such as lenses, triangles, and blocks that can be positioned on a computationally sensitive table or white board. The chips on board the tangible building block can be programmed to respond in various ways. Placing an object in a specific location allows the agent within the tangible artifact to communicate with other agents (Ishii & Ullmer, 1997). To illustrate one application, triangular objects can be loaded with an information set that contributes to a story (Gobert, Orth, & Ishii, 1998). The triangles have picture cues on them that suggest ideas and topics in a story, for example, Cinderella. Children can play with the triangles to compose different sequences and structures, for instance juxtaposing characters in the story. Each triangle is equipped with magnetic sensors so contact between triangles and the electronically sensitive playing board can be detected, allowing the triangles to communicate. The information possessed by each triangle appears on a screen as each one is brought into contact with the others;

hence a story (e.g., interactions between the characters) emerges in line with the composition of the physical structure.

TUIs extend VR toward ubiquitous computing; rather than placing the user in a virtual world, the computer is placed into a variety of artifacts within the real world. By wiring the real world, users can interact with software-empowered artifacts to create applications for learning, group working, and entertainment. This theme is returned to in chapter 7.

Having reviewed architectures and design issues for multisensory UIs, the next step is to define exactly what multisensory user interfaces are and how they relate to multimedia, VR, and multimodal communication.

DEFINITIONS AND TERMINOLOGY

Multimedia and VR essentially extend the range of interaction beyond the GUI (Graphical User Interface) paradigm. Multimedia does so by providing a richer means of representing information for the user by use of video, sound, speech, and so forth; VR extends representation into a 3D world in which users can be immersed. However, exact definitions of multimedia and VR are not easy. Some views of what constitutes a taxonomy of multimedia can be found in Heller and Martin (1995) and Bernsen (1994). Bernsen proposed a distinction between analogue and discrete media, which he called modalities, as well as between visual, audio, and tactile dimensions. Heller and Martin took a more conventional view of image, text, video, and graphics for educational purposes. The following definitions broadly follow those in ISO Standard 14915 on Multimedia User Interface Design (ISO, 1998). The starting point is the difference between what is perceived by someone and what is stored on a machine.

Communication concepts in multimedia can be separated into the following:

- *Message*—The content of communication between a sender and receiver.
- *Medium* (plural *media*)—The means by which that content is delivered. Note that this is how the message is represented rather than the technology for storing or delivering a message. There is a distinction between perceived media and physical media such as DVD, CD-ROM, and hard disk.
- *Modality*—The sense by which a message is sent or received by people or machines. This refers to the senses used such as vision, hearing, touch, and, less commonly, smell and taste.

Hence, a message is conveyed by a medium and received through a modality. A modality is the sensory channel that we use to send and receive messages to and from the world, essentially our senses. Two principal modalities are used in human–computer communication:

- *Vision*—This is all information received through our eyes, including text and image-based media.
- *Hearing*—This is all information received through our ears, as sound, music, and speech.

In addition we use two other modalities:

- *Haptic*—This is information received via the sense of touch. This is closely related to motor-based action with computer devices, for example, keyboard, mouse, and joystick. A subdivision of haptics is the kinesthetic or proprioceptive sense, that is, our sense of body posture, position, and balance.
- *Gustatory–Olfactory*—This is received through chemical sensors; so far, the use of our sense of taste and smell has been of limited use with computers.

Modality characteristics are illustrated in Table 1.1.

Vision is a broadcast modality but is not directed unless a highlighting technique is used. We only see something if it is in our field of vision and our attention is attracted to it. Audio, however, is directed and we receive if we are in hearing range. Paying attention to audio also depends on salience effects, for example, loud noise. Olfaction is the third broadcast modality, but unlike vision and audio it is not instantaneous. Smells diffuse slowly. Gustation is narrowcast because it has to arrive on our tongue via a discrete carrier. Likewise, the haptic sense is located in a discrete area of our fingertips. Finally, proprioception is an internal sense that monitors body posture and position. Action or manipulation is not strictly a modality; however, this mode of interaction does integrate strongly with vision, proprioception, and haptic senses for effective motor control.

Outbound multimodality combines two channels with different media, for example, a voice explanation of a diagram. Inbound multimodality occurs when we communicate with a computer using two channels, such as speech and pointing. Outbound modality concerns multimedia presentation scripting, whereas inbound modality raises problems of dialogue design. Input multimodality also raises a timing problem; for example, should pointing come after, before, or during speech? Two forms of multimodality are possible:

- *Asynchronous*—This is when communication in one modality must be before or after the other. Inbound modalities are usually asynchronous, although some synchronous interaction, such as speaking while pointing, is possible.
- *Synchronous*—This is when input from both modalities may occur at the same time. This is common in outbound communication.

TABLE 1.1

Comparison of the Modality Characteristics

Modality	Transmission	Information Content	Integrates With
Vision	Broadcast. Users attend to the message if within field of view.	High and flexible image detail and text.	Audio. Tends to dominate other modalities
Audio	Broadcast, linear; user has to attend to it.	High, but less detail than complex images.	Vision.
Proprioception, kinesthetics	Internal to self; feedback by pressure or force transducer.	Limited to self-orientation and position.	Haptic. Vision for motion detection.
Haptic	Narrowcast. Feedback by vibrational deformation of a tangible surface.	Surface properties: roughness, viscosity, heat, pressure.	Proprioception for pressure. Vision.
Olfaction	Broadcast, but by slow diffusion. Feedback by evaporating and burning chemicals.	Limited number of chemicals discriminable.	Gustation.
Gustation	Narrowcast. Needs access to chemical solution.	Limited number of chemical combinations discriminable.	Olfaction.
Action, manipulation	Directed. Limited by limbs and body.	Robotic devices or force feedback.	Vision, haptic, proprioception.

Synchronous multimodality is more difficult to process in computer dialogues because the input messages have to be integrated, but it is natural in human terms.

Physical Media Formats and Storage

Unfortunately, defining a medium is not so simple, as what is conveyed depends on how it has been stored, how it was captured in the first place, and how it was designed. For example, a photograph can be taken on film, developed, and then scanned into a computer as a digitized image. The same image may have been captured directly by a digital camera and sent to a computer in an e-mail message. The way the image was captured may make no difference to the perceived medium, as the user just sees an image that looks real, but in some cases the physical medium may have an effect. The resolution of the scanner may have degraded the image quality such that a difference is noticeable.

At the physical level, media may be stored by different techniques. Indeed, a single medium is often represented in different ways. Text, for example, may be encoded as 7-bit ASCII or 8-bit EBCDIC. Images are stored either as pixel arrays or as vectors. Pixel storage represents images as a series of dots (or pixels, "picture cells") that have different qualities of grayness on a black and white scale. An image is composed of many pixels (1,024 × 1,024 for most high-resolution computer screens). For color, the red, green, and blue properties of each pixel are encoded. This becomes very expensive in storage, as 24 bits are necessary for high quality color. Compression may lead to perceptible loss in image quality because the constraints on disk storage or bandwidth in transmitted moving images over networks encourages designers to compress moving images into manageable file sizes. To reduce storage demands, various encoding algorithms have been invented which only code necessary information, such as differences within an image rather than areas that are the same. The JPEG and MPEG (Joint and Moving Pictures Expert Groups) algorithms are now widely adopted by most computer systems for compressing and decompressing images to economize on storage. Vectorized images are more economical to store as the whole image is not represented; instead, shapes which compose the image are encoded by the algorithms that drew them, for example, curved lines, polygons, cylinders, and so forth. Vector graphics are effective for drawings but less useful for realistic images where pixels are necessary for details of texture, shading, and color. Vector graphics are more common in VR, where requirements are designed as polygons that can be drawn to compose an image. Multimedia, in contrast, tends to use pixel formats in PICT, GIF, or JPEG files.

If storage is a problem for still images, then for moving image it becomes severe. Moving image on film or videotape, encoded in an analogue medium, is bulky to store as videotapes or film spools, and cannot be manipulated by computers except via an analogue playing device such as a projector or VCR. Computer-based moving image has to be digitized into pixel format, and this is when the storage demand becomes huge. A short clip of film will contain more than 30 separate images per second, so 10 sec worth would consume 200 to 300 megabytes of disk space uncompressed. This assumes 307,200 pixels per frame with 640 × 480 VGA resolution using 24 bits per pixel for good color coding gives 921,600 bytes per frame, so at 30 frames per sec (NTSC American video standard; 25 per sec for European PAL), this needs 23,040,000 bytes. Compression is essential, and algorithms adopted by the MPEG are now used by most systems. These algorithms work in a manner similar to still image compression by looking for the changes within an image and, over time, between two or more images. Algorithms may be either "lossy," so that when the movie is decompressed some of the detail is lost, or "lossless," if all the detail is preserved. Not surprisingly, lossless algorithms achieve lower compression on storage, about 10 times reduction, whereas lossy algorithms can achieve 20 to 30 times reduction. Even so, storing more than a few minutes of moving image consumes megabytes. The usability trade-off is between the size of the display footprint (i.e., window size), the resolution measured in dots per inch and the frame rate. The ideal might be full screen high resolution (600 dpi) at 30 frames per sec; however, with current technology, a 10 cm window at 300 dpi and 15 frames per sec is more realistic. Physical image media constraints become more important on networks, when bandwidth will limit the desired display quality. Sound, in comparison, is less of a problem. Storage demands depend on the fidelity required for replay. Full stereo with a complete range of harmonic frequencies only consumes 100 kilobytes for 5 min, so there are fewer technology constraints on delivery of high quality audio.

In view of the large storage demands made by multimedia, special devices are necessary. Most multimedia is stored on CD-ROM. These are optical disks that are written by lasers burning digital code into the disk, which is then read by another laser. Once written, the data cannot be changed. Some read–write optical disks do exist and will become more common in the future. Currently, CD-ROMs store around 550 megabytes per disk, but disks can be stacked in platters and multidisk reading devices called jukeboxes, raising the storage capacity to many gigabytes. More detail on the physical storage and systems architectures for multimedia can be found in Crowcroft (1997) and Morris (2000).

Logical Media Definitions

The following definitions focus on the logical level of how the message is presented to people, rather than the physical level of how the message is stored inside a computer. Perceptual media types are related to modalities. For example, image media are conveyed by the visual modality, although images can be presented on a variety of different physical media, for example, printed on paper, displayed on a VDU or a LCD screen. Speech and sound use the audio modality unless they are sent via the visual modality in which case the perceived medium is different: speech is printed as text; sound might be portrayed as a diagram of the frequency distribution or an image of a sonogram recording. The message in text and speech may be the same; however, it may be delivered either in a printed form by a visual modality or in a spoken form by audio modality. The main point to bear in mind is that the definitions are from the user's viewpoint, that is, how people perceive a medium. Media classifications have had many interpretations (Bernsen, 1994; Heller & Martin, 1995; Vetere, Howard, & Leung, 1997). This classification focuses on the psychological properties of the representations rather than the physical nature of the medium (e.g., digital or analogue encoding in video). Note that these definitions are combined, so speech is classified as an audio, linguistic medium, whereas a cartoon is classified as a nonrealistic (designed) moving image. Seven media categories can represent information, as detailed in Table 1.2.

The first distinction is between linguistic and nonlinguistic media. Linguistic media, text, and speech represent language-based concepts and facts. Nonnatural symbolic languages of mathematics, science, and engineering (e.g., circuit designs in electronic engineering) also belong to this category. Nonlinguistic media are everything else: images and sounds from the natural world. The second distinction is between media designed by people, for example, drawings, text, and those captured from the real world by microphones or cameras (e.g., natural sound, photographs). Diagrams pose an interesting boundary problem; in one sense they are symbolic languages, but informal sketches have few conventions and most people would say they are (semi) natural representations of the world. Speech is created by people and therefore falls within the designed category. The third distinction is between static and dynamic media. Static media persist over time; they are inspectable and viewable, for example, text, or still images. Dynamic media, in contrast, are played continuously and once finished are not inspectable without replay controls (e.g., moving image, sound, and speech). These distinctions are important because of two psychological properties. Dynamic media attract our attention and are difficult to ignore (try to avoid listening to the radio and concentrate on reading a newspaper instead). By virtue of their attention-grabbing powers, dynamic media engage our reasoning. The disadvantage is that dynamic media continually overwrite working memory. The reason why you can't remember more than 10% of a university lecture is that you have to make sense of one sentence, and store your understanding before the next sentence floods in. For the same reason, we only remember the gist (top-level story line) and a few vivid scenes in a film. So we need static media to act as an external memory during problem solving.

Text, numeric displays, and graphics are static media in the sense that they have no time dimension. Design constraints are a consequence of addressability of components that lead on to limitations for control and navigation. For text, individual characters are addressable, because the representation is stored in a processable format as ASCII code. As word processors become more complex, the encoding of text makes it less transferable between computers; for instance RTF (Rich Text Format) is the interchange

TABLE 1.2

Characteristics of Media Types

Media Type	Description	Example
Nonrealistic, designed	Content created by human action rather than being captured from the real world. Designed media vary in the formality of their semantics.	Diagrams, graphs, cartoons.
Realistic, natural	Content perceived by users to have been captured from the natural world rather than being explicitly designed.	Natural sounds, photographic images, film showing people and natural scenes.
Audio	Any medium received by the audio channel (hearing), sounds.	Dog barking, music, traffic noise, speech.
Linguistic	Language-based content; text, spoken language, and symbols interpreted in linguistic terms.	Alphanumeric text, hieroglyphics, symbols, and signs.
Moving image	Visual media delivered at a rate that is judged by the human viewer to be a continuous image.	Video, film, animated diagrams, and simulations.
Still image	Visual media that are not presented continuously (although frames may be shown in a sequence).	Photographs, drawings, graphs.
Interactive	Any medium that affords action and two-way conversation. Implies design of an agent or device that can be interacted with, using a variety of media types to communicate with the user.	Microworld simulation of an ecosystem, virtual environments. Avatar, conversational agent.

Note. More detailed definitions are given in chapter 4.

standard for text, but Microsoft Word files contain embedded format codes and macros that are lost in RTF. However, text might not be directly addressable at all if a page has been scanned and the physical medium is a PICT or PDF (Portable Document Format) file. Addressability in images also depends on physical medium for the representation. The ability to address and hence interact with part of an image depends on the ability of the computer's object management system to discern and interpret shapes. Thus, images stored as arrays of pixels such as PICT files can only be processed as a single unit. Individual objects (e.g., a nose in a face) cannot be active objects because the physical medium does not encode the topographic area that corresponds to the nose. In contrast, components in a drawing created by a graphics package in vector graphics (e.g., AutoCAD) format can be manipulated because the computer stored a representation of the object when it was created. Semantic encoding involves giving image subcomponents an identifier and descriptive attributes, so they can be treated as separate objects.

The ability to change a medium depends on the storage format and the capabilities of the presentation device. Text formats can usually be changed in a variety of ways such as size (point) and shape (font, bold) because the medium is encoded at the lexical (individual character) level. Drawings created by graphics packages also allow considerable scope for manipulation, such as resizing, changing, and inverting shapes. However, the ability to change images that are scanned in is restricted to actions on the whole image. Images can be scaled by zoom in and out and some semiselective editing can be carried out by changing contrast or color palette in a display. To edit subcomponents of the medium, they must be made addressable as areas that can be treated separately. In complex images with depth perspective, this becomes a complex task, that graphics packages solve by modeling the image in a series of "depth" layers. Even if the format does not support addressability, captions and images can be overlaid to give the designer more freedom in planning interactive effects between media and to show links between different messages.

Design may also be constrained by the compression encoding of media. In text this is rarely a problem, apart from the time consumed in decompressing zip files. With images, compression can be a problem for high quality displays. The encoding process does lose some visual quality because subtle differences (e.g., shading) will be lost. In some applications, the fidelity of the encoding process can be controlled so that users can make a trade-off between image quality and size of the disk file. When the image is decompressed, there is usually little noticeable degradation in quality, but if the image is expanded or printed on a high quality printer, then the effects of compression may become apparent.

The temporal dimension marks these dynamic media apart from other forms, because the designer has to consider addressability and possibly synchronization. Components in dynamic media can have two interpretations, both of which have implications for design:

- Components within the content that have *meaning* to people; for instance we can distinguish a single note in music, a phoneme in speech, but little in background (white) noise. In moving images, we can name objects within a single frame if it is paused.

- *Time-ordered* segments of the media stream, in which an external referent is used to describe arbitrary components such as "first 5 min."

As with static media, the addressability of the perceived medium depends on its encoding in the computer. Some media may have component-level encoding, such as music notes and words in speech that can be dynamically generated by music and speech synthesizers. These media can be searched and addressed at the component instance level. Component-level encoding in moving image media is less common, although avatars in VR, animated cartoons, and drawings can be generated by scripts that act on logical descriptions of components. Dynamic media can be addressable either directly or indirectly. Direct addressing is achieved by format codes within the medium, whereas the indirect addressing uses an external referent to locate the approximate position of components in a media stream, for example, frame numbers on a film allow access to frame 101, and so forth. Indirect addressing may use a clock if no format markers are present in the medium itself, hence going to the second movement of a Mozart symphony is achieved by starting to play the sound 9 min and 30 sec from the start, having identified the start position.

The physical format may also constrain the flexibility of time controls for a medium. Most formats and devices allow the speed of presentation to be changed by controls that follow the metaphor of VCR technology: fast forward, rewind, freeze frame, stop, and start. Controls for moving image may allow a trade-off between the number of frames per second that can be displayed and the image resolution. First there is the frame rate: playing movies at a slow frame rate is one way of avoiding bandwidth restrictions on the Internet, but display rates of 12 to 15 frames per sec (50% normal speed) are not very natural. Display rate is less of a problem for CD-ROM multimedia. Second, there is the display footprint: expanding the window in which the movie is shown may make compression degradations very noticeable because an image that was compressed at low resolution or from a small original footprint is being displayed on a larger area with more pixels. The loss of subtle boundaries becomes apparent when the display area is enlarged.

Time varying media present a particular problem in synchronization; for instance, the sound channel for a movie or subtitle texts have to be coordinated with the display rate of frames in a movie. The SMIL (Synchronous Multimedia Interface Language; W3C, 2000, 2001) multimedia standard and reference architectures recommend the controls that should be available and the effects that implementing such controls should have.

SUMMARY

Multisensory UIs cover multimedia and VR technologies. These extend the range of devices and representations for human–computer communication. Multimedia adds image, sound, and video; VR provides a 3D interactive graphical world that immerses the user. Multisensory products need improved usability to ensure competitive advantage in design. Usability is a multilevel concept, composed of operational or how-to-drive-it usability, information delivery, and learning. The latter two are vital concerns for multimedia in particular. Multimedia forms an information-rich part of the general process of human–computer communication. Outbound from computer to human, presentation of information is the main design concern, whereas inbound from users to computers, choice of communication modality is more important. Media can be defined according to how they are perceived by users. Dynamic media change over time and have different properties from static, nonchanging media. Media may also be categorized according to the modality of communication, essentially visual or audio. Different media types have implications for human perception.

Dynamic media attract our attention, but we remember little content because we have to process the continuous media stream. Static media, in contrast, give us more freedom in processing. Dynamic media and images do make considerable demands on disk storage and network bandwidth. Compression algorithms reduce these demands but at the penalty of loss of quality. Image media and audio have to be indexed if components in the medium are interactive. Addressing components may be direct or indirect via a time marker on video and audio.

2

Cognitive Psychology for Multimedia Information Processing

This chapter introduces the psychological background to multisensory user interaction. An overview is given using a model of human information processing covering the role of memory, attention, and the processes of perception and comprehension. The aim is to provide background knowledge that is useful in the design process in its own right, as well as forming the basis for many guidelines.

The overview starts with perception, the process of receiving information from the outside world, followed by cognition, the mental activity we describe in everyday terms as reasoning and problem solving. The boundary between the two is blurred because as we receive information, we also interpret it. The receptive processes for multisensory interaction are examined first.

PERCEPTION AND MODALITIES

We perceive the world via a variety of senses, although the dominant senses for interacting with each other and computers are vision and hearing.

Vision

Vision is our dominant sense and this has many implications for multimedia. Visual perception poses three problems:

- Receiving an external stimulus, in this case the electromagnetic radiation as light.

- Translating the stimulus into nerve impulses in a manner faithful to the stimulus.
- Attaching meaning to the stimulus.

Visual acuity, that is, the ability to resolve just noticeable differences, is influenced by several factors. There is the complexity of the image itself, the intensity of the light, and image color. Low light intensity makes images difficult to resolve. Absolute human visual sensitivity is remarkable, as the human eye can see in almost complete darkness, although the threshold of vision, that is, the smallest quantity of light that can be seen, decreases with age. Although people can see light at low intensities, they can resolve little detail and for normal working good illumination is required. The advantages of good luminance in image displays follow:

- Acuity increases with better luminance and with increased foreground or background contrast.
- Better luminance means a smaller aperture in the eye which increases the depth of field. In the eye, aperture is controlled by the iris; the effect is the same as reducing the camera stop from F5.6 to F8, which gives a better depth of focus.

On the minus side, increased luminance makes VDU flicker more obvious and direct glare may become uncomfortable. Visual flicker is caused by the eye discriminating changes in an image in a short time period. If the change happens quickly enough, the eye assumes a continuous state and does not differentiate between each image. This quality, called the flicker fusion frequency, happens at approximately 32 images per sec, and the continuity illusion is exploited in motion picture photography. People will tolerate but notice lower refresh rates, so movies displayed at 20 frames per sec are annoying because the frames are visible. Below 15 frames per sec, movies become harder to process as animation. This is because we treat each image as a still snapshot and do not automatically make the join between frames that is necessary to understand motion. Flicker fusion becomes a problem in VR systems when the graphics software cannot refresh the whole 3D world quickly enough. This leads to the world appearing to judder, and it may result in motion sickness caused by mismatch between vision and sense of balance. In multimedia, low frame rates are annoying but more tolerable.

Human visual acuity is quite remarkable but individually very variable. Most people can resolve gaps of 2 mm at a distance of 2 m, but this tells us little about how people see meaningful shapes. More important for multimedia design is resolution of more complex shapes and letters. The optician's test measures optimal visual ability as resolving letters 20

mm high on the bottom row at 6 m, although average ability is only capable of resolving 40 mm letters. Few people have perfect vision, so display
design should accommodate average human abilities. One design implication is for the size of text characters. The size of printed letters is measured in points, a point being roughly 1/72 of an in.; thus, 10-point type
has letters with an approximate height of 10/72 or 0.14 of an in. Printed
text usually ranges between 8- and 18-point; anything smaller than
10-point is difficult to read for a long period of time. Text displays, where
the reading distance is 0.5 m, need to be 12 point; however, text for over-
head projectors, when the reading distance is 2 to 5 m, should be 18 to 24
point. Serif fonts (such as the Times New Roman font you are currently
reading) have additional graphical embellishments that help readability
compared with plainer sans serif fonts. Color sensitivity varies between
individuals and between colors. Most people can see yellows better than
reds and blues; however, color blindness should also be considered. Approximately 9% of the male and 2% of the female population have some
color blindness, with the inability to discriminate reds and greens being
most common.

Human perception of light rarely bears a close relation to its actual physical properties. Consequently, brightness of light in our everyday opinion is
not just its physical intensity but is conditioned by the difference between
light intensities in an image. We see differences in illumination very well and
this helps us discriminate boundaries and edges of objects. We are sensitive
to contrast in illumination, which is measured by the difference in luminance between two surfaces. Generally, dark surfaces absorb more light;
light ones absorb less light, so white objects appear to be brighter. Luminance, as measured by photographic light meters, is expressed in candelas
per square meter (cd/m), whereas contrast is the difference in luminance between two surfaces and is expressed as a ratio:

$$\text{Contrast} = \frac{\text{Lmax} - \text{Lmin}}{\text{Lmax} + \text{Lmin}}$$

The Lmax/min formula gives a measure between 0 and 1 for low to high
contrast. Hence, to make an object stand out in an image, a high overall luminance is desirable (Lmax) and a large difference between the object and
background. This matches with our intuitive feeling of high contrast of dark
shadows in bright sunlight. On VDU screens, displayed characters should
have a high contrast with the background.

Contrast on VDU screens is not as good as on a printed page, so readability
of text is worse on-screen. To exacerbate matters, the image of a text character is not as sharp as its printed counterpart because of the limitations of current raster displays. Hence, text which may be readable on paper, when

scanned and clipped into a multimedia presentation may be very difficult to read. Designers need to allow for some reduction in readability when using text media and this becomes worse when text is displayed in virtual worlds.

Visual Processing.   Our eyes have specialized receptors for black and white and for color. These have an irregular distribution in the retina, with black and white receptors being concentrated around the periphery whereas color receptors are more concentrated at the center (the fovea), which is the natural point of focus on the retina. We can see quite a large area in front of us about 80 degrees either side of our nose, but we can only see detail in a small area on which we are focusing (central vision). In the rest of our peripheral vision, we cannot discriminate detail but we are aware of shape, color, and especially movement. Peripheral vision is more like a monitor, very sensitive for detecting movement and change in an image but poor at detail. In immersive VR, we see the virtual environment with peripheral as well as central vision leading to a sense of being within the world; in contrast, desktop VR does not give us the same sense. Our eyes scan images in rapid movements called saccades, alternating with jumps between different areas. Generally the eye is programmed to look at complex areas of images where the detail is denser. Eye tracking records (see Fig. 2.1) show dense patches of scanning (fixation) interleaved with rapid movements (saccades) between certain objects. These movements are automatic and not within our conscious control. What we look at depends on surface level perceptual properties of the image such as complex, odd, and irregular shapes; color; and contrast boundaries. However, we are also influenced by priming effects, our knowledge of the domain, and motivation. Eye movement is therefore controlled by a complex integration of low-level (perceptual) and higher-level (knowledge, memory) factors. However, the dominant effect of movement will attract central vision to any movement detected in the periphery.

Before images are transmitted to the brain, the eye does a considerable amount of image enhancement. The human visual system is much better at dealing with variation in light intensity than even the most sophisticated camera. This is because the eye has an automatic intensity adjustment device which turns sensitivity up in dark conditions and down in bright light. Another example of preprocessing is treatment of boundaries. The retina has feedback circuits that enhance boundary detection. The consequence is that our eyes pick up edges, especially moving edges, very well indeed. Further abstraction of image qualities is carried out in the next stage, which is image interpretation.

Image Interpretation.   The whole process is still not completely understood; however, the basic principles were analyzed by Marr (1982), who

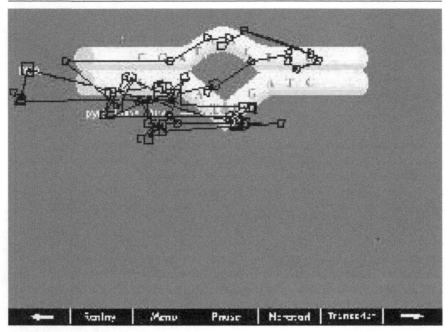

FIG. 2.1   Eye tracking record in a multimedia application. The squares indicate fixations where the eye movement came to a brief halt before moving rapidly to the next fixation point.

described the process of extracting shapes in an image to build sketches with increasing complexity. Receptor cells have specialized roles responding to different primitive components within the image such as edges, corners, bars, and gaps. By combination of many thousands of receptors, an image is built up as a composite of primitive features that define the shapes that we see. Contrast boundaries are accentuated so that shapes can be detected.

The optic cortex in our brain receives a mass of information encoding different qualities of the image. The cortex then has to create visual meaning, the image we see, out of this information. It does so by referring to past records in memory, using an object–property matching process (Treisman, 1988). Object identification usually works very well but sometimes what we see is not what is there, but rather our interpretation of what is there based on memory. The process makes a mistake and we see a visual illusion. Visual illusions use two tricks to fool the eye and brain: ambiguity and suggestion. Ambiguous images are ones that are open to two or more interpretations. Different people will see different images because they have different memories to fit the clue, and that creates an illusion of what is there. Only on closer examination does a contradiction become apparent. Suggestion can also work by supplying insufficient information in an image and then giving an extra clue verbally. People instantly see something in an image that they couldn't see beforehand (see Fig. 2.2).

Information is extracted by detecting boundaries that segment the image into shapes to create a 2.5D sketch (Marr, 1982). Depth cues enable us to see perspective, because our eyes have slightly different right and left angles of vision. This creates stereoptic vision, when our brain integrates the two viewpoints so we can use cues of shadows and occlusion of shapes to see in perspective or 3D. Depth perception becomes important in virtual environments where projection of separate right and left eye images gives the illusion of true depth, whereas VDUs in desktop VR give only a partial illusion of 3D, much as an artist can convey by use of perspective in a painting.

We preferentially recognize certain patterns in images, as demonstrated by the Gestalt psychologists, such as areas and boundaries, groups of objects that share the same attributes, objects in close proximity treated as groups, symmetry both bilateral and radial, and closure (completeness in boundaries). Other salient stimuli that can be added are complexity, dense areas, areas of bright color, areas separated by high contrast, and odd, unusual shapes in images. Although it is difficult to give an exact rank order for the attentional salience of image components, an approximate ordering is vivid color, odd shapes, complex areas in a simple background, high contrast, and then the Gestalt properties.

Interpretation of images also depends on an attentional process, so what we extract from an image depends on what we look at. Just what will be fixated in an image is controlled by several factors, such as the user's intention and background knowledge, and properties of the image itself. As central vision moves around an image, we are aware of objects in an attention spotlight (Kosslyn, 1980). Certain objects will maintain their salience in memory as landmarks that we reference to construct a spatial map of the world we see. In multisensory user interfaces, we often want to direct the user's attention to make an object or message salient within an image. Attention can be controlled by changing visual properties of objects with the image, a point developed in chapter 4. Interpretation generally occurs only when objects are focused in central vision; however, we also process some information in peripheral vision. This *preattentive* processing is an automatic activity not under our conscious control, but it can have important implications for the direction of conscious attention. Movement is the most salient effect that automatically attracts our attention. However, we also perceive shape and color in peripheral vision to an extent, so objects may be partially recognized, allowing us to notice things that are not in our central vision. Preattentive processing has important implications in immersive VR where the 3D graphical world covers central and peripheral vision.

FIG. 2.2   Visual illusions. People see a cow in the image when prompted; alternatively a Dalmatian (spotty dog) can be seen. It depends on the cue and individual opinion.

The implication of visual interpretation is that images are open to misinterpretation, because each person attaches their own meaning to what they see. Visual comprehension can be summarized as "what you see depends on what you look at and what you know." Multimedia designers can influence what users look at by controlling attention with display techniques such as use of movement and highlighting objects. However, designers should be aware that the information that people assimilate from an image also depends on their internal motivation, what they want to find, and how well they know the domain. For instance, a novice may not see an interesting plant species in a tropical jungle, whereas a trained botanist will be able to pick out individual plants in a mass of foliage. Selection of visual content therefore has to take the user's knowledge and task into account.

The user's viewing and reading sequence differs between media. Video and speech have to be processed in sequence; similarly, text enforces a reading order by the syntactic convention of language. However, what the user looks at in a still image is less predictable. Attention-directing design effects can increase the probability that the user will attend to an image component, although no guarantee can be given that a component will be perceived or understood. Ultimately, the order of viewing objects in a still image depends on the user's task, motivation, knowledge of the domain, and designed effects for salience.

Implications for Multisensory UI Design follow:

- Do not expect people to attend to detail in several different areas of an image at once; although users can scan images rapidly, they only extract detail from small areas at any one time.
- In multimedia systems, only one moving image should be presented at once; users cannot attend to a still image and a video at the same time because of the dominant effect of movement on visual attention.
- Use of movement is a highly effective means of alerting users and drawing their attention in peripheral vision.
- What the user will see and comprehend in an image is difficult to predict; it depends on prior knowledge, priming effects, and motivation.
- Users should be familiar with the contents of an image for comprehension to be successful.
- Extracting information from images can be cued by priming effects if a topic is introduced in one medium and then elaborated in another medium; text prompts, for example, alert the user to the contents in a following diagram.

Audio Modality: Hearing and Speech

Although vision is the dominant sense for human–computer communication at present, hearing assumes at least equal importance in multimedia. As with vision, what we hear is not just a matter of the sound we receive but also how we interpret it with reference to memory.

Receptors in the inner ear show a similar specialization to the optical system. Some are activated by particular frequencies of sound; others respond to the amplitude (power of the sound) at a particular frequency. A sound composed of many frequencies is converted into a pattern of nerve impulses representing its various features. The frequency range for deciphering speech is approximately 260 Hz to 5600 Hz; however, the region of 2 to 3 KHz (2000–3000 Hz) is most important. Telephones only transmit from 300 to 3000 Hz, yet we can hear speech quite adequately, and people are able to extract useful information from very poor quality audio. Our overall auditory acuity is in the range of 200 to 20,000 Hz, but the range decreases with age, and individual abilities differ considerably.

Hearing receptors have narrower bandwidths at lower frequencies with progressively wider bandwidths at higher frequencies, so the ear is tuned to extract more information from lower frequency sound. Our ability to attend selectively to certain frequency combinations enables us to filter out background noise and listen to conversation in spite of considerable interference, a phenomenon known as the cocktail party effect. Because our ears are positioned on either side of our heads, sound from many sources arrives at slightly different times in right and left ears. This difference, together with our ability to selectively discriminate between frequencies, gives the binaural sensation of being surrounded in a soundscape. Quadraphonic sound projected in virtual environments helps to maintain this.

The ear has to extract certain sounds mixed in with background noise. The relation of sounds to background noise is expressed as decibels (dB), a logarithmic ratio of the power of the sound to background noise, usually referred to as the signal-to-noise ratio. Thus, not only does the ear have to be sensitive to the overall frequency range, but it also has to resolve small frequency components within noisy input. Very loud sounds are painful to the ear, although what people find unpleasant and what causes actual harm are not always the same. Higher pitch sounds are usually considered more unpleasant whereas lower pitch and loud sounds (e.g. rock bands) are actually more harmful.

Interpreting Sound and Speech.   The properties of audio are intensity (amplitude), timbre, pitch (frequency components), dynamics, and register. In addition, when music is being considered, rhythm and melody are important. Pitch alone is a pure frequency and not very interesting; however, when other harmonics are added (higher and lower complementary frequencies), a sound has timbre. Pitch and intensity interact in a strange manner; at less than 2KHz, increasing intensity increases the perceived pitch, whereas above 3KHz increasing intensity decreases the perceived pitch (Brewster, 1994). Blind users can make accurate judgements of spatial dimensions using pitch and timbre in a musical scale together with amplitude, and further coding can be achieved by use of musical instruments to give additional dimensions of timbre (Alty, 1997). These properties can be combined into earcons or designed descriptive sounds which the user learns to associate with particular commands or events (Leplatre & Brewster, 1998). Ambient and natural sounds or auditory icons can also be used to convey information about states and events, as demonstrated from research into sounds from a bottle plant to present information about the state of the plant (e.g., lines active or inactive, speed of bottling). Although earcons and auditory icons are not as effective a speech in identifying events, users often prefer to have sound as a supplementary modality (Portigal, 1994).

To interpret sound, the auditory system has to classify the input into three categories: noise and unimportant sounds which can be ignored; significant noise, that is, sounds which are important and have meaning attached to them such as a dog's bark; and meaningful utterances composing language.

The hearing system, like vision, makes use of past experience when interpreting input. Spoken language is full of mispronounced words, unfinished sentences, and interruptions; furthermore, it happens quickly (160–220 words per min), so the interpretation mechanism has to keep pace with the input.

Language recognition starts by discovering the basic sound units of language called phonemes. These sounds can then be matched to the basic units of written language, called morphemes, which correspond approximately to syllables, suffixes, prefixes, and so forth, and thereby words (e.g., fo-ne-emes). Interpretation, however, does not use phonemes alone. It is a layered and integrated approach that makes use of language syntax (the grammar), semantics (the meaning of words and sentences), and pragmatics (knowledge of the context of communication) to decipher meaning.

People supply a significant amount of what they hear on the basis of expectancy. This can be demonstrated by experiments asking people to identify a sound masked by a cough in the middle of a sentence. Speech recognition suffers from illusions in a similar manner to the visual system, but the timing of perception is more critical and as a result the tolerance of speech interpretation mistakes is higher; consequently, illusions in speech are not referred to as such. Evidence of verbal suggestion is demonstrated by an experiment in which one word, "eel," is heard as four different words depending on the sentence context:

It was found that the •eel was on the axle
It was found that the •eel was on the shoe
It was found that the •eel was on the table
It was found that the •eel was on the orange

The sound "eel" is heard as wheel, heel, meal, and peel, respectively, in the four sentences (Warren & Warren, 1970). Natural speech has many subtle variations in frequency and amplitude, which, although they are not essential for understanding, are noticeable by their absence. Voice tonality, called prosody, is important in speech synthesis. We can understand synthetic speech but it sounds artificial because of the difficulty in getting computers to generate tonal variations that come naturally to people.

Implications for design follow:

- Only part of the auditory range is necessary for speech. People will tolerate poor sound communications unless quality is vital, such as high fidelity music.
- Background noise should be reduced for effective communication, although the human ear is good at suppressing superfluous noise.
- Sound is very effective as a means of alerting and warning. Sound is an environmental change we are tuned to pick up.

- Sound is a broadcast medium, so beware of annoying other users by overuse of warning sounds; and high pitch sounds tend to be uncomfortable for most people.
- Speech is interpreted by the rules of grammar and reference to memory. We automatically correct many imperfections in spoken language.

Proprioception

Proprioception is the sense of balance and position. It depends on two separate systems: first, a set of receptors embedded in our muscles that detect the position of our limbs from muscle tone, that is, whether the muscle is contracted or relaxed. Second is the vestibular system in each middle ear that gives our sense of balance and motion.

Proprioceptors signal the position of limbs and our body by registering the muscle tension, and like most human sensors they are tuned to signal change rather than steady state. These signals are interpreted by integration with vision to give the sense of posture and position we take for granted until it is disrupted in VR. We maintain a mental map of where our limbs are independently of our visual sense; hence, complex movements of limbs can be coordinated in the dark. Proprioception also gives the sense of pressure and weight when we pick up objects. Heavier objects require more muscle power to lift, so we can judge weight via this sense. In virtual environments, the lack of force feedback makes us more dependent on visual input to judge movement and force, although force feedback devices that mimic the mass of objects by applying resistance to limb movement are being researched to restore proprioception.

The sense of balance comes from three semicircular canals in our middle ear oriented in each of the three dimensions: horizontally, vertically, and planar. These fluid-filled canals have tiny hairs suspended on top of sensitive nerve cells enabling them to act as the human equivalent of accelerometers and gyroscopes. As we move, the tiny hairs become displaced because they are more massive than the surrounding liquid. The nerve cells signal the rate of displacement and our brain calculates a complex integration of signals from all three semicircular canals to interpret our relative motion and acceleration. Continuous change in direction and acceleration, as experienced in a car being driven quickly along a bendy road, can overwhelm our sense of balance leading to motion sickness. In virtual environments, the mismatch between visual feedback on motion and the lack of any corresponding change in the balance system also causes sickness.

Haptic Sense: Touch

The haptic sense is a collection of receptors in our skin that signal properties of surfaces, that is,. roughness, stickiness, plasticity, elasticity, viscosity, the pressure applied (strictly proprioception), and temperature. Our ability to distinguish a wide range of surface properties of solids and fluids by touch is concentrated in our fingertips. Sensations are created by integration of change of stimuli over time as our fingertip travels over an object; thus roughness or smoothness approximates to deflections caused by a surface, plasticity depends on pressure deflections, and elasticity, stickiness, and viscosity have time-dependent interpretations of contact duration and deflection. Our haptic sense is closely integrated with proprioception and these senses are often treated as one. Integration of these senses is essential for effective action. The sensation of grip is an interpretation of where our arms and fingers are, the muscle tone applied, and the deflection detected in the gripped object. In virtual environments, we have to interact without the benefit of this feedback, which makes precise manipulation very difficult. Some cross-modal substitution is possible, such as using color hue and audio tones to represent pressure, but we have to learn to interpret these new forms of feedback.

Olfaction and Gustation

Although the senses of smell and taste may appear dissimilar, they are both based on detecting dissolved chemicals by nerve cell sensors. The difference lies in how the chemical arrives. Smell detects airborne chemicals that dissolve in a thin aqueous film in our nose, leading to smells that we describe as mixtures of basic smells such as spicy, fruity, resinous, burnt, flowery, and putrid. Our ability to discriminate certain chemicals in low concentrations is remarkable; skunk odor (Ethyl mercaptan), for example, can be detected in a dilution of 0.5 ml dispersed in 10,000 L of air. We can identify 15 to 30 common stimuli (coffee, paint, fish, etc.) and can also discriminate a large number of different chemical combinations, but the sense of smell has to be trained to get to performance levels of expert parfumiers. For most people smell is an underdeveloped sense, and human olfaction is poor in comparison with most of our mammalian relatives. Interestingly, the sense of smell is better in women than in men.

The taste stimulus arrives on our tongue either as a liquid or by dissolving chemical solids when we lick an object. The properties of taste are similar to those of smell. Taste receptors are tuned to dimensions of sweet, sour, hot (peppery), and acid. Our ability to detect very low concentrations of certain chemicals is good (one part per million in quinine) and we can identify a huge range of different chemical combinations. However, taste has to be trained to achieve the expert performances typical of wine tasters; for most of us it is another underdeveloped sense. Both taste and smell are limited in current multisensory interaction by the lack of emitter or generator devices.

Delivering taste requires action by the user that may limit its appeal to specialized circumstances.

Sensory Integration and Motor Coordination

We rarely detect and interpret our environment by one sense alone. Instead, our brain creates an integrated impression of the world via all the senses, although the extent to which the senses can be integrated differs. Integration is important in three key contexts: taking action in the world, locomotion, and communication.

Sensory Integration For Action. The senses of proprioception, haptics, and vision are closely coupled for action. To grip, manipulate, and move objects, we rely on feedback from our proprioceptive and haptic receptors to adjust muscle power, and finger position to grip and manipulate objects; vision is necessary to steer the motion of our limbs and interpret the effect of action. If any of these senses is disrupted by VR, or by weightlessness in space flight that alters proprioception because we don't need muscle tone to maintain our posture against gravity, then precise manipulations are impaired.

We use our senses, especially vision, to direct movement of our limbs. Although we are capable of very precise movements using our hands, speed and accuracy of movement falls off with distance. This ability is summarized in Fitt's law:

$$\text{movement time} = a + b \log_2(\text{distance/size} + 1)$$

where a and b are empirically determined constants that depend on the display and interactive technology. The implication is that our ability to hit a target quickly and accurately falls off as a log function of distance; hence small, distant targets in VR are hard to select, especially as the display fidelity and manipulation device may give higher (adverse) values for a + b.

Locomotion. Moving is not as simple as it seems. The reason why human babies spend 6 to 12 months or more learning how to walk efficiently is learning how to integrate visual proprioceptive and balance senses. As we move forward, our sense of balance detects acceleration and change in body posture; this is integrated with proprioceptive information about change in limb position as we step forward. These senses are integrated with haptic information from the foot about the nature of the ground (rough, smooth, pliable or not) and finally with visual feedback as some objects in central visual come closer and lateral objects disappear into peripheral vision. The visual sense of objects changing in proportion and relative location during locomotion was called the ambient optical array by Gibson (1986), who drew attention to our ability to interpret a stream of objects moving toward us in terms of relative motion. The effect is very strong and overrides sensory integration to provide the sensation of motion in immersive VR, when in fact our movement is restricted. When the optical array is not present in peripheral vision, as in desktop VR, we still interpret change in a 3D image as our relative motion through an environment.

Communication.   The audio modality dominates communication in speech; however, we also use nonverbal communication. Body posture, head nods, and gesture all contribute either to reinforce what has been said or occasionally to contribute information independently. Communication is also influenced by the context in which it takes place, so all the senses are important in creating a visual, olfactory, and possible gustatory environment that may change our interpretation of what is being said. Speech is also coupled with visual feedback of lip movement. If this departs from the spoken phoneme (speech segment) by more than 0.5 sec, we notice something is wrong, as in a dubbed film.

To summarize, we perceive the world via a variety of senses, but memory plays a crucial role in interpreting the world for most senses and especially in vision and hearing; consequently, the role of perception in receiving information and cognition in understanding and using external information cannot be meaningfully separated. This leads to an investigation of how memory works and how it is used in the processes of understanding and reasoning.

COMPREHENSION AND COGNITIVE MODELS

To explain how perception and comprehension are related, it is necessary first to introduce a simplified model of human cognition. Information processing models describe human perception, cognition (i.e., thinking, reasoning, comprehending), and memory using a computer-like analogy. Cognitive models are useful because they illustrate the advantages and limitations of the human machine. In the following section, perception and cognition will be explored using an information-processing model (the Model Human Processor, MHP; Card, Moran, & Newell, 1983).

According to the model, each perceptual sense has a processor and associated short-term memory (STM). These memories form the input and output buffers of the human system. Meaning is generated when information in the input short-term memories is passed on to the central cognitive short-term memory for interpretation. The cognitive processor is responsible for object identification. This is effected by matching the incoming information with past experience and then attaching semantic meaning to the image or sound. To complete the model, the cognitive processor has an associated STM that is used for storing temporary information. The collection of short-term memories is often referred to as *working memory*.

The cognitive processor performs most of the actions that are considered in everyday language to be thinking. The results of thinking are either placed back in working memory, stored in long-term memory, or may be passed on to the motor processor to elicit behavior. The motor processor is responsible for controlling actions by muscle movements to create behavior, for example, running, talking, pointing, and so forth. Speech output is a special case that requires a separate output processor and buffer of its own.

Some critical limitations in our ability to process multimedia can be illustrated with these models. Selective attention means that we can only attend to a limited number of inputs at once. Although people are remarkably good at integrating information received on different senses, there are cognitive resource limitations because information delivered on different modalities (e.g., by vision and sound) can compete for the same resource. For instance, speech and printed text both require a language understanding; video and a still image use an image interpretation resource. The MHP (see Fig. 2.3) shows that certain media combinations and media design will not result in effective comprehension because they compete for the same cognitive resources, thus creating a processing bottleneck.

As shown in Fig. 2.3, capacity overflow (1) may happen when too much information is presented in a short period, swamping the user's limited working memory and cognitive processor's capability to comprehend, memorize, and use information. The design implication is to give users control over the pace of information delivery. Integration problems (2) arise when the message on two media is different, making integration in working memory difficult; this leads to the thematic congruence principle. Contention problems (3) are caused by conflicting attention between dynamic media, and when two inputs compete for the same cognitive resources, for example, speech and text require language understanding. Comprehension (4) is related to congruence; we understand the world by making sense of it with our existing long-term memory. Consequently, if multimedia material is unfamiliar, we can't make sense of it. Finally, multitasking (5) makes further demands on our cognitive processing, so we will experience difficulty in attending to multimedia input while performing output tasks. To illustrate bottleneck (2), imagine listening to the radio while the television is on. Even if the sound is turned down, trying to make sense of what is going on on both the radio and TV at the same time is nearly impossible. You have to maintain a thread of two topics in working memory and swap between them. Because the topics are unrelated you cannot chunk them or discover common themes, hence the working memory bottleneck limits your ability to process two unrelated media streams.

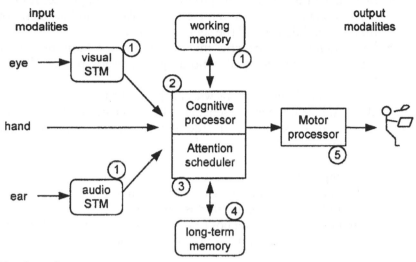

input
modalities

working
memory

output
modalities

eye

visual
STM

①

hand

②

Cognitive
processor

①

Motor
processor

Attention
scheduler

⑤

①

ear

audio
STM

③

④

long-term
memory

Bottlenecks
1. Capacity overflow: information overload
2. Integration: common message?
3. Contention: conflicting channels
4. Comprehension
5. Multi-tasking input/output

FIG. 2.3 Approximate model of memory and reasoning components using "human as computer" analogy, adapted from the model human processor.

Another, more sophisticated, model is Interacting Cognitive Subsystems (ICS) developed by Barnard over a number of years (Barnard, 1987, 1991; Duke, Barnard, Duce, & May, 1998). This describes a cognitive architecture of resources that are recruited to process inputs and carry out mental activities. Unlike the MHP architecture, it does not distinguish between working and long-term memories, but posits a collection of different temporary memories that hold the inputs and outputs from cognitive processing. The subsystems of ICS that contain memories and associated processor components follow. The abbreviations are used in subsequent discussion.

- *Morphonolexical*: Morph, Aud take audio input and extracts phonemes of speech and meaningful sounds.
- *Visual*: Vis is low-level image processing and scene segmentation.
- *Object*: Obj processes visual input to extract objects and identify them by reference to memory.

- *Body-State:* BS contains the proprioceptive and haptic senses that detect body posture from muscle tone, balance, and acceleration from the middle ear and the sense of touch.
- *Propositional:* Prop attaches meaning to input stimuli by matching them to memory; also holds propositions retrieved from working memory.
- *Implicational:* Implic reasons with propositions to create high-level abstractions and memory schema. The implication subsystem undertakes more of the higher-order reasoning, both analyzing input and planning action in the world.
- *Articulatory:* Artic is responsible for speech generation. Planning and composition of utterances are carried out at the Implicational and Propositional levels, leaving generation of speech via the vocal cords and shape of the lips to this subsystem.
- *Limb:* Lim represents the position and posture of limbs. Motor actions create movement by acting on the Limb subsystem.

Appropriate resources are recruited according to the nature of input and reasoning processes being carried out. These resources will depend on the knowledge held by the user, so novices require explicit processing by each subsystem in turn whereas experts will have automated some processes thereby skipping some subsystems. ICS assumes memory is distributed across the different subsystems with a spreading activation model. That means chunks which have been used recently will receive more activation than others; furthermore, where memory structures exist, activation will spread along links. Thus, if I am reasoning about the ICS architecture in Fig. 2.4 (after Teasdale & Barnard, 1993), the subsystems will be active chunks in memory, as will the implications about a distributed processing or memory model. The activation of chunks may then spread to memory schema I already possess about chunks and working memory. Distributed memory models see working memory and long-term memory as a continuous structure with a focus determined by activation.

To illustrate how the model works, when the user is manipulating an object in a virtual environment (VE) the following processing sequence is invoked. Visual input is perceived and interpreted (Vis→Obj→Prop subsystems) so the user is aware of the properties of the object and the VE. The user then plans what to do (pick up the object) and carries out the action. This involves preparing the plan (Prop→Implic) to form a mental model of the VE and task, possibly retrieving from memory the plan and specific action of what to pick up in the VE (Implic→Prop) and then translating this plan into motor movements (Prop→Lim) to drive the hand and grip. However, this also involves targeting movement via

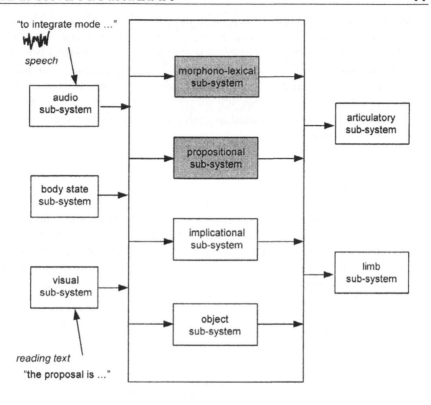

FIG. 2.4   ICS architecture, showing subsystems and connections.

the visual sense (Vis→Obj→Prop→Lim); note that no higher-order Implication subsystem involvement is required because visio-motor coordination is automatic. The Body-State system is also involved to deliver feedback as the arm moves and grips the object (BS→Prop→Lim), but here we have a mismatch between reality and virtual environments. The feedback from the Body-State system will be inaccurate when the hand grips the object because no haptic feedback is present and the hand passes through the object, contrary to expectation in the user's memory. This will cause confusion at the Propositional level which will have to be resolved at the Implicational level with visual feedback to adjust the grip.

Thus, the initial semiautomatic action (BS→Prop→Lim) becomes much more complex (BS→Prop→Vis_Obj→Prop) to detect the mismatch, then (Prop→Implic) to reason about why a mismatch has occurred, (Implic→Prop) to revise the planned action, and then many cycles of (Vis→Obj→Prop→Implic) to judge whether the object has been gripped using visual feedback alone. This example demonstrates how cognitive models can be used to understand the underlying issues in VR and multisensory UIs.

MEMORY

Working Memory

In spite of the different views between the ICS and MHP models, most psychologists agree that short-term or working memory has important implications for human information processing. The capacity of working memory is not clear, but for vision it must be at least the contents of one visual field, that is, what we can see at any one point in time. The contents decay rapidly in about 100 msec and are continually overwritten by new input; consequently, when you close your eyes the visual image vanishes quickly; any transient "after image" is your visual working memory. The visual input buffer has to be overwritten because the quantity of data in an image is vast and images change continually; so storing even a few images would take a vast amount of memory. This has implications for multimedia; for instance, if images are not held on screen long enough we will not be able to extract much information from them. A consequence for video or film is that we remember the gist of what happens but rarely any detail within individual scenes. Speech input has the same overwrite problem, because speech working memory too has a limited capacity of only a few words or sounds.

Working memory has at least two subsystems: one deals with language-based data, the other with visio-spatial information. The linguistic subsystem functions as a list but access is like a hybrid LIFO (Last In First Out) queue. We tend to remember the last and first few items in the list and forget the middle. Speech memory is like a conveyor belt in which words are placed to compose sentences.

Some key features of working memory follow:

- Rapid read and write access time: 70 msec.
- Memory decays quickly: 200 msec unless refreshed.
- Storage capacity can be increased by abstracting qualities of raw information into "chunks."
- Capacity is limited to 7 ± 2 chunks, but depends on the level of abstraction.

- Immediate memory for details in complex images is poor.

The concept of "chunks" is difficult to define. Chunks are related to learning. Any abstraction, structure, or categorization you impose on basic data will create high-order chunks. For instance, grouping telephone numbers helps memorization: 0161–200–3324 rather than 01612003324. Showing trends as a graph rather than a series of numbers establishes the more abstract concept <trend, increasing, rainfall>. Working memory evades its capacity limitation by storing higher-order abstractions rather than detail. How it does this is complex, but in simple terms a tag to the abstraction is held in working memory that activates links to long-term memory for any necessary interpretation. Working memory is one of the key limitations in human information processing. When we receive media streams (video, speech and sound), we encounter the problem of working memory being continually overwritten as we try to process information. We have to recognize and interpret images and sounds, while comprehending their implications. Even if we have several working memories at different levels of abstraction, as in the ICS model, overloading happens rapidly, so we can only extract a fraction of the detail contained in dynamic or time-based media. Working memory limits our ability to process information during tasks and holds a limited number of facts for current processing; its counterpart, long-term memory, stores the knowledge which we have learned and is used to help us understand what we perceive.
Implications for design follow:

- Beware of overloading working memory, both in terms of quantity of information and time span of retention.
- Input from dynamic media rapidly exceeds the capacity of working memory; only the high-level gist will be retained.
- Working memory has to be refreshed; keeping the information available in persistent media allows rescanning of text or images.
- Structuring (chunking) information helps memorization.
- Memorization of detail from image is limited.

Long-Term Memory

Long-term memory is memory in the everyday sense of the word. Putting facts into memory (memorization) is generally more difficult than getting facts back (recall). Retrieval of facts from memory can be remarkably fast, especially for frequently used items and procedures. Often, remembering a fact is not instantaneous; instead, it comes back some minutes after the original effort to retrieve it. Retrieval from memory is a two-phase process; first you recognize something as being familiar, reflecting the initial activation of a memory access path by cues; then you recall: the actual retrieval of the information itself when activation spreads down to the actual memory contents.

In frequently used memory, both recognition and recall are so quick that no difference is noticed. However, it appears that memories are found by a process of activating a search process, "spreading activation": remembering one fact often helps the recall of other related items. It is rather like a large net of interconnected facts that becomes sensitized by use.

Sometimes we do not remember all at once but have the "tip of the tongue" feeling that we know what is required but cannot exactly remember it. Partial recall is probably caused by spreading activation as the cue starts the search process through the memory network. If the network is not well formed or the cues are weak, then the activated search only progresses to a limited depth, and finds general rather than the specific facts.

Memorization fails because an access path either decays through lack of use or was poorly constructed in the first place. Similar facts can interfere with recall, so well-recognized and distinct access paths prevent recall errors. Distractions during the memorization process also cause recall errors, because the access path is liable to be incomplete. Thus, if attention is diverted during memorization, for instance by a noisy environment, memory performance will suffer. In multimedia this happens when dynamic media are played during memorization.

Memory is an active process. We memorize facts more effectively if we have to think about them. This is known as depth of encoding and can be approximately summarized as "the more effort you put into memorization the better you will learn." Not all learning is hard. Some things we memorize automatically (e.g., memories of significant events); however, for most learning, more effort helps. This has important implications for tutorial systems. Memorization is helped by interaction and problem solving, so it is better to construct interactive, multimedia simulations (i.e., microworlds of the problem domain) that the users can explore. Interactive multimedia that challenge the user to explore and solve problems will be more effective for training than simple presentations with a quiz at the end: the drill and test paradigm. Memorization and recall are also helped by context effects. We store memories associated with the context in which they were made, that is, the time of day, location, and possibly our emotional state. Recall is improved if the associated state is present, so feeling happy, on a sunny morning on a holiday beach, helps recall of memory laid down in similar circumstances. In multimedia, the affect or emotive impact of images and sounds can have important effect on memorability and how attractive we find a particular presentation.

Memory is one of the critical limiting factors of human information processing. We understand and memorize complex information by breaking the complexity down into simpler components using a hierarchical approach. The more structure we can put into a body of information, the easier it is to learn. Although building many cues into memory helps, the disadvantage comes when the cues are similar, leading to interference when the wrong item is recalled. This can be a considerable problem when software versions change the interface; your memory for the old version is fine but the update is slightly different. Relearning the new version can be difficult unless interference can be avoided.

Organization of Memory

There are several forms of long-term memory that resemble diagram conventions and common approaches to organizing knowledge. This is a good illustration of how external representations have been designed, or may have naturally evolved, to fit with human abilities.

Semantic Networks.   The basic organization of long-term memory consists of linguistically-based concepts linked together in a highly developed network (see Fig. 2.5). The organization of human memory is far from clear, although most evidence favors the view that all storage is finally of the semantic associative kind, with several different formats. External representations of semantic networks appear as conceptual models or "mind maps" that give informal associations between facts, propositions, and concepts (Eden, 1988).

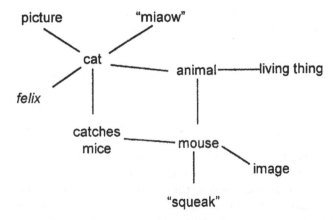

FIG. 2.5   Semantic network with type-instance nodes. This forms a reusable knowledge structure for a common concept of a cat with associated facts.

Episodic Memory.   This stores events, scenes, and contextual information in realistic detail. Episodic memory, in contrast to semantic memory, is composed of more detailed facts about the world, anchored to a particular episode. This memory can store images, sounds, and physical detail of an episode that is particularly salient; for instance, eyewitness memory of accidents. However, as studies of eyewitness testimony have shown, episodic memory is highly selective and can be inaccurate (Baddeley, 1986). Memorization tends to be automatic and linked to the emotions: pleasure, enjoyment, or fear. In VR, episodic memory can give rich details of events and scenes for interpreting virtual environments, so cuing tasks needs to be sensitive to episodic memory, for example, the appropriate virtual tool is set in a scene that the users would expect. However, designers have to beware that people's episodic memory is highly selective so their interpretation of events and characters in a virtual world may be biased by a personal viewpoint.

Categorial Memory.   This is memory of objects and their groupings, familiar as classes in library systems or in object oriented design. There is evidence that we organize the world not into discrete nonoverlapping categories but in a more fuzzy manner, with core and peripheral members (Rosch, 1985). To illustrate the idea, most people have an idealized concept of a bird. A robin fits this core or prototypical image by having the properties: round, feathered, sings, lays eggs, and so forth. In contrast, a penguin is a more peripheral member of birds because it does not share all the attributes of the prototype image and it has additional nonstandard attributes, for example, it swims, but can't fly (see Fig. 2.6). This concept works well for concrete physical objects, but the situation for more abstract concepts (e.g., religions) is less clear. Although people tend to agree about concrete facts taken from the real world, consensus on more abstract categories is harder to achieve. Categorial memory is helped by structuring information into abstract layers, that is, class hierarchies.

Procedural Memory.   This is knowledge of actions and how to do things. Computer programs, macros, and scripting languages are sequences of instructions or procedures. Action-related memory is held in two different forms: declarative or rule-based knowledge and procedural knowledge (Anderson, 1985). When we start out knowing little about a subject, we acquire fragments of declarative knowledge as rules. This knowledge, however, is not organized, so to carry out a task we reason with declarative knowledge fragments and compose them into a plan of action. As people become more familiar with a task, fragments of declarative knowledge become compiled into procedures that can then be run automatically. When carrying out a familiar task, we simply call the procedural knowledge of how to perform it automatically. Scripts (Schank, 1982) are a form of procedural

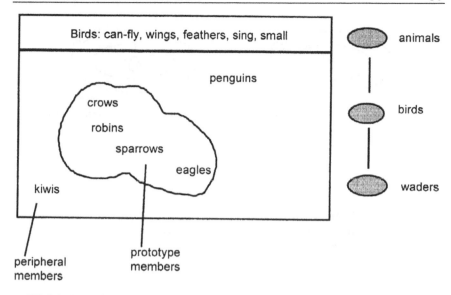

FIG. 2.6   Natural category prototype and peripheral members. Categories are usually organized in three-level hierarchies.

memory that encodes a sequence of events and their context that we have learned from experience. They represent prototypical "stories" of what we expect to go on in a particular context; for example, when we enter a restaurant the usual sequence of events is to receive the menu, order a meal, eat it, pay for it, and leave.

Analogical Memory.   Analogical memory links two sets of domain knowledge that on first sight are unrelated. When the knowledge has been used in reasoning, further abstract links are created in memory to store the relationships. The concept is best explained by example. Take two domains, astronomy and chemistry, and their knowledge structures, one representing the relations among the sun, planets, gravity, and orbits and the other representing atoms, nuclei, electrons, electromagnetic forces, and orbits. The linking analogy is the abstraction of satellites revolving around a central node on orbits determined by forces (Gentner & Stevens, 1983; see Fig. 2.7). Analogy is a useful way of exploiting existing memory by transferring it to new situations. Analogical memory is closely related to abstraction in computer science. Metaphors in GUIs and virtual worlds depend on leveraging analogies; for instance, organizing information hierarchically maps to a virtual library represented as streets, buildings, floors, and rooms.

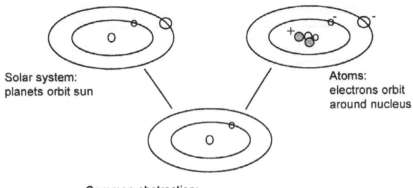

Solar system: Atoms:
planets orbit sun   electrons orbit
                                                                       around nucleus

Common abstraction:
objects revolve around central object;
forces determine orbits

FIG. 2.7   Analogical memory schema and the application of analogies in problem solving.

Two general principles for memorization and learning are structure and consistency. The more consistent something is, the easier it is to perceive patterns within it and hence to learn its structure and characteristics. Memory is always helped by recency and frequency; the more often we re-call and use a piece of information the easier it is to learn it.

Implications for design follow:

- Effectiveness of recall is correlated with the depth of processing. More effort and problem solving help memorization by creating a richer semantic network with better access paths.
- Recall is helped by unique cues and the distinctiveness of the item in relation to other items stored with the same context or cues.
- Distraction causes forgetting of recently learned material. Even a small number of simple chunks of information are lost if there is dis-traction during input.
- Very similar inputs impair recall. Supplying closely related items during memorization makes recall worse (interference effects).
- Recall suffers if one cue is used for many different objects (cue overload).
- Recall is better for an image presented with text than for text or im-age alone (cue integration). Presentation of similar information in different media helps learning and recall by reinforcing the message.
- Recall is better if the context of remembering fits the context of memorization (episodic match).

- Similar items should be grouped in categories and structured to help recall (chunking).
- Memorization can be helped by enriching information during learning. Reasoning and understanding what is being remembered helps. Interactive multimedia microworlds and simulations improve learning better than static displays.
- Structured information techniques can be used to create extra recall cues to retrieve items, for example, keywords, acronyms, spatial memorization, and so forth.
- Consistency in structure and associations creates better contexts for memorization and recall.

THINKING AND PROBLEM SOLVING

Interaction in the real world or in virtual environments poses problems of understanding how something will work. Problem solving is something we do every day of our lives when we come up against the unexpected. It may be defined as "the combination of existing ideas to form new ideas." An alternative view focuses on the cause: problems arise when there is a discrepancy between a desired state of affairs and the current state of affairs and there is no obvious method to change the state. Simon (1973) laid the foundations of problem-solving theory by distinguishing between the problem and solution space. The former is a model of the problem before its solution; the latter consists of facts describing the solution. Problem solving progresses through several stages. The names of stages vary between authorities on the subject, so the following scheme is a generalization:

1. *Preparation or formulation*—The goal state is defined and necessary information for a solution is gathered to create the problem space.
2. *Incubation or searching*—Anticipated solutions are developed, tested, and possibly rejected, leading to more information-gathering and development of alternate hypotheses.
3. *Inspiration*—The correct solution is realized to complete the solution space.
4. *Verification*—The solution is checked out to ensure it meets the goals and is consistent with the information available.

Interaction is a form of problem solving. The UIs should help us to form the problem space (e.g., the virtual world contains relevant objects) and provide guidance toward the solution (e.g., controls and functions appropriate for the user's task). An important concept to help the incubation phase is affordances. The term *affordance* was coined by Gibson (1986) as a visual feature that suggests the effect of an action. Norman (1998) developed the concept in terms of physical features in the world that suggest appropriate action, for example, door handles should be designed to indicate pushing or pulling actions. Transferring the analogy to UIs has caused some confusion about the term. In GUIs, affordances are graphical metaphors that indicate action; for example, a tab suggests a pull-down menu. Another interpretation is organizing information to facilitate problem solving; for example, timeline bar chart data visualization helps solve progress-tracking problems. This interpretation is closer to a cognitive affordance. Finally in VR, objects and virtual tools should prompt action by their physical appearance. The essence of affordances is that they have a physical manifestation that prompts appropriate action either by metaphor or concrete suggestibility. Design therefore has to help users solve the problem of interacting with computers as well as problem solving in the external world task.

People use a wide variety of problem-solving strategies, but are naturally conservative in their approach to problem solving, and adopt the methods they are used to. We solve problems by building a presentation of the necessary facts in working memory as a mental model of the problem space.

Mental Models

Mental models are important because we construct our view of problems as a set of facts and relationships held in working memory. The limited capacity of working memory is partially solved by our ability to abstract the essence of a problem and disregard the details. We also form mental models of the system, based on our previous experience (see episodic and analogical memory). The designer needs to create a model in the system that will be compatible with the user's mental model and if this succeeds interaction becomes intuitive.

The explanation of cognitive processes by mental models has been advocated by Johnson-Laird (Johnson-Laird & Wason, 1983) and this work has had a wide influence on cognitive psychology. Mental models may be either physical or conceptual, and represent abstractions, propositions, and truth-values about objects and their relationships. Positive facts are held in memory without difficulty but negative facts pose problems; representing that something does not exist does not come so naturally and consumes more chunks. This leads to a "confirmation bias," which means we look for positive evidence that actions have had the desired effect and hence were correct, but we rarely look for evidence to prove it is incorrect; for example, that our actions have resulted in a dangerous side effect, or that a counter example exists as illustrated by the vowel/odd numbers card problem.

You are given four cards; on each card there is a number on one side and on the other a letter. A rule states that if there is a vowel on one side then there must be an even number on the other. Which two cards should be turned over to prove the rule true or false?

E   K   4   7

Most people go for cards E and 4. Logically, this is not correct because the rule states a vowel-even number link and not the converse, so finding a consonant on the reverse of 4 proves nothing. The correct answer is E and 7 because if 7 happens to have a vowel then the rule is wrong. The rule says nothing about consonants (K) and nothing about even numbers always having vowels on the opposite side.

Some of these problems can be alleviated by use of external memory to represent the problem, but there is no substitute for careful thought to ensure that a mental model of the domain is as complete and accurate as possible. Limitation on working memory and mental model formation can be reduced by use of external memory representations, as diagrams, sketches and lists; UI metaphors and affordances for action in virtual worlds can suggest appropriate mental models of the system to the user.

Levels of Reasoning

The way we reason is critically determined by memory. The more we know about a problem the easier it is to solve it. The influential model of problem solving proposed by Rasmussen (Rasmussen, 1986) has three modes of reasoning according to experience of the domain. If we have never come across the domain before then we have to reason from first principles, general rules of thumb, or heuristics. After some experience, partial problem solutions are stored in memory as rules or declarative knowledge. Reasoning still requires some effort, as rules have to be organized in the correct order to solve the problem. Finally, after further experience has been gained, rules become organized in memory as procedures, that is, runnable programs that automatically solve the problem. In this case, we have solved the problem and stored it in memory. Recognition of the correct calling conditions then invokes the automatic procedures (or skills) that consume less effort. People tend to minimize mental effort whenever possible so there is a natural tendency to use skills and to automate procedures with practice. Hence, if we can recognize a previous solution to the problem in hand (e.g., via analogical memory), we will try to reuse it (Sutcliffe & Maiden, 1992). This is the human equivalent of running programmed and precompiled knowledge.

Acquisition of skill is influenced by the same factors as memorization. Frequent, regular learning sessions help skill acquisition whereas gaps without practice cause forgetting; positive feedback during task performance helps automation, as does presenting a clear model of the task. Redundant feedback only confuses.

Skill and automatic processing are important because they enable parallel processing to occur, reduce the need to attend to external stimuli, and decrease the load on working memory. The penalty we pay is that sometimes automatic procedures are triggered in the wrong circumstances, even when environmental cues obviously contradict the course of action. In such situations we make errors. Errors may be either slips that are attention failures in carrying out a correct sequence of actions, or mistakes when the plan of action was misconceived in the first place (Reason, 1990). Slips are usually caused by a distraction or failure in attention so that a step is missed out or not completed. True mistakes, however, are either a failure in matching the correct procedure to the problem or incorrect reasoning at the rule-based level. The implications for UI design are that functions and manipulations should be structured to help users solve problems and that we need to design UIs that anticipate or prevent users' slips and mistakes. This is particularly important in safety critical systems. We need to consider how users will reason when they are using the computer system, and help the user to construct a clear mental model by building on appropriate parts of the user's experience. For instance, if they know little about the domain (novice users), then the designer should provide ways of learning procedures from rules.

A summarization of the design implications of reasoning and mental models follows:

- A clear mental model of the domain can be promoted by using familiar metaphors, virtual worlds, animated diagrams, or interactive simulations to engage the user in active problem solving. This encourages better depth of encoding in memorization.
- UIs should prevent or contain human error, both slips and mistakes. This involves detecting errors, containing the consequences of errors, and helping users correct the situation.
- The allocation of functions between people and machines, and the degree of automation, should be informed by analysis of how people will reason within a domain. Skilled procedures that are deterministic are candidates for full automation, whereas domains with rule-based reasoning suggest decision support rather than full automation.
- The poor ability to hold negative facts in mental models increases confirmation bias and leads to mistakes when we assume all is well without seeking evidence to the contrary. Clear feedback on positive and negative (side effects) of action can help.
- We reason by applying procedures to memorized facts and environmental information. Domain knowledge and reuse of previous solutions is important for learning new user interfaces. Designers need

to beware of inconsistency between applications, and negative transfer effects when metaphors or affordances in virtual worlds do not suggest appropriate actions because the user's previous experience clashes with the system model.

- Problems are formulated as mental models that are a collection of facts and their relationships held in working memory. The limitations of working memory can be partially alleviated by external representations in the UI, for example, cues, prompts, and memory aids.

- Reasoning is heuristic in situations when little is known about the problem. The early stages in learning a new system are the most difficult, when we know little about the problem. Experience leads to the results of reasoning being stored, first as declarative, rule-based knowledge, and then as automatic procedures. We can reuse knowledge of previous systems to short-cut the learning process, but the old and new designs have to be consistent for effective transfer of knowledge.

- Automatic procedures, or skills, have calling conditions. Mismatch between memory of a previous application and the current system can lead to inappropriate reuse and usability errors. Failures can lie in analogical memory, poor cues for retrieving previous solutions in metaphors and object affordances in virtual worlds.

Attention

The information-processing model (see Fig. 2.3) demonstrated that several input/output channels compete for the resources of the cognitive processor and working memory. Visual and auditory input competes with other senses, for example, touch, smell, and pain. In addition, the cognitive processor has to find time to access memory and control output to the motor processor and speech buffer.

Attention enforces a sequential process and limits our ability to do two or more mental tasks concurrently. Try reading a newspaper and listening to the radio at the same time; either the radio or the newsprint will be remembered but not both. Attention is selective; the best we can do is to time-slice between channels so we remember part of what the radio announcer said and a few things from the newspaper article. In spite of our considerable capacity for concurrent processing, there is a limiting sequential bottleneck in cognitive processing. Resource rationing has to occur and like a computer this is controlled by scheduling with interrupts for important events. If little of interest is happening in the environment, we pay little attention to sensory input. The instant something unexpected happens, for example movement in peripheral vision, our attention is immediately switched to the sensory input. Our attentional apparatus is finely tuned to ignore constant states and pick up changes in the environment. Attention is also affected by motivation. This is the internal will of an individual to do something, which can be influenced by physiological factors (e.g., hunger, sleepiness), psychological factors (e.g., fear), and social issues such as companionship and responsibility.

The demands on attention are considerable. Take a scenario of listening to another user's instructions while trying to carry out a task in a virtual environment (such as surgery training mediated over the Internet). Audio input is coming from the instructor at the same time as sound input from the VE (sound of patient's heart or breathing), so the user has to separate the speech from other significant audio and understand them both. All speech and important sounds have to be understood with the help of long-term memory and the results held in working memory. Meanwhile, the user is visually scanning the VE to pick up cues about the locations of objects to plan what to do next. Visual information also has to be held in working memory. On top of this considerable load, the user is running a cognitive process to analyze what the instructor has said, to plan and interact in the virtual world, and invoke motor processors to control the user's hands to create action in the VE. Furthermore, the attention scheduler may also have to control further processes that look at the instructor, and decide to reply if they have two-way voice communication. Thus, up to 10 separate processes may be running just to listen to an instructor, monitor change in the virtual world, as well as planning and carrying out action within it.

The only way we can deal with so many separate threads is by time-slicing between each process, just as a multitasking computer operating system gives a little processor time to each task. Our brain polls each input channel and runs some processes in background while one is in foreground. Computers have very fast processor cycles to enable multitasking. People are also good at multitasking but there are limitations. The aforementioned scenario is close to the limit. Most people find listening, planning, and acting while speaking very difficult.

Care has to be exercised that multisensory interfaces do not produce too many competing demands for attention. For example, attention tends to be diverted by change; hence dynamic media such as film, animation, and sound will dominate static media such as pictures and text. Because speech and video overwrite working memory in a continuous input stream, we find it difficult to extract much detail, so important facts need to be recorded in static media, that is, text and diagrams. If too much information is presented at once the attention scheduler cannot cope, leading to information overloading and exceeding our capacity to understand and then either memorize the important facts or make notes. Information overloading leads to breakdown of human information processing, the symptoms of which are manifest in stress and task failure.

Implications for design follow:

- Dynamic media contain change by definition and these attract attention more strongly than static media.
- Change in static media (e.g., highlighting) will attract attention.
- Two or more dynamic media will compete for the user's attention, and this can lead to stress and fatigue.
- Media presentation has to be under user control or designed to avoid information overloading.
- Limit multitasking, unless skilled procedures are involved.

Motivation and Arousal

Motivation is a complex phenomenon that affects task performance, decision making, and attention. It can be decomposed into arousal that tunes our senses to attend to certain stimuli; intrinsic motivation that reflects factors internal to the individual's own will; and extrinsic motivation linked to properties of an external stimulus. Attention is influenced by the difficulty of the task, by distraction in the environment, and motivation of the individual. More difficult tasks hold attention better than mundane ones, which explains why most people will read a good book without degraded attention but watching a blip on a radar screen soon becomes boring and performance suffers. However, content plays a more important role. We rapidly find a boring politician's speech de-motivating because of the topic or the way it is delivered in a monotonous voice. Motivation is important in task design. Designers should try to motivate users by giving them the appropriate level of interest, responsibility, and reward for performance. Of course, these variables interact; for instance, if we are hungry (intrinsic) and smell cooking with garlic (extrinsic stimuli) and have had previous good experience of garlic-tasting food (arousal effect by priming), then our motivation to seek out and buy the food will be increased.

Arousal is poorly understood. Dynamic media (video, speech) are generally more arousing because we find these stimuli harder to ignore than static images or text. Natural images such as landscapes have calming effects and tend to reduce our arousal; in contrast, images of designed artifacts and usual objects stimulate our curiosity and tend to be arousing. Space rockets apparently have a particularly arousing effect. Arousal is influenced by our good or bad reaction to content, termed valence by psychologists. Dangerous, threatening (chased by a tiger), gory (mutilated body), and erotic content all increase arousal, whereas pleasant images (e.g., flowers, sunset) tend to decrease it, that is, have calming effects (Reeves & Nass, 1996). Arousal also affects memory. We remember events after unpleasant incidents more effectively than events beforehand (proactive inhibition). Unpleasant events become highly salient memories, but proactive inhibition often suppresses what led up to the event, making eyewitness testimony unreliable (Baddeley, 1986). The interaction between arousal, motivation, and attractiveness is complex. If we try to predict why someone should be motivated to look at a Web site and then purchase a product, the variables involved are numerous. The layers of possible influences on motivation follow:

- *Media*—Image, especially moving image, attracts attention and increases our arousal. However, too much animation can rapidly become annoying and distracting.
- *Aesthetic design*—This is significant if the visual image conforms to our idea of a pleasurable image. However, defining what is pleasurable for different people is not easy, as the history of modern art demonstrates.
- *Information and content* play a key role in several ways. First, information can persuade the user that a multimedia Web site is useful, or that a product is worth purchasing. Second, the Web site might project the image of the owning organization to motivate the user by engendering trust.
- The *design* may have preselected the user to match their needs (intrinsic motivations) with the content, product, or service on offer (extrinsic motivation). Rewards can be offered to maintain the user's motivation, for example, loyalty bonuses.

The links between arousal, motivation, and attention are illustrated in Fig. 2.8. Each cognitive component has some influence on all the others. Selective attention controls our response to external events. This is partly an automatic process triggered by moving stimuli, but we also have conscious control of our attention. Arousal interacts with the attentional mechanism by tuning our responses to stimuli as well as making events more memorable (proactive and retroactive inhibition). Arousal increases what we generally call excitement, and this increases our curiosity to investigate events and take action. Motivation in turn is influenced by our intentions and the task. Goals prime our attentional mechanism to search for particular information within media input, and memory also influences the process of comprehension. Finally, motivation and prior knowledge affect our arousal and responsiveness to certain content; for instance, memory of a lover increases the probability of our attention to a photograph of him or her.

The links and interactions are complex and still poorly understood in psychological theory. The nature and strength of these influences is still a subject of active research. Motivation can be divided into short-term extrinsic motivations that are triggered by environmental stimuli, and intrinsic motivations that resemble long-term goals or needs. Motivations can be ranked

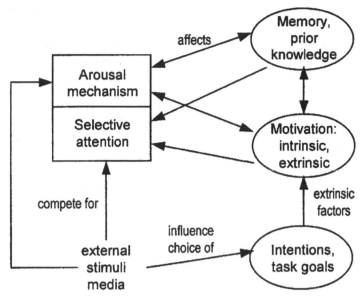

FIG. 2.8 Components of cognitive architecture associated with attention, motivation, and arousal.

in a series of satisfiability (Maslow, Frager, McReynolds, Cox, & Fadiman, 1987), from basic survival needs (hunger, thirst, shelter), to reproductive drives (sex, find a partner), curiosity (learning), individual self-esteem (job satisfaction), societal influence (power, politics, possessions), and altruism (benefit for others). Once basic motivations have been satisfied, other motivations come into play, but they have large interindividual differences. Sex (and reproduction) is one of the more powerful motivations, demonstrated by the rapid growth of pornographic Web sites that match high intrinsic motivation (more strongly but not exclusively for men) with the necessary content. Once basic food purchasing has been satisfied, motivations for self-esteem, curiosity, and power come into play in subtle combinations. Motivation becomes critical when we want to attract users with multimedia; unfortunately, it poses a severe user-modeling problem. Although some motivations (sex, hunger) are predictable basic needs, other motivations are complex and individually different. Furthermore, our motivations change with experience and over time. The advertising industry has been trying to analyze motivations of audiences for many years with only moderate success at the level of groups of people. In UIs, the growth of personalization will make new demands on our ability to understand each other's motivation.

Emotion

Emotion is the visceral feeling that is closely linked to motivation and arousal. Emotion controls our behavior, our interpretation of situations, and strongly influences memory. In physiological terms, it can be considered as activation tags on memories that, when activated by events, cause feelings. At a cognitive level, a useful taxonomy of emotions from Ortony, Clore, and Collins (1988) distinguishes three types of emotion: reaction to events, perception of attributes, and response to agents (see Fig. 2.9). Emotions may also relate to oneself or feelings about others. Most emotions can be mapped to appropriate words in English, but this is not always true. For instance, anticipation of a future undesirable event might evoke worry at a low intensity and fear at a higher intensity. If the event doesn't happen, we will feel relieved; however, if it does, we don't have a good description for "fear confirmed."

Emotions can play important roles in the design of avatars and animations via the expression of gesture, body posture, and facial expressions. Furthermore, emotion is reflected in dialogue content and prosody in speech.

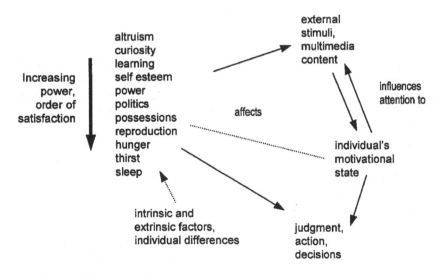

FIG. 2.9   Types of emotion (after Maslow).

Reactions to agent emotions such as sadness, joy, reproach, or guilt are important motivations for dialogue planning. Reaction to objects may also influence avatars' or agents' behavior, but these emotions (like and dislike) can be manipulated by design for attractiveness in multimedia.

Stress and Fatigue

Fatigue may result from continuous mental activity in over-long, mundane tasks and from intense concentration in tasks demanding difficult mental reasoning. In either case, rest is required for the human attention system to readjust itself. Fatigue can be caused by repetitive tasks containing no break points. Long, continuous tasks should be broken up by rest periods in which the user is allowed to do a mental reset. These break points, called "closure events," should be placed at natural intervals during a task. The more complex a task, the more demanding and potentially fatiguing it will be; consequently, break points should be planned with task complexity in mind.

Task complexity, however, does not always lead to increased fatigue. People find stimulating but demanding tasks interesting. Complexity may hold their attention and delay the onset of fatigue for some considerable time, although highly demanding continuous activity should be avoided because users may be unaware of their tiredness and make mistakes. Mundane, nonstimulating tasks are liable to cause fatigue precisely because they do not stimulate interest and hence hold attention. Such tasks should best be avoided but if they are necessary, a high frequency of break points helps to combat the strain of enforced attention.

Fatigue can also be caused by sensory factors. Strong stimuli, such as bright colors, intense light, and loud noises, all cause sensory overloading as they bombard the perceptual system and demand attention. If exposure to such stimuli continues for a long time, the cognitive system will try to ignore the steady state in the environment; however, such strong signals are not easily ignored. This sets up a conflict in the attentional process that can become fatiguing.

This concludes the brief review of the psychological background to design. In the next section, the implications from psychology are summarized in the form of design principles for multisensory UIs, that amplify and extend those proposed for more general UI design, for example, ISO 9241, part 10 (ISO, 1997).

PRINCIPLES FOR MULTISENSORY USER INTERFACE DESIGN

Principles are high-level concepts that are useful for general guidance, but they have to be interpreted in a context to give more specific advice. A more complete list of the multimedia design principles in ISO 14915, part 3 (ISO, 1998) is given in Appendix A.

General Multimedia Principles

- *Thematic congruence*—Messages presented in different media should be linked together to form a coherent whole. This helps comprehension as the different parts of the message make sense by fitting together. Congruence is partly a matter of designing the content so it follows a logical theme; for example, the script or story line makes sense and does not assume too much about the user's domain knowledge—and partly a matter of attentional design to help the user follow the message thread across different media.
- *Manageable information loading*—Messages presented in multimedia should be delivered across modalities at a pace that is either under the user's control or at a rate that allows for effective assimilation of information without causing fatigue. The rate of information provision is a function of the quantity of information present in the message, the effectiveness of the design in helping the user extract the message from the media, and the user's domain knowledge and motivation. Some ways of avoiding overload of the user's information-processing capacity are to avoid excessive use of concurrent dynamic media and give the user time to assimilate complex messages.
- *Ensure compatibility with the user's understanding*—Media should be selected that convey the content in a manner compatible with the user's existing knowledge; for example, the radiation symbol and road sign icons are used to convey hazards and dangers to users who have the appropriate knowledge and culture. The user's ability to understand the message conveyed influences selection of designed image media (diagrams, graphs) when interpretation is dependent on the user's knowledge and culture.
- *Complementary viewpoints*—Similar aspects of the same subject matter should be presented on different media to create an integrated whole. Showing different aspects of the same object, for example, a picture and a design diagram of a ship, can help memorization by developing richer schema and better memory cues.
- *Consistency*—Help users learn an interface by making the controls, command names, and layout follow a familiar pattern. People recognize patterns automatically, so operating the interface becomes an automatic skill. Consistent use of media to deliver messages of a specific type can help by cuing users with what to expect.

- *Reenforce messages*—Redundant communication of the same message on different media can help learning. Presentation of the same or similar aspects of a message helps memorization by the frequency effect. Exposing users to the same concept in a different modality also promotes rich memory cues.

Principles for Virtual Reality Applications

Multimedia principles are augmented by the following list for VR applications that reduce the user's learning burden and make virtual worlds more predictable. Some principles are directly motivated by psychology and encourage design that helps users to learn (compatibility, natural expression), or accommodate the cognitive limitations (close coordination); others are motivated by the need to foster a sense of presence or naturalness in VEs. Some principles owe their heritage to Nielsen's (1993) general GUI design heuristics, for example, clear entry and exit points. Principles for VR applications follow:

- *Natural engagement*—Interaction should approach as far as possible the user's expectation of interaction in the real world. Ideally, the user should be unaware that the reality is virtual.
- *Compatibility with the user's task and domain*—The virtual environment and behavior of objects therein should correspond as closely as possible to the user's expectation of real-world objects and their tasks.
- *Natural expression of action*—The representation of the self or presence in the VE should allow the user to carry out tasks and exploration in a natural manner and not restrict normal physical actions.
- *Close coordination of action and representation*—The representation of the self-presence and behavior manifest in the VE should be faithful to the user's actions. Coordination of action and feedback without delay is important to avoid disrupting skilled behavior.
- *Realistic feedback*—The effect of the user's actions on virtual world objects should be immediately visible and conform to the laws of physics and the user's expectations.
- *Faithful viewpoints*—The visual representation of the virtual world should map to the user's normal perception, and change in the view by head movement should be rendered without delay.
- *Navigation and orientation support*—The users should always be able to find where they are in the VE and return to known, preset positions; unnatural actions such as flying through surfaces may help but these have to be judged in a trade-off with the naturalness heuristics.
- *Clear entry and exit points*—How to enter and exit from a virtual world should be clearly communicated to the user.

- *Consistent departures*—When design compromises are used they should be consistent and clearly marked, for example, cross-modal substitution and power actions for navigation.
- *Support for learning*—Active objects should be cued and if necessary explain themselves to promote learning of VEs. Base the layout of the VE on the user's episodic memory.
- *Clear turn taking*—Where system initiative is used it should be clearly signaled and conventions established for turn-taking.
- Sense of presence—Multimodal cues and immersion of peripheral vision give users a better sense of being in the virtual environment.

Conventional HCI Principles

Besides the aforementioned multimedia and VR specific principles, there are other general HCI principles that are applicable to multisensory interfaces. Briefly, these principles follow:

- *Compatibility*—This is the goodness of fit between the user's expectation and the reality of an interface design. This principle follows on from consistency to state that new designs should be compatible with, and therefore based on, the user's previous experience. If this is followed, recognition is enhanced, learning is reduced, and the interface should be easier to use. Compatibility relates to the concept of users' models; the essential concordance is between the user's mental model of the task and the operational model embedded in software.
- *Predictability*—The interface should always suggest to the user what action is possible. This may be by messages, prompts, and so forth, or information may be contained in metaphors and icons in GUIs. Predictability has a subprinciple of observability, which states that the current state of the system should be made explicit to the user. An example would be highlighting a graphical object with "handles" showing that it has been selected.
- *Adaptability*—Interfaces should adapt to the user in several ways. The user and not the computer should be in control, so the interface adapts to the user's speed of work and does not enforce continuous attention. Also, the interface should adapt to individual user characteristics, skill levels, and so forth, as to do otherwise would offend the compatibility principle. Adaptability, however, must not be overdone, otherwise the consistency of the interface is reduced.
- *Economy and error correction*—Interface designs should be economic in the sense that they achieve an operation in the minimum number of steps necessary and save users work whenever possible.

Shortcuts in dialogues, setting defaults, and not allowing the user to get into states causing damaging errors, for example, deleting all files without backups, are examples of this principle.

- *User control*—The interface should function at the user's pace and according to the user's commands, and should not attempt to control the user. This principle is related to predictability, as users should be able to forecast what to do next from a system's current state. A subcomponent, reversibility, states that users should be able to backtrack at will when mistakes are made. Reversibility is manifest in "undo" commands and should be possible for most actions in VEs.

- *Structure*—Interface designs should be structured to reduce complexity. We deal with complexity in the environment by imposing order on it. Classification and structuring of information are consequences of this propensity to organize. Structuring should be compatible with the user's organization of knowledge and not overburden memory. This leads to a subcomponent of simplicity and relevance; information should be organized so that only relevant information is presented to the user, and in a simple manner.

SUMMARY

Perception is the process of seeing and hearing. Our vision is divided into a small area of central vision where we see detail and much larger peripheral vision where movement is detected but no detail is seen. We scan images by rapid eye movements using central vision. Images and sounds are received and coded in an abstract form. Memory may supply a considerable amount of what we see and hear which creates illusions in some circumstances. Human information processing is composed of sensory, cognitive, and motor processors with associated short-term and long-term memories. Short-term or working memory has limited capacity that may be expanded by increasing the level of abstraction of information. Information in short-term memory is held in chunk form and has to be refreshed frequently. Long-term memory has an infinite capacity and can be thought of as a highly networked database. Memory is essentially semantic, and has several different forms of organization, for example, procedural, categorial, analogical, and script- or event-based memory.

Problem solving involves steps of formulating, searching, and verifying problem solutions. It consists of forming a mental model as a network of goal substeps, each of which has tests associated with it. Various methods are used by people to solve problems. Human reasoning is not strictly logical; instead, we form mental models of problems and reason by association. Problem solutions are stored as skills and automatic processes which are called by a context. Mismatch of calling context and automatic behavior can cause errors.

Human information processing is essentially sequential although considerable concurrent processing occurs. Information processing models describe architecture of the human mind. Two influential models are the Model Human Processor (MHP), which is composed of processors for input, cognitive, and motor functions with working and long-term memory, and Interacting Cognitive Subsystems (ICS), which proposes a distributed processing model. Sequential scheduling is controlled by attention that directs the resources of the cognitive processor. Attention is related to arousal and motivation. Arousal can be considered the level of excitement created by input stimuli, whereas motivation is a complex processing of matching internal needs and goals with external stimuli and opportunities for action to satisfy our needs. Attention has important consequences for task design. Fatigue affects attention and sensory processes and should be considered in task design. Arousal and motivation have important consequences for user interface design via choice of media, selection of information content, design for attractiveness, and aesthetics. Emotion controls our feelings and reactions to situations. Emotions are governed by our reaction to events, agents and objects, and have a good or bad valence and an intensity. Emotions have important design implications for agent-based dialogues.

From knowledge of psychology, seven general principles of interface design can be drawn: consistency, compatibility, adaptability, predictability, economy, user control, and structure. Multisensory interfaces add thematic congruence, manageable information loading, ensuring compatibility with the user's understanding, complementary viewpoints, consistency, and reinforcing the message. VR principles are natural engagement, compatibility with the user's task and domain, natural expression of action, close coordination of action and representation, realistic feedback, faithful viewpoints, navigation and orientation support, clear entry and exit points, consistent departures, support for learning, clear turn-taking, and sense of presence. These principles should increase the effectiveness of interface design that may be measured in terms of attractiveness, efficiency, task fit, and usability.

3

Models of Interaction

Designing multisensory interfaces poses complex problems not found in designing graphical user interfaces. Interaction can be mediated by different devices, speech, and natural language. Information can be presented in a complex mixture of image, sound, speech, and so forth. Furthermore, we interact within interfaces in virtual worlds, whereas in "ubiquitous" computing, the interface is distributed among various devices. In multisensory systems, the interface itself may not be a recognizable entity, as virtual environments become so realistic that we don't notice the computer. In ubiquitous computing, the interface may vanish in wearable computers. However, the design problem does not go away. To achieve effective and transparent interfaces we need to design interaction to fit with the user's expectation of action in the world.

Design could rely on guidelines and principles derived from psychology, but that doesn't help to plan dialogues and UI services in an integrated manner. To help integrate knowledge from psychology within the design process, a set of models describing interaction is proposed, to link the cognitive resources and design features required at different stages of interaction. The starting point is Norman's (1986) model of interaction that is already familiar to many and has served well as the underpinning for cognitive walkthrough methods for usability evaluation (Wharton, Reiman, Lewis, & Polson, 1994). Norman's model describes goal-directed action in general terms but it doesn't account for exploratory, opportunistic behavior that is commonplace in complex multisensory interfaces; it also does not describe behaviors in reaction to external stimuli. Hence an extended model is necessary, not only to deal with these aspects but also to link psychology to design so that we can predict the design features that should be required in a particular task context (Sutcliffe, 2000).

65

Ideally, theory should underpin all design. Although this has been a holy grail for HCI researchers, success in connecting theory and design has not been realized in the general case. This chapter is a modest contribution to this debate, so before embarking on an explanation of the theory, it is necessary to situate this endeavor within the wider field of HCI theoretical contributions.

Psychological theories of human–computer interaction are extensions of more general cognitive models of reasoning and problem solving. Preeminent among these is the ACT–R/PM model created and refined over a number of years by John Anderson and colleagues (Anderson & Lebiere, 1998). ACT–R is a computational model of cognition that predicts how people reason and problem solve. It consists of components that model working memory, long-term memory, and reasoning, with an attention scheduling mechanism. Problems have to be described in a propositional form of facts and goals to be achieved. ACT–R will then predict learning and problem solving, including typical errors that people make when working memory's capacity is exceeded. Various cognitive phenomena such as the Stroop effect can be faithfully reproduced. The weakness of ACT–R is that all input had to be coded in propositional form. This has been partially alleviated by PM (Perceptual Motor extension), but that still requires preprocessed input. ACT–R/PM does not have an image, speech, or audio processor so configuring the model to process even a simple interface such as a menu takes considerable effort.

Other cognitive theories that model perceptual cognition, such as LICAI (Kitajima & Polson, 1997) and EPIC (executive process input controller; Kieras & Meyer, 1997), provide mechanisms for an architecture of perceptual and cognitive processors with rules that predict the user's attention, recognition, and understanding of UI features. However, these models also required propositional input, so dealing with complex multimedia UIs involves considerable effort in converting a UI into a detailed, abstract description. Inevitably, there are many subjective judgements involved in this process, so the theory may only predict behavior within the ambit of the input provided by the analyst.

Theoretically EPIC and ACT–R/PM might be able to answer questions about user behavior with multimedia applications, but they depend on preprocessing of complex multisensory input. The cognitive architecture has to be supplied with a list of objects attributed with perceptual properties to represent a computer display. The motivation to invest preprocessing effort will depend on the perceived payback in answering industrial-scale design questions. More effort may be expended in modeling the user than is justified by the benefits gained in predicting the affordances that should be designed.

Barnard (1991; Barnard & May, 1999) has argued for families of theoretical models that address different aspects of users' cognition and interactive system designs with a means of exchanging knowledge between different theories and models. Modelers from cognitive, artificial intelligence, and software engineering backgrounds can contribute solutions to design problems from different perspectives using design rationale to summarize design issues and modeling recommendations (Bellotti, Buckingham Shum, MacLean, & Hammond, 1995); however, this study did not show how knowledge could be exchanged between models from separate academic traditions, although some progress has been made on linking cognitive and software engineering models (Harrison & Barnard, 1993). Unfortunately, design rationale has little to offer in organizing the semantics of knowledge exchange, so more rigorous definitions of HCI issues and arguments are required to create a lingua franca for designers and researchers. Barnard and May (1999) provided a partial answer in Transition Path Diagrams (TPDs), which are derived from running a computational cognitive theory (Barnard's ICS augmented with task or domain knowledge to create a Cognitive Task Model; CTM). TPDs represent snapshots of the user's mental model during interaction with a specific design created by a CTM analysis; however, understanding the design recommendations from TPDs still requires understanding the CTM analysis in some depth.

In an attempt to escape from the trap of small-scope applications, this chapter follows Barnard's called for families of theories that address UI design, either by contributing to different aspects of the problem, or by connecting detailed cognitive mechanisms to more broadly-scoped models of interaction (Sutcliffe, 2000). The theory builds on an intermediate-level model of cognition proposed by Norman (1986), and links this model to Barnard's Interacting Cognitive Subsystems (Barnard et al., 2000).

The following models are based on collaborative research with my graduate students who investigated cognitive resources for multimedia interaction (Faraday & Sutcliffe, 1997b, 1998b, 1999) and a theory of interaction in VEs (Kaur, 1998). The models have been revised and extended in light of validation experiments (Kaur, Maiden et al., 1999; Sutcliffe & Kaur, 2000) and improved in subsequent research.

MODELING MULTISENSORY INTERACTION

The theory of interaction predicts the resources the user will require and the features the design should contribute to enable successful interaction. Three components constitute the theory:

- A set of *cognitive resources* that the user contributes in solving the problem of interaction.
- A set of *design features* that the design should ideally contribute to facilitate solving the user's problem of interaction.

- A *model of interaction* that predicts the user's resources and design features that are necessary at each stage of interaction.

The models act as a bridge between cognitive theories of behavior, such as ICS that was described in chapter 2, and design guidelines. They facilitate design decisions by first indicating the design features that should be present for a usable interface, and suggest trade-offs between user abilities and design requirements, so that designs can be tailored for particular user requirements.

MODELS OF MULTIMEDIA INTERACTION

I begin with multimedia to present a simplified model before progressing to the more complex theory that addresses VR and all multisensory interfaces. The multimedia model is illustrated in Fig. 3.1.

The action side of the model is not significantly different from Norman's (1998) original model that was extended to cover GUI interaction by adding a stage for locating appropriate controls and functions (Sutcliffe & Springett, 1992). However, because multimedia are frequently information-intensive systems, interaction can be interpreted from two viewpoints:

- Information retrieval in which the users' actions are primarily directed toward navigation and browsing through an information space.
- General task-directed interaction that is similar to other UIs.

The system resources (generalized design properties) and user resources for each interaction stage are given in Table 3.1.

At the start of the cycle, the user's resources are task and domain knowledge; the system features are clear metaphors for suggesting actions, followed by comprehensible prompts, cues, and icons for action specification. Information intensive multimedia systems make considerable demands on navigation so system features are required to represent a clear structure of the information content, possibly as a visual map (Sutcliffe & Patel, 1996; Card, Mackinlay & Shneiderman, 1999). Navigation pathways are necessary to indicate where the user might locate the information he or she needs, with hints and prompts along the way, following the concepts of information scent proposed by (Furnas, 1997; Pirolli & Card, 1999). Other navigation support features are familiar in many interfaces, for example, waymarks (bookmarks in Web browsers). Controls such as the video player metaphor of fast forward, stop, and play help navigating in dynamic media streams; zoom, pan, and scroll controls support exploration in static media. Action execution requires that controls are easy to operate and within the normal human bounds of motor precision.

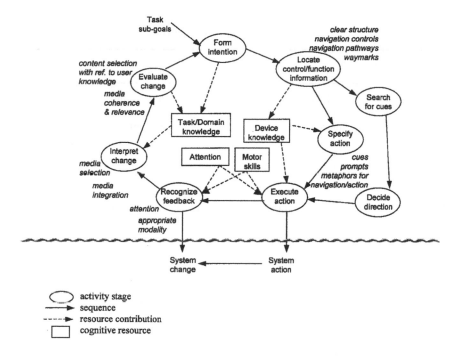

FIG. 3.1   Model of user behaviors in multimedia interaction, adapted from Norman's (1988) model of action. The stages of action are shown in circles (Norman's originals plus Locate). Design contributions for each stage are in italics.

On the feedback side of the cycle, the picture is more complex. There are two possible contexts:

- *Navigation and control*—Interpreting the effects of action.
- *Information assimilation*—Interpreting the information supplied by the system as a consequence of user requests.

Navigation and control actions involve recognizing and interpreting the effect of action on objects and evaluating change in the context of the user's task. Interpretation and evaluation depend on the user's knowledge of the navigable space and how well the system indicates the user's location therein, for example, current position. When interpreting information feedback, the user contributes domain and task knowledge to understand the perceived content, but the design needs to support the limitations in user attention or assimilating information, prevent working memory overload, and

TABLE 3.1

Generalized Design Properties

Task-Action Stage	User Resources	System Resources (GDPs)
Form intention	Task knowledge; articulate information need.	NC1 Feature hints; control cues and functions. NC2 Task-related information.
Locate information and control	Task and device knowledge.	NC3 Metaphors, information maps. NC4 Prompts, cues for command.
Search for cues	Task and domain knowledge.	NC5 Information scent cues. NC6 Lists, diagrams, thesauri to organize information.
Decide pathway and direction	Domain knowledge.	NC7 Navigation pathways on maps, waymarks.
Specify action	Device and task knowledge.	NC8 Operational affordance metaphors. NC9 Clear controls and command identifiers.
Execute action	Motor coordination.	NC10 GUI commands and controls within human abilities, links.
Recognize information and feedback	Attention, perceptual abilities.	FP1 Clear feedback. FP2 Appropriate modality, location. FP3 Highlighting and salience effects for key information.
Interpret information and change	Domain and task knowledge.	FP4, FP5 Contact points to integrate themes. FP6 Appropriate media and content selected. FP7 Congruent messages. FP8 Thematic integration.
Evaluate information and change	Domain and task knowledge.	FP9 Reinforce message. FP10 Augment viewpoints. FP11 Content appropriate for user's knowledge. FP12 Change matched user task.

Note. Generalized Design Properties (GDPs) state usability requirements and user resources necessary for each stage in multimedia interaction. The GDP numbers cross-reference to a more detailed description in appendix B. NC = navigation and control; FP = feedback and presentation.

promote comprehension and learning. At the "recognize feedback" stage, the design should first ensure the user can perceive the feedback in an appropriate medium; for example, audio feedback cannot be heard in a noisy environment. Then the design should draw the user's attention to key facts and items within the content. Selective attention can be directed by judicious use of highlighting and emphasis in different media. At the next stage, information on different media streams has to be integrated to enable interpretation at the propositional level. The design should direct users' attention by making the reading and viewing sequence apparent so that users can recognize thematic links between different media. This is effected by highlighting and attention-directing effects between media to form contact points (Faraday & Sutcliffe, 1998a, 1999; ISO, 2000). Media integration also requires the design to deliver messages on appropriate media so that comprehension is efficient. Media selection and combination guidelines play a role at this stage. Finally, when the integrated message is evaluated in context, the role of content design becomes critical. The script and selection of content should be matched with the user's existing task and domain knowledge so that he or she incrementally builds up memory schema. In training and educational applications, this is often termed scaffolding (Kolb, 1984). The new content fits into a topic or theme that the user already knows so he or she can incrementally develop his or her memory schema.

MULTIMEDIA CONVERSATIONS

Our reaction to multimedia usually treats the content of presentation as information; however, when speech and images of people are used, something strange happens. We treat the computer as a person rather than a machine. This has been known ever since Eliza fooled people into talking to a computer as if it were a person (Weizenbaum, 1983). It appears that we context switch from receiving information and acting in the world to conversational interaction with another person, although we are still clearly communicating with a computer (Reeves & Nass, 1996). The psychological reasons for this context switch are not well-understood; however, empirical evidence demonstrates we are very suggestible, so if a machine speaks to us we automatically grant it human-like status. Speech seems to be the most powerful trigger, so when we design multimedia with speech output and human image, the natural laws of dialogue have to be respected. There are still many interesting research questions about how robust this effect is; for example, the illusion of conversation rapidly disappears when the machine makes an error, and most of us are only too aware of voice-mediated telephone menu systems. Nevertheless, Reeves and Nass's (1996) experiments have demonstrated that people attribute computers with human properties although they will report that they deny consciously doing so. This has some important consequences for design. The model for conversational interaction with multimedia is illustrated in Fig. 3.2.

This model approximates closely to human–human conversation. Indeed, if speech recognition and natural language generation or speech synthesis are available, in theory there should be no difference between human–human and human–computer conversation. In the current reality, natural language understanding and speech synthesis systems are far from perfect, although quality is improving. When encountering a multimedia UI, our reaction is governed by an automatic mode or context switch. Three decisions are possible:

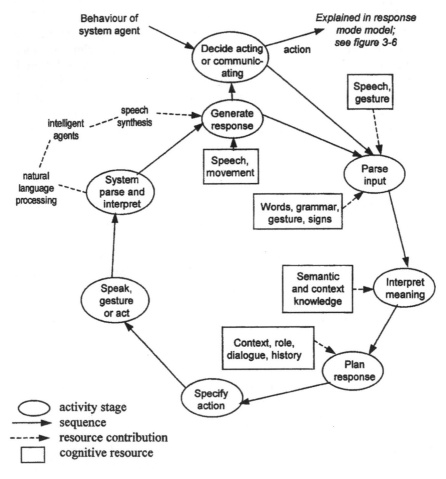

FIG. 3.2   Model of conversational interaction. See table 3.2 for details.

- The other agent is clearly inanimate and we therefore treat it as a machine. Conventional user-system interaction with GUIs and most multimedia fall into this category.
- The agent has a human-like appearance (i.e., photograph or mannequin) and is manipulating objects, so we observe the agent acting and reason about any implications. This mode is dealt with in the section on VR.
- The agent communicates by speech and/or has a human-like presence for gesture-based communication. This switches us into conversation mode.

When speech or natural language output is received, we enter conversational mode and treat the other agent as a surrogate person. The laws of human dialogue apply and we expect a polite conversation following Grice's maxims (Grice, 1975). The resources required for conversational interaction are summarized in Table 3.2.

First, we have to understand the speech output, possibly accompanied by gesture and nonverbal communication such as facial expressions. The next step, interpreting meaning, takes us into the semantics and pragmatics of natural language processing. First, we interpret meaning using linguistic, semantic knowledge, and then that meaning is refined with knowledge of the conversational context. This pragmatic knowledge consists of our awareness of whom we are conversing with, any previous history of interaction with that person, and the conversational setting and time that it is taking place. Thus, we interpret a reply to our question "How do I get to the railway station?" with knowledge about where we are (the starting point), what we can see (navigation cues), the time (how long it will take us to get to the station), and our assumptions about the person we asked. We will probably trust the reply of a friend more than that from a complete stranger. Conversational interaction is governed by pragmatic knowledge of the context, a shared common ground of understanding, and assumptions about a cooperative purpose (Clark, 1996). Conversations are built up by developing a shared common ground of understanding between the two parties. Dialogue progresses toward a common goal by an action ladder of stating propositions, explaining and clarifying the proposal, and leading to agreeing action. The design problem is how to communicate shared intent and how the system can understand the human user's goals. This is a difficult problem for artificial intelligence to solve, but it can be finessed by restricting the dialogue to a known domain.

When we plan our response, we employ pragmatic knowledge, and then articulate our response in language or action. If the system has natural language processing capabilities, it has the same problem of interpreting our utterance in context. This takes considerable common sense and specialized

TABLE 3.2

User and System Resources in Conventional Interaction

Conversation Stage	User Resources	System Resources
Decide action or communication	Task and domain knowledge, dialogue history, knowledge of other agent.	Clear communication of action or speech.
Parse input	Language lexicon and grammar (Morph, Artic subsystems in ICS).	Render speech, text, or animate image of agent's gesture or action.
Interpret meaning	Task and domain knowledge, language semantics, dialogue history, context, agent's role, personality.	Not applicable, unless intelligent agent with image and natural language understanding.
Plan response	Task and domain knowledge, context, agent's role, personality, discourse plans.	Dialogue history, explanation of agent's intentions, attitudes.
Specify action	Device and task knowledge, language semantics, and syntax.	Not applicable.
Speak, gesture, or act	Speech generation, motor coordination.	Receptor devices: microphones, image analyzers, gesture and action capture devices.

Note. The system's parse and interpret stages have been omitted because they require the same resources as the user's parse and interpret stages. ICS = Interacting Cognitive Subsystems.

domain knowledge. Not surprisingly, machine capabilities for true multimodal communication are limited to narrow, domain-specific sublanguages where the interpretation problem is tractable.

In multimedia, we have an increasing ability to personalize computer conversations. This can be implemented in several ways. Video can show a person speaking to the user; a synthesized image or avatar can represent human presence with facial expressions and gestures; or speech may be used to talk to the user. To hold a real person's attention, we have to be polite, interesting, and helpful. Computers that adopt human properties are going to have to follow the rules of polite conversation. When we address another person, we look at them to make eye contact. Averting the gaze signals attention to another task and breaking off a conversation. At the beginning of an exchange, we show interest and give a subconscious greeting by raising eyebrows. Verbal greetings when we meet people and take our leave (hellos and goodbyes) should also follow the conventions of politeness (Brown & Levinson, 1987). The content of speech can dramatically effect how we react to the content; for instance, praise from a computer will make us more favorably disposed to a following suggestion. These issues are elaborated in chapter 4.

Finally, we need to note that context switching is related to multitasking. From skill-based learning, we know that people can switch contexts rapidly when multitasking; swapping between conversing with a passenger while driving a car is a case in point. This review of multimedia interaction leads into the next stage where we consider multisensory interaction theory in more depth. First, the set of cognitive resources supplied by the user are described in more depth.

COGNITIVE RESOURCES

These are divided into a set of knowledge structures the user should possess and a set of more general resources in which demands are made on interaction. The latter are better considered as limitations of human information processing that may lead to mistakes and errors if the design does not take them into account. Some cognitive resources are general requirements for interaction so they are not strongly associated with any particular interaction stage or context; however, other user knowledge resources can be associated with interactive contexts. Knowledge structures are memories employed by the user to solve the problem of interaction. Naturally, these will change with experience as the user becomes familiar with the system; furthermore, each knowledge structure will improve incrementally with experience. However, even experienced users may have partial models of some parts of a system so knowledge structures are rarely perfect. For design purposes, a stereotype simplification has to be assumed with novices possessing minimal knowledge and experts having richly developed memories. Knowledge structures are classified as follows:

- *Task knowledge* is composed of plans, procedures, and actions. A good description of task knowledge can be found in Johnson's Task Knowledge Structures (Johnson, 1992). Briefly, tasks are composed of goals organized in a hierarchy. Upper-level goals form the task plan. Lower-level subgoals are decomposed into procedures that are in turn composed of actions organized in sequences with control constructs of alternatives (if-then-else) and iteration (do-while).

Task knowledge is generally assumed to be well-developed in expert users, and represents the skill they bring to operating the system. Learning how to operate a system and to adapt to the design is a critical aspect of learning a new system. Task knowledge should integrate with device knowledge, so learning to use a system flows naturally as an extension of the known task.

• *Domain knowledge* is composed of objects organized in class hierarchies, with attributes describing objects and relations. Domain knowledge structures complement task knowledge as actions change the state of objects (Johnson, 1992); however, domain knowledge will also include the user's spatial and episodic memory, as well as more abstract knowledge of the domain in categories and semantic networks. Novices (in device knowledge) may bring good domain knowledge to interaction, which the design should exploit by appropriate metaphors and representations of the domain in VEs.

• *Device knowledge* represents the knowledge the user has accumulated about the system. This, initially, will be nil or minimal, but increases as users learn the system. Device knowledge has the same components as task and domain knowledge: procedures, actions, objects, and so forth; indeed, it is an extension of both task and domain knowledge. When users learn to operate a new system, they extend their task knowledge to include procedures for operating the UI controls. In a perfectly designed VE, interaction would require no extension of task knowledge; the user just operates the virtual tool as a real-world one. Unfortunately, that is rarely the case in practice, and the designer's job is to minimize the amount of learning imposed on users. Although users will have little initial device knowledge, it is rarely nil. Most people transfer their experience of previous systems to a new UI. Unfortunately, we have adapted to certain styles of GUI interaction (e.g., menus, palettes, etc.) that may not transfer so well to multisensory UIs, so device knowledge may cause learning interference effects.

• *Status knowledge* is knowledge of the current state of interaction, so unlike the previous knowledge structures that are retrieved from long-term memory, status knowledge is held in working memory. It describes the user's current model of interaction and the interactive world, and where he or she is within it, and may be viewed as the subsets of task, domain, and device knowledge recruited to working memory at a point in interaction.

• *Motor skills* coordinate precise action with multisensory feedback. Ideally, real-world skills should transfer into virtual worlds; however, lack of haptic feedback means that manipulation skills have to be relearned. Motor skills are an extension of device knowledge.

The system design should encourage the development of device knowledge, easy maintenance, and update of status knowledge. Design has a paradoxical role; on one hand, device knowledge needs to be minimized so that the computer becomes invisible, but on the other hand, technology may change the way we work for the better, in which case the design has to be explicit and help the user learn new actions and procedures. In tutorial applications, the design actually needs to impart domain and task knowledge to the user. In this case, although the device knowledge should be easy to learn, the role of the design may need to make learning effortful to be effective, because active problem solving helps depth of encoding (see chap. 2). There will be other trade-offs that have to be made, as we shall see later.

The second set of resources are the general cognitive facilities required by the user during interaction. These are subdivided into perceptual resources for receiving input, cognitive resources that will utilize knowledge structures in memory, and action resources necessary for the user to act on the world or communicate with others. Cognitive theories like ICS can be interrogated as "tools for thought" with different scenarios or snapshots of interaction to determine which subset of the following list of cognitive resources will be necessary. The appropriate component of the ICS model with the resources is given in parentheses and are identified as follows (the first list consists of perceptual resources, the second list consists of cognitive resources, and the third list consists of action resources):

- *Vision*—The ability not only to recognize but also interpret the image (Vis, Obj).
- *Audio*—Hearing and sound interpretation (Aud).
- *Speech recognition* (Morph).
- *Tactile ability* to detect properties of surfaces and temperature (BS).
- *Proprioceptive* sense of balance and muscle tone for posture (BS).
- *Selective attention*—The automatic control of perceptual resources between competing stimuli.

- *Working memory* to hold status knowledge and subsets of task, domain, and device knowledge.
- *Language processing ability* to understand the content of spoken or written language (Prop).
- *Comprehension* to interpret change in visual and other sensory inputs and make sense of the integrated input (Obj, Prop).
- *Problem-solving abilities*—Understanding the causation of perceived events and reasoning (Implic).
- *Planning*—The ability to organize and rehearse future action and communication (Implic).

- *Attention and concentration*—The ability to continue problem solving and learning how to interact without becoming distracted or giving up.
- *Motivation*—Internal volition which underlies attention and concentration.

- *Planning movement* in detail (Implic, Prop).
- *Locomotion*—The ability to move (Lim).
- *Manipulation of objects* by grip, hand, and limb movements (Lim).
- *Speech generation* (Artic).
- *Gesture*—A generation of gestures with head, arms, and body, including facial expressions (motor).

The combination of resources used will depend on the user's experience and level of knowledge. Experienced users need a combination of perceptual and action resources but they do not have to exercise conscious control over them because they run as precompiled skills. In contrast, novice users have to actively analyze perceptual input and control motor output at a higher knowledge- or rule-based level. This requires more cognitive processor resource at the implication and propositional level, which makes interaction slower and more error prone. The use of cognitive resources can be illustrated by the example of interpreting the multimedia image in Fig. 3.3. This is taken from a tutorial sequence that explains how cancer cells divide and invade other tissues. The design aims to increase the user's domain knowledge about human biology by giving a causal explanation. The cognitive resources (using ICS subsystems) are understanding the image (Vis→Obj→Prop), making sense of the speech track that accompanies it (Aud→Morph→Prop), and then integrating the message on both modalities (Prop→Implic). At the basic resource level, the design does not seem to present any problems; however, when the role of attention is considered, a potential problem arises. First, animation is used selectively for some parts of the explanation. The sequence should have transferred the following domain knowledge:

- Cancer cells multiply in the epidermis (skin).
- Cancer cells invade the body by chemically attacking the basal lamina and entering blood vessels.
- Cancer cells are transported through the vascular system.
- Cancer cells invade the liver and other tissues by dissolving cell walls.

Animation focuses the user's attention on the movement part of the explanation (cells invade liver via blood vessels) to the detriment of other key facts (chemical attack) that appear only in the speech track. Hence, the (Prop→Implic) cycle will be unlikely to integrate all the information that was presented. The concept that cancer cells invade by chemical attack is less likely to be learned (Faraday & Sutcliffe, 1996). Besides the role

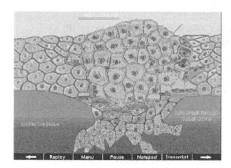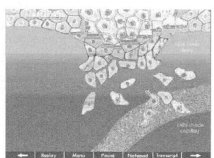

FIG. 3.3   Multimedia screenshots from cancer sequence.

of attention, the use of visual and audio (speech) media will reinforce the explanation of cell movement because two media streams come together with a single proposition for the movement sequence (skin→blood ves‑ sels→other organs). The user's mental model of the explanation is not constructed effectively because the necessary background information is not given to describe how the cancer cells invade other organs. A more ef‑ fective strategy would have been to establish the cancer cells' means of at‑ tack first (by chemical assault on other cells) and then build the explanation while visually cross‑referencing where the attacks take place (on the basal lamina, blood cell walls, and liver membrane). One may ar‑ gue that this omission was a failing in content selection or pedagogical de‑ sign by the authors, and indeed that may be true. However, the point of modeling is to make that omission explicit. A more general mapping of in‑ teraction stages to ICS processes and other cognitive resources is illus‑ trated in Table 3.3.

In the gulf of execution parts of the Norman (1988) cycle (Plan–Spec‑ ify–Execute), the ICS processes transform plans as implications to prop‑ ositions and then to limb and detailed motor actions. In the gulf of evaluation side (Recognize to Evaluate), sensory input is transformed in the opposite direction from multisensory input into propositions and im‑ plications. Sensory and motor skill resources are needed in the Execute and Recognize stages; long‑term and working memory are necessary for other stages. Attention is a necessary resource throughout the cycle; however, it is more critical in the Specify–Execute–Recognize–Interpret stages where slips and lapse errors result from attentional failure.

Another example of resource analysis involves the sequence of inter‑ action in a VE illustrated in Fig. 3.4. This involves resources for planning

TABLE 3.3

Associations Between Interacting Cognitive Subsystems (ICS)
Process Stages in the Interaction Models and Cognitive Resources

Stage	ICS Processes	Other Cognitive Resources
Form intention	Implic	Memory retrieval, LTM task knowledge, motivation, reasoning.
Locate information and control	Vis→Prop→Implic Morph→Prop→Implic	Central and peripheral vison, attention control, memory.
Search for cues	Implic→Prop→Vis Vis→Obj→Prop→Implic	Attention, visual scan, search strategy, central vision.
Decide pathway and direction	Implic	Working memory, LTM, reasoning.
Specify action	Implic→Prop	Working memory, skill in LTM.
Execute action	Prop→Lim→Morph→Artic	Motor skills, visio-motor coordination.
Recognize information and feedback	Vis→Obj→Prop	Attention, visual and audio acuity, working memory.
Interpret information and change	Prop→Implic	Attention, LTM domain knowledge, working memory.
Evaluate information and change	Implic	LTM domain knowledge, reasoning, working memory.

and specifying action as well as interpreting feedback. In the screenshot shown in Fig. 3.4 the user has to find out how to alter the position of the drawing board. In reality, there are several controls that change angle and tilt, but in VR, only one is active so the user receives inconsistent feedback from trying affordances. Thus, the user's domain knowledge does not transfer to the virtual world device knowledge. Because the rule that a device which suggests action (an affordance) will respond to manipulation is not generally applicable, either the user has to substitute the impaired domain knowledge by testing all or possibly some interactive objects, or the design should indicate which objects are active by vi-

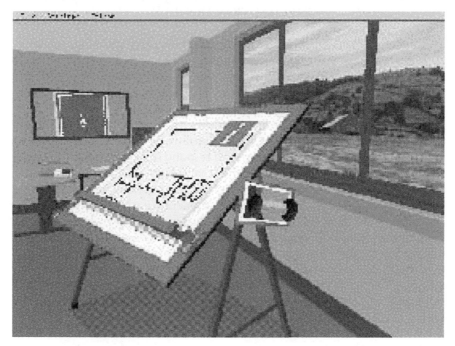

FIG. 3.4   Drawing table example from business park Virtual Environment. Image courtesy of Virtual Presence Group.

sual cues. Imposing the sampling load on the user overloads working memory and attention resources. First, working memory is strained by the need to remember which objects should be and have been sampled; this distracts attention from the user's task, and hinders planning. Memorizing which specific objects are active does not allow any general rule to be learned, so the user's device knowledge will only increase slowly. Learning interaction by a few general rules is easy, whereas devices with many specialized rules impose a worse memory burden, as demonstrated by TAG (Task–Action Grammar; Payne & Green, 1989).

Even if the system did signal that the object was active, when manipulation was attempted the lack of haptic feedback would create two contradictory input channels: (Vis→Obj→Prop) indicates an affordance for action whereas (BS→Prop) does not give a sense of touching a handle because no tactile feedback is built into the system; hence the user is forced into concentrating on visual control of manipulation. This shows how the user's resources and knowledge structures can be integrated with the ICS model to analyze potential usability problems; however, we can refine this analysis by considering models of interaction.

INTERACTION MODELS

The model is composed of three cycles or submodels. The most important cycle is task-based activity, when the user is trying to achieve a goal. Subordinate to this cycle is navigation and exploration, when the user's intention is simply to find his or her way around the VE. In some cases, exploration may become a task goal in its own right. We distinguish between goal-directed exploration and serendipitous browsing in which the user's goal is not clearly formed. The third cycle describes system initiative when the user's role is to interpret actions taken by the system and respond to them when initiative is returned, or interrupt and seize initiative from the system if necessary. System initiative may be a manifestation of action by other users represented as avatars in collaborative VEs; and multiparty interaction in shared virtual worlds. The models describe behavior during normal interaction. Errors occur when the necessary cognitive and system resources are not present at any particular stage of interaction. Errors introduce a behavior subcycle of error recognition, diagnosis, and remediation that may occur at any stage when users make mistakes. First, normal error-free behavior is described; error prediction and recovery is introduced to use the models for usability evaluation in chapter 6. Each model is now described in more detail.

Task-Action Model

Fig. 3.5 illustrates the main task–action cycle. The task–action cycle is driven by the goals in the user's task model. There are two loops: an outer one which starts with goal formation from which the user forms an intention to achieve a task goal or subgoal and retrieves the appropriate procedure from memory; and an inner one that runs through each action in the procedure. Procedures are scripts of actions that achieve the task goal, so the user will commence interaction with an intention to carry out the first action in the procedure. The first step is to scan the immediate environment for any affordances for action. Affordances are any design feature that matches the user's intention and suggests how to act; for instance, a handle on a coffee cup indicates that it can be picked up. If the objects necessary for the first task–action are not visible, then the user has to search the environment for them. This leads into the navigation subcycle and exploration until the necessary objects are found or the user gives up. The next step is to specify action. How an action is specified depends on the modality choice available to the user. Modality selection depends on the ease with which the modality or device matches the user's goal. Speech may be efficient for commands and invoking automated procedures, but for movement and precise manipulation, physical interaction will be necessary. Modality choice may also be influenced by habit. We are used to interacting physically with com-

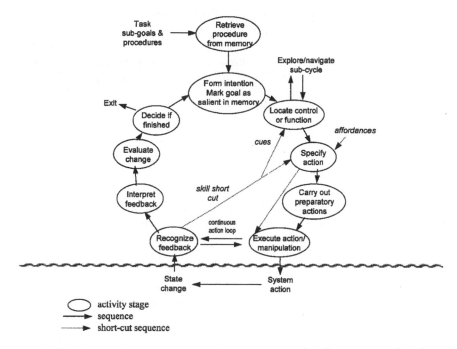

FIG. 3.5   Stages in the task-action cycle, adapted from Norman (1988), and Kaur et al. (1999).

puters, so swapping to speech can be inhibited unless users are trained to use speech in particular circumstances.

Assuming that manipulation has been chosen and a familiar part of the VE is found with the necessary objects, then the user has to locate the objects, approach, and orient his or her self-representation in the correct position for interaction. This may invoke movement for the preparatory action. With simple shapes and large objects in an uncluttered environment, this step may not be necessary. For traditional GUI features, the action specification step is simplified to finding the appropriate control or UI feature that triggers an action.

Specifying action is followed by executing action. Actions may be simple controls, manipulating objects in virtual worlds, or operating virtual tools. Actions that involve movement to a target become progressively more difficult as the size and proximity of the target decrease. This relation is expressed in Fitt's Law (see chap. 2). Actions are followed by feedback from the environment, or the effects of tools on the environment. In continuous actions, manipulation and feedback are interleaved as the user may adjust action in light of feedback. First, the user must receive and recognize the feedback and then interpret the change. Problems may arise if the change is not immediately perceivable; for example, feedback may be given in an inappropriate modality or in a location not expected by the user. Interpreting and evaluating change involves making sense of the perceived input (ICS propositional and implicational level). Once an action is complete, the user may continue to the next specify–action by loading the next action from procedural memory. However, if interaction has caused change in the VE that obscured the necessary objects, then the user may have to search for affordances, reorient, and approach again. Alternatively, if the end of a procedure has been reached, then the user proceeds to the next task goal and the cycle resumes.

Specification of action may be determined by retrieving task procedures from memory or by problem solving in response to the environment. Action specification is shaped by what is available via display-based cognition (Kitajima & Polson, 1997), in which the user's perceptions of affordances shape action. Hence, the task model stage is not completely sequential: location, intention, and action specification may overlap. The main connotation of the procedure-driven versus display-based cognition is that the VE needs to shape intention and action more directly. Because there is considerable evidence that users specify action using environment cues (Kitajima & Polson, 1997; Reiman, Young, & Howes, 1996), by following menu cues and graphical icons, display-based interaction is likely to be the dominant mode in VEs.

Pathways through the model will change with experience. Novice users will progress through each stage under conscious (knowledge-based processing) control. This will invoke longer resource cycles in the ICS model chaining from the top implication level to action and back up to implication as feedback is interpreted. The chain of processing for novices and experts with shortcuts in the task-action model are illustrated in Fig. 3.6.

Skilled knowledge short circuits the cycle between interpret change and specify action. The user simply checks that the effect of action conforms to the expectation of the procedure (see script and procedural memory) and then continues with the next action. In highly skilled procedures, action may become an unconscious activity that loops between recognize feedback and execute action. The disadvantage of skill is that slip errors can occur (Norman, 1988). When the user is familiar with the device, procedural memory has been laid down that specifies the necessary action, so simple memory-fetches shortcut the need for implicational processing. Once the task commences in response to an event trigger, the appropriate rules and procedures are retrieved from memory. The degree of automation will depend on the detail of the user's procedural memory. In a perfect case, the user memory contains the location of actions and their specification, thus leading directly to execution.

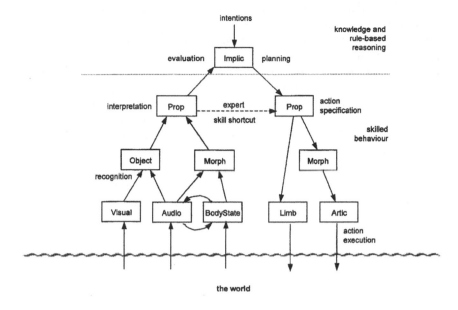

FIG. 3.6   ICS architecture (see figure 2.4) re-interpreted to map Norman's (1988) model of action and Rasmussen's (1986) levels of reasonings.

However, if some aspect of the environment does not accord with memory (e.g., an object has been moved), then conscious rule-based processing intervenes for approach and orient. Similarly, skilled action may relegate feedback recognition to an automatic process so that interpretation and evaluation are not necessary. Unfortunately, although skilled operation is cognitively efficient, it can easily lead to errors from slips in attention or failure to recognize unexpected feedback.

System Initiative Model

Reacting to events and behavior of other agents in VEs, or when the system takes control, is described in the system initiative cycle. The importance of reactive behavior was highlighted by Suchman (1987), who made the case for considering most user behavior as reactive or situated action; however, the proportion of reactive behavior depends on the task and application. In some domains, planning and task-driven interaction will be the norm; in others (e.g., games), situated action will predominate. Reactive or opportunistic behavior may either require reasoning at the knowledge-based level if the stimulus and its context are unfamiliar; or, if it has been encountered before, a preplanned automatic response can be triggered.

System initiative may occur at any stage in task–action when an event interrupts the user's action. If the system initiative is communicated by speech, or action involves human-like presences in the virtual world, then we will switch into conversational mode (see Fig. 3.2). In conversational systems this cycle may become the dominant mode of interaction as the user monitors the behavior of other agents (or their avatars) and then responds to their messages. Behavior in this subcycle (see Fig. 3.7) reverses the task–action cycle. First, change is observed, evaluated and interpreted, and then action is planned in response. Planning may involve deciding what to do by reasoning at the knowledge level if the situation is unfamiliar or retrieving procedures from memory and running

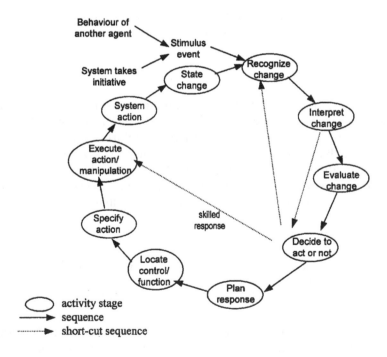

FIG. 3.7   Stages in the system iniative cycle. Dotted lines indicate shortcuts while the user monitors an event sequence before responding; the dashed line shows the skilled response shortcut.

these precompiled responses. The user may allow the system to retain the initiative until the action sequence terminates, or to interrupt. In the former case, the observe–interpret loop continues until the system action ceases, when the user plans a response and carries it out. If the user decides to interrupt and regain the initiative, action is specified and executed, and the subsequent effects will be recognized and evaluated to determine success. Action may then transfer back to the task–action cycle; however, in groupware applications, interaction will continue as an interlinked set of conversational turns between different users, each taking the system initiative. Expert behavior depends on possessing memory of the triggering stimulus and the appropriate response, whereas novices have first to analyze the implication of the system's behavior and then actively plan a response.

Exploration and Navigation

System exploration is frequently embedded within task–action or system initiative cycles when the user needs to find information or discover parts of the interactive world. Exploration, illustrated in Fig. 3.8, has two main modes. In serendipitous exploration, the user has no specific goal in mind, so interaction is composed of a series of scan environment→specify direction→navigate→recognize and interpret change loops. If interesting objects or information are encountered, these may be memorized for subsequent use or explored further by manipulation, which is modeled as goal-directed exploration. The main difference between goal-directed and serendipitous exploration lies in the interpretation and evaluation part of the cycle.

In goal-directed exploration, the user decides what to find and then forms a plan about how to find it. If the environment affords no clues about where to look for the search target, the user may resort to guesswork. Interaction proceeds by a loop of scan→navigate→interpret; the interpretation is whether the user has found, or is closer to, his or her goal. Serendipitous exploration follows the same cycle but omits planning as the user follows cues that look interesting. Interpretation may be cursory if the new location does not evoke interest; however, if it is does, then further exploration cycles may be invoked. The dividing line between goal-directed and serendipitous exploration is finally one of degree. Hints of interest encountered during browsing may lead to goal-directed navigation; locating a target object may stimulate exploration of its immediate environment. Exploration reverts to the task–action cycle when the appropriate part of the environment is found and evaluated to be relevant. In some applications, goal-directed exploration is the main user task, so interaction may reside primarily within this subcycle.

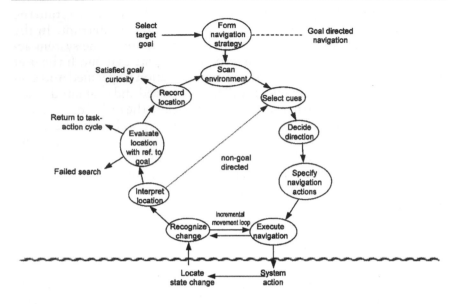

FIG. 3.8   Stages in the navigation–exploration cycle. The dashed line illustrates serendipitous exploration shortcut and continuing cycles before the target is found.

Novice–expert differences are reflected in different pathways through this cycle. Complete expertise is interpreted as the user knowing the desired location and going directly to it; for example, direct access facilities help expert users by navigating directly to an address. Other interpretations of partial expertise range from some knowledge of the search environment, so that the user does not need to form a plan or scan the environment for cues, to knowledge of search strategies but with little knowledge of the environment. This case is closer to novice behaviors where navigation becomes a conscious planned process.

The models of interaction are general descriptions of how user action should occur for a novice user. With expert users, stages in the cycle will become increasingly automated and unconscious, so navigation becomes a closely coupled loop of action interleaved with feedback.

Context Switching

The theory proposes that we act and react in virtual worlds in different modes. The link between these modes will not be consciously recognized, so if users are asked to think aloud while interacting in VEs, they are unlikely to report any perceived change between navigating and task action. Nevertheless, modes have powerful effects on how we act. This is because we load different goals and knowledge into working memory when we make the transition across a mode boundary. The nature of these transitions is depicted in Fig. 3.9.

The first mode switch is between immersed and nonimmersed interaction. This is not dealt with explicitly in the models because it is a property of display. Immersive interaction with head mounted displays or CAVE technology fills our peripheral vision with the virtual world. We are less aware of the computer and its interface, hence the virtual world becomes the context for interaction. In contrast, desktop VR presents us with two contexts, one virtual world displayed by the computer and the external world. Our sense of presence is reduced and the illusion of acting in the virtual world is not so powerful.

The second mode switch is between conversational and traditional interaction. Transitions across this boundary are mediated by speech and display of human image. This mode has a powerful effect on our interpretation of the information communicated by the other party. When conversation is generated by people and mediated by computers, as in chat rooms, MUDS, MOOs (multiuser dungeons, multiuser object oriented systems) and virtual world implementations thereof, the interface should become invisible be-

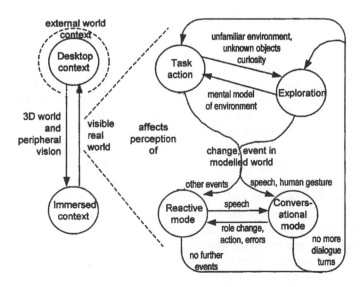

FIG. 3.9   Context switching between the interaction models.

cause interaction is governed by the laws of human discourse. When faced with speaking avatars, we react according to our expectations of human–human discourse and treat the avatar as a person, irrespective of whether it is visibly a computer agent. This mode exerts a powerful effect because we load very different assumptions into working memory when we converse as opposed to when we act.

The boundary between exploration and task-action is rarely noticed, as we often have to investigate objects and explore virtual worlds to achieve task goals. Although we can switch rapidly between these modes, there is still a cognitive effort in context switching while we refocus attention on task goals in working memory. The switch between task-exploration and reactive mode is more dramatic and noticeable. This is because the flow of reasoning is reversed. In task-action and explore mode we are engaged in a plan-act-interpret cycle (Implic→Prop→Lim→motor in ICS terms); whereas in reactive mode, the flow is switched to interpret-plan-react (Obj→Morph→Prop→Implic→Prop→Lim). Sometimes when we are deeply engaged in a task or exploration, we fail to notice messages and don't make the appropriate switch to reactive mode.

DESIGN FEATURES

UI design features are the third component of the theory. Because these change as technology advances, generalized usability requirements are specified. These are called GDPs: Generalized Design Properties, which can be mapped to more concrete design components that implement them. To effect this mapping, the knowledge representation schema of claims analysis and the task-artifact theory may be used (Carroll & Rosson, 1992; Sutcliffe & Carroll, 1999).

GDPs are organized into groups motivated by general design issues in VR and multimedia, and usability support requirements implied in the interaction models. The first and second groups record general usability requirements. The third group involves supporting action planning and specification, and facilitates user navigation in its various forms. The fourth group supports execution of action and interpreting feedback, and the final group supports reactive behavior. The GDPs selected for an application depend on the communication modality, user's knowledge, task, and the naturalness constraints imposed by the domain. For example, in multimedia systems, facilities for navigating through complex information structures are necessary and these may be manifest as maps, metaphors, and visualizations of classification structures. In contrast, for a VR training application, a realistic representation of the domain will be necessary so that the user can encounter all aspects of the system although some features may not be easy to learn. In many VR applications, the need for natural representation may override adding artificial features that could improve usability (e.g., wayfinding maps). Appendix B describes GDPs with correspondence rules linking them to appropriate stages in each cycle.

Design features put in place the third component of the theory. The next step is to integrate the models, cognitive resources, and design features to produce a model of design requirements for normal interaction, and then to explore errors that result from any departures from the normative model.

INTEGRATING RESOURCES AND ACTION

Knowledge sources, design features, and user behavior are integrated by rules that predict the requirements for successful interaction. The theory balances the cognitive resources possessed by the users with the facilities that should be supplied by the system. Some cognitive resources are general throughout interaction (such as working memory limitations); however, knowledge resources change. Users start as novices with little device knowledge but become experts with comprehensive device knowledge. As users learn the system, their needs for support change. To deal with the problem of adaptivity, the theory adopts the stereotype solution of proposing two rule sets, one for novices and one for experts.

The general form of the rules follows:
@ ModelStage(x)
   IF UserResource(a) is present and DesignFeature(GDP–b) is present
   THEN interaction will be successful
   ELSE UsabilityErrorType(c) is probable.
Resources and features complement each other to deliver effective use but their interaction depends on the level of user knowledge, so specialization of the rules is given for novices and experts.

Novice rules have the general form:
@ ModelStage(y)
   IF ResourceKnowledgeStructure(x) is minimal
   THEN Features(GDPs a, a^1, a^{11}) should be present.
Expert rules have a similar form:
@ ModelStage(y)
   IF ResourceKnowledgeStructure(x) is complete
   THEN Features(GDPs a, b, b^1) should be present.

Some example rules follow:
Form Intention Stage
Expert

IF Task Knowledge is complete
THEN GDPs IAS1 (system services), IAS2 (information),
    IAS3 (modalities), should be present
ELSE functionality mismatch error.

Novice

IF Task Knowledge is minimal
THEN GDPs IAS4 (tutorial), IAS5 (task maps) should be present
ELSE goal formation error.

Locate Feature Stage

Expert

IF Domain/Task Knowledge is complete
THEN GDPs IAS6 (layout), IAS7 (expected location) should be
    present
ELSE hidden functionality error.

Novice

IF Domain/Task Knowledge is minimal
THEN GDP IAS8 (feature search) should be present
ELSE goal formation error.

Experts will share some system features with novices but new ones will be necessary such as power effects, and ability to change and customize interaction. Rules are instantiated to predict novice requirements for more supportive and error-preventing design features; in contrast, experts require more powerful features with less support. Departures from the expected expert (or novice) profile will result in a usability problem, and this theme is taken up in the "Error Diagnosis and Recovery" section. The current section deals with normal interaction. Application of GDPs has to be judged in light of HCI principles; for instance, in VEs the naturalness principle overrides GDPs that recommend system initiative to help the user. Indeed, there is a more general trade-off between helping the user by representation, metaphor, and affordances, in contrast to system initiative, wizards, and assistive agents (Shneiderman, 1998). GDPs do not apply exclusively to a single stage, but may be inherited by subsequent stages. For instance, GDPs that support goal formation will usually be relevant to the locate command–function stage, and possibly to the action specification stage. The rules recommend when GDPs should be deployed during the interaction cycle; however, when they are removed depends on the designer's judgment. In most designs, GDPs in the goal to action side of the cycle (i.e., gulf of execution) will be replaced by a different set for feedback in the gulf of evaluation.

GDPs specify the requirements for usability. In some cases they recommend specific design features, but more usually the general requirements have to be interpreted by the designer in the context of the application. Each rule indicates one or more GDPs so the designer still has to interpret the theory's predictions in light of the task and domain requirements. For instance, one filter is to eliminate GDPs that recommend intrusive design features, when naturalness of the VE is required by the task. Another limitation on GDPs is the ability to analyze the user's task and intentions accurately. If the user's intentions cannot be captured, then plan-related or system initiative GDPs cannot be deployed. Listing rules can make for laborious reading (see Appendix B for details), so the working of the model will be illustrated by two scenario walkthroughs: one for a multimedia system and one for a VE.

Multimedia Interaction

Interaction with multimedia systems is simpler in terms of action but involves complex navigation and evaluation. The user's task is to make a reservation to see a play by Shakespeare, so the application involves information searching and then transaction processing to make a booking. The screen in Fig. 3.10 shows the search screen to choose a play.

At the *planning* stage, the user has to decide how to search for a play. The user has good domain knowledge about Shakespeare's plays and knows what he or she wants. Task knowledge for searching and making a booking is not complex and can be considered to be complete. However, because we assume a novice user, device knowledge will be low. The system should provide one or more of the goal formation GDPs, such as task-related cues and feature hints. The system gives two options, search by browsing a time line of what is coming in the next few months, or search the theater's catalogue for current and future productions. Appropriate commands are listed in a top-level menu so that interaction can proceed.

The user has to *locate* the play he or she wants, and the interface needs to provide GDPs to help the user locate the appropriate search function. This is supported by GDPs (clear prompts, information scent) that recommend search facilities to find information, as well as browsing along a time line display that adopts an appropriate metaphor for the underlying information. This gets the user to the decide direction stage. The user decides to select a play from the time line, which supports the action specification, followed by action-execution stages. The system highlights the play and the duration of its run (recognize and interpret the feedback stages) and provides highlighting and feedback GDPs to implement perceivable effects of change, and structures the plays in a time line schedule to ensure that changes match task and domain knowledge.

The user progresses to the next goal in his or her task, *making a booking*. The first subgoal is to establish the prices and availability of seats. The system supports this by a menu option (GDP feature hints) that the user selects; this leads to display of a seating plan (GDP appropriate media for the message) highlighting the available seats according to the selected date

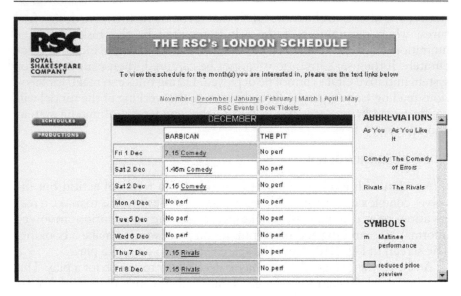

FIG. 3.10   Theater booking: multimedia search screen to choose a play. Reprinted with permission by the Royal Shakespeare Company.

(GDP direct attention to key information). The user chooses a date, then selects a seat leading to a system response of displaying the price but also showing the viewpoint of the stage from that location (GDP augmented viewpoints). The user selects the seat and the dialogue continues with payment and confirmation of the booking; these steps are dealt with by a standard form-filling dialogue that will not be described further.

Virtual Reality Walkthrough

The application is an exploratory VR that demonstrates the facilities of buildings in a business park; however, embedded within the exploration are discrete tasks where the user has to operate virtual equipment to assess its suitability.

   Task-Action Cycle.   The user's task in this case is to operate a virtual drawing board in an architect's office. The links between action-cycle stages, user knowledge, and selected GDPs are given in Table 3.4, with index numbers that point to the more detailed description in Appendix B.

This cycle commences with *retrieving the appropriate* procedure from memory for the current task goal. Two problems may arise at this stage: user memory failure or inadequate task knowledge. This can be alleviated by GDPs for task maps that provide a browsable aide-memoire or a searchable task list. In the next step, *form intention*, the user loads a goal into working memory to execute the procedure. This could be supported by a status indicator to remind the user which subgoal is currently active. In the next stage, the user needs device knowledge to locate the control. To help the user, GDPs are suggested for clear structure, consistent layout, and meaningful labels, familiar advice from HCI guidelines (e.g., ISO, 1997); however, system initiative may also be deployed to actively suggest appropriate controls for the user's current task goal or to initiate the appropriate tool. However, the application demands naturalness because the user is assessing the usability of a real design in a VE, so no GDPs are added beyond natural representation of the domain.

Action specification involves detailed planning about how to act, and draws on the user's device knowledge. GDPs are for clear operational metaphors and perceivable affordances (Norman, 1988). Design of affordances depends on mapping from past experience and features that suggest specific actions (e.g., door handles that indicate push rather than pull; tool grips that suggest twisting operations). At this stage, if power tools are available they need to be explained to the user because such effects cannot be predicted from task-domain knowledge. In VR applications, preparatory actions may be necessary to approach and orient the user's self-representation into a position to operate a control. GDPs in this stage are for accessible controls and snap-to effects to help orientation without haptic feedback. *Execution of action* should be supported by visible controls that do not make above average demands on human sensio-motor coordination. The *effect of action* should be signaled by precise feedback and mapped to the physical forces expended, for example, visual feedback for contact and force; the demands of naturalness may inhibit adding these GDPs to the design. Returning to the drawing table shown in Fig. 3.4, only one control is active to tilt the table and this is not clearly indicated; other control features are located underneath the table and are hard to access. The design, therefore, does not supply GDPs clear affordances and consistent controls.

To *recognize and interpret feedback*, users need domain knowledge. The GDPs recommend locatable and perceivable feedback. This may be a problem when the effect takes place in a remote part of the virtual world, where the user is unaware of it. In these circumstances, active notification by speech or audio may be necessary. The locus of objects that have changed should be portrayed in sufficient detail to allow the change to be interpreted and feedback messages should be meaningful. The *evaluation of change* relies on the user's task and domain knowledge; however, deficiencies may be

TABLE 3.4

GDPs and User Resources Associated With Task-Action Cycle
Stages for Novice User (Cross-Referenced to Appendix B)

Task-Action Stage	Generalized Design Properties	User Knowledge
Retrieve procedure	IAS1 Task map, list of search facilities.	Task knowledge, retrieval cues, procedural skill.
Form intention	IAS2 Necessary information and status indicator.	Current task goal.
Locate control	IAS6 Clear structure and consistent layout. IAS7 Layout matches user's model.	Domain and device knowledge, virtual environment, layout and organizing, and metaphor and menus.
Specify action	IAS9 Clear affordances; power tools and controls. IAS10 Active objects, clear operational metaphor.	Device knowledge, control and operational, metaphor.
Perform preparatory actions	MA3 Accessible controls.	Domain and device knowledge, motor skills.
Execute action	MA5 Visible control. MA7 Consistent controls. MA8 Acceptable movement and precision. MA10 Precise effects commensurate with user action. MA15 Indicate proximity. MA17 Object selection by snap-to effects.	Device knowledge, motor skills.
Recognize feedback	FI1 Locatable, perceivable feedback. FI3 Active notification. FI4 Discriminable detail.	Domain knowledge.
Interpret feedback	FI6 Meaningful messages. FI7 Observable state change.	Domain knowledge.
Evaluate change	FI16 Explanation of change. FI17 Comparison of states.	Domain, task, and status knowledge.
Decide if finished	IAS2 Task completion indicator.	Task and status knowledge.

Note. IAS = intention and action specification; MA = manipulation-action; FI = feedback interpretation.

remedied by active explanation of changes and facilities so that before and after effects can be compared. The final stage of determining whether the *task is complete* can be helped by the aide-memoire status indicators, and then the cycle continues if more actions and goals are present. Changes in the position of the drawing table reflect manipulations in the real world but without any haptic feedback to represent the force exerted on the surface. The GDP modal substitution recommends use of visual feedback to signal touch and force. In the real application, usability errors were observed because this GDP design feature was absent.

Navigation-Exploration Cycle

In this example, the user's goal is to explore the buildings in the virtual world and test electrical equipment contained within the building. The task is goal-directed navigation, so the first step is to select the *navigation strategy*. The user has little domain knowledge of the buildings and their layout, or necessary task knowledge for operating switches. Task knowledge for searching is assumed, e.g., sampling strategies, random search, and so forth. The sequence of navigation cycle stages, user knowledge, and necessary GDPs is illustrated in Table 3.5.

The GDPs that the system should provide at the select navigation strategy stage follow:

- Clear metaphor and system structure.
- Guided tours.
- Overview map.
- Reusable searches.
- Explanation of the navigation controls.

In this case, the virtual world is based on the real world, so the first and third GDPs do not apply. If the representation of the building is a reasonably faithful rendering of the real world, then navigation strategy selection can rely on the user's task knowledge; e.g., search each building systematically, random sample, and so forth. Note that if the user's knowledge is deficient, then system initiative GDPs may be deployed to compensate. For instance, the system could propose strategies for navigation, or take the user on a guided tour, or provide reusable histories of previous searches. A systematic search is adopted to visit each building in turn.

The next stage, *scan environment*, only requires that the VE is visible and has sufficient detail to be discriminable. The ability to change the user's viewpoint could help scanning. This is followed by *select cue* that should be implemented by highlighting appropriate cues, landmarks, and indications of pathways. If the user's knowledge is poor, the interface can compensate

TABLE 3.5

Navigation Cycle Stages With Associated Contributions
From User Knowledge and Design Features

Navigation Cycle Stage	Generalized Design Properties	User Knowledge
Select navigation strategy	NV5 Explain navigation controls, virtual compass. NV2 Metaphor for organization, map. NV3 Reusable searches. NV5 Guided tours.	Task knowledge and search strategies, device knowledge and available facilities.
Scan environment	NV6 Perceivable detail, change viewpoint.	Domain knowledge—layout and features.
Select cues	NV7 Faithful representation. NV8 Highlight cues, landmarks.	Domain knowledge—target features.
Decide direction	NV10 Clear structure, overview map. NV11 User location. NV13 Clear pathways.	Domain knowledge—topology and status.
Specify navigation actions	NV15 Maps. NV16 Power movements. NV17 Flexible motion.	Device knowledge—controls.
Execute movement	NV19 Natural direction and orientation controls. MA8 Visible and accessible controls. MA10 Precise effects.	Device knowledge.Motor skill.
Recognize change	FI1, FI2 Locatable and perceivable feedback. NV6 Discriminable detail.	Domain knowledge.
Interpret location	NF3 User location. F13 Active notification. FI6 Meaningful messages. MA14 Proximity indicators.	Domain and status knowledge.
Evaluate change	FI16 Explanation of modes. NF5 Track/movement history. NF6 Explanation of context.	Domain and task knowledge.

Note. The navigation cycle GDPs are marked NV (navigation–planning–action stages) and NF (navigation–feedback stages). Other GDPs are inherited from the task-action model: MA = manipulation-action; FI = feedback interpretation GDPs.

with directions to the search targets depicted as highlighted pathways and landmarks, but this assumes that the user's knowledge of the domain can be captured beforehand. The naturalness compromise and lack of knowledge about the user's intentions inhibits explicit design of these features for this application. *Decide direction* is based on the user's perception and interpretation of cues with domain knowledge. GDPs in this stage recommend indication at the current location as well as pathways and landmarks for course setting. In this case, commonsense knowledge of doors indicates the direction and pathway for entering the building and rooms within it. At the *specify navigation action* stage, the user changes from domain to device knowledge. The user has to translate the desired direction and speed into action using the available navigation devices. These may be gestures with a virtual hand, operating controls on a 3D mouse, or selecting a hypertext link. Execute movement will follow, assuming that the control is visible, easy to use, and gives precise control.

Once motion is underway, it needs to be tuned with feedback to adjust course and speed until the destination is reached. Movement, recognizing, and interpreting change in location become a closely coupled loop that should be supported by perceivable and incremental feedback, clear representation of the self position, movement history where appropriate, and meaningful messages from the system. In the buildings example, feedback accords with the natural sense of motion through the virtual world as objects become closer or recede during the user's progress through the building. Domain knowledge is vital for interpreting feedback. If the user's knowledge is poor, some help can be given by explanation of any hidden states, modes, and objects within the new context. For example, as the user approaches the electric switches (see Fig. 6.10), hover text labels explain their properties and operation.

System Initiative Cycle

The GDPs selected for system initiative are influenced by the nature of the initiating event. If it represents communication from another user or an intelligent software agent masquerading as a person, then the response will follow the conversational mode. The GDPs invoked in this path support understanding, planning, and generating a natural language dialogue. If the event signals a possibly dangerous state from the environment, then interpretation and planning response actions are more important. The event may signal a change in system initiative, in which case the user has to interpret whether this is acceptable. The GDPs and user resources for the system initiative cycle are given in Table 3.6, and for interaction with intelligent agents in Table 3.7.

TABLE 3.6

GDPs and User Resources Associated With the System Initiative Cycle, Assuming a Novice User and Response to Environmental Events

System Initiative Cycle Stage	Generalized Design Properties	User Knowledge
Stimulus event	SI1 Clear message, hazard warning.	Domain knowledge.
Recognize change	FI1, FI2 Locatable and perceivable event. FI3 Active notification.	Domain knowledge—identification.
Interpret and evaluate change	FI12 Explain role and status of event source. FI18 Explain event context.	Domain and status knowledge—causal analysis.
Decide to act	SI3 Automatic response to hazard. SI6 User-system override.	Domain and status knowledge, history, roles, and attributes of agents.
Plan response	SI7 Implications of event. SI8 Diagnose hazard. SI9 Pre-planned responses.	Task knowledge—proceduralized responses.
Locate control and function	IAS6 Clear structure, consistent layout. SI10 Suggest and auto-select controls. IAS3 Appropriate modality.	Domain knowledge. Device knowledge.
Specify action	MA7 Consistent operation. SI3 Automated responses. IAS9 Perceivable affordances.	Device knowledge, agent controls, scripts.
Execute action	MA6 Visible control. MA8 Acceptable movement and precision.	Device knowledge, motor skill.

Note. SI = system initiative GDPs; FI = feedback interpretation; IAS = intention and action specification; MA = manipulation-action.

TABLE 3.7

GDPs and User Resources Associated With the System Initiative
Cycle, Assuming a Novice User and Conversational Interaction
With Intelligent Agents

System Initiative Cycle Stage	Generalized Design Properties	User Knowledge
Recognize message and action by other agent	CV1 Sender identity. CV2 Clear message, audible speech, visible gesture and action.	Role of sender, task and domain context.
Interpret message	CV4 Comprehensible semantics in gesture and speech, action in context.	Identity, role, and context of sender, dialogue history.
Evaluate message	CV5, CV7 Information on context of event. CV9 Sender's intention, social context.	Domain and status knowledge; task context of communication.
Decide to act	CV5 Status authority of sender. CV6 Conversation history. CV10 Speech generation, gesture, gaze, movement controls.	Domain and context knowledge. History, roles, and attributes of agents.
Plan response	CV6 Conversation and event history. CV12, CV13 Preplanned messages, signals, and actions.	Knowledge of language and signs (semiotics).
Locate control and function	SI10 Suggest and auto-select controls. IAS3 Select modality.	Domain knowledge of agents. Device knowledge.
Specify action	MA7 Consistent operation. SI10 Automated responses. IAS9 Perceivable affordances.	Device knowledge.
Execute action	MA6 Visible control. MA8 Acceptable movement and precision.	Device knowledge, motor skill.

Note. CV = conversation response; SI = system initiative; IAS = intention and action specification; MA = manipulation-action.

The cycle is initiated by the stimulus event that may signal that the system has taken the initiative, or it may be an external event from the environment or communication from another user or automated agent. The GDPs at this state indicate that the design should make the event clear and ensure it is perceived as a warning if it signals danger. For "recognize change" the user employs domain knowledge to identify the event and understand its content. The GDPs point out that the event should be locatable and perceivable and that active notification may be necessary for hidden events. Interpretation attaches significance to the event using domain knowledge to infer a causal explanation about why the event occurred. Planning a response will be necessary if the event or situation is unfamiliar and diagnosis of the implications of the event precedes the response decision. In safety critical systems, this gets into a considerable debate about allocating automated or human mediated responses (Hollnagel, 1998).

Alternatively, if the event emanated from a human-like agent, then it is interpreted as a communicative act and this invokes different GDPs to supply information about the identity of the originating agent, their role, character, and intentions. The decision whether to react builds on the causal and intentional analysis of the speech act, but it also requires more information about the history of the conversation and status, role and authority of the sender agent (Clark, 1996). Planning a response to an agent requires knowledge of the agent's personality. In the absence of specific information, people attribute artificial agents with human properties; for instance, they trust older personalities more than younger ones (Reeves & Nass, 1996). Locate control and specify action depend on the available communication modality: speech, gesture, or movement response.

Planning a response depends on the user's prior experience of similar events and their context. For conversational dialogue, this depends on knowledge of the sender agent, so planning is usually conscious at the knowledge-based level. For events originating in the environment and system initiative signals, explanation of the event's implications and context may be necessary, as well as access to any appropriate preplanned responses. This stage draws on the user's task and domain knowledge for proceduralized responses. If these are minimal, the system may have to take the initiative in responding automatically to hazardous events. A specialization of this is to initiate an automatic response with a user override. Alternatively, a list of appropriate preplanned responses could be provided from which the user could choose.

The next three stages have GDPs shared with the other cycles, although "locating controls" has additional GDPs for selecting the modality for response, which is important for conversational interaction; automatic selection or suggestion of controls may follow from a preplanned response.

Having integrated the models, GDPs and resources, we can now put the theory to work in design and usability evaluation. The next section describes prediction of user errors and usability problems with the models.

ERROR DIAGNOSIS AND RECOVERY

Usability problems will arise if user resources or design features are inadequate. Errors are predicted when one or more contributions for successful interaction are absent, so the rules can be used to predict errors:

IF user knowledge or system feature is not present THEN ActionStage(x) may fail.

Errors may be the responsibility of the design or the user. Design errors are manifest as usability problems during interaction, but the dividing line between user and designer's responsibility can be fine. If one user in a population experiences an error but all the others encounter no problems, then the user is probably (but not always) at fault, and training to increase device knowledge may be the cure. In contrast, if several users experience the same problem and sufficient training has been given, then the designer is responsible.

In this section, the causes of human error described in chapter 2 are revisited in the context of models of interaction. Classification of user errors follows Reason's (1990) categorization of slips, failures in attention that can be quickly corrected; and *mistakes* that arise from incorrect plans and errors in knowledge-based reasoning. *Slips* and mistakes are refined into error types that help diagnosis of usability problems by forming a bridge from observation of users' problems in interaction to pinpointing their cause in a UI design feature.

Errors may occur at any stage in the normal cycles of action. The types of possible error and their location are shown in Fig. 3.11 for the task-action model, Fig. 3.12 for system initiative, and Fig. 3.13 for navigation. In the *goal formation* stage, errors may be caused by absence of functions or services to support the user's task. These are requirement analysis failings. However, the function may be present but not visible to the user. In complex interfaces, access paths have to be provided to functions so cues support user navigation to locate the function. If preparatory actions are necessary, problems may arise from inaccessible objects and inability to navigate and orient the user presence into the appropriate position. *Action execution* has to take account of the limitations of human sensory–motor coordination. Controls that are poorly tuned or make excessive demands on human coordination cause problems at this stage. In the *feedback* stages, design-induced errors will arise from inadequate or missing feedback, and presentation of feedback in a manner that does not make sense in the user's context. Sometimes observation of a problem is not located with the cause. This is common in mode errors when the user's mental model is not consistent with the system state. An example is being puzzled when graphical objects automatically align them-

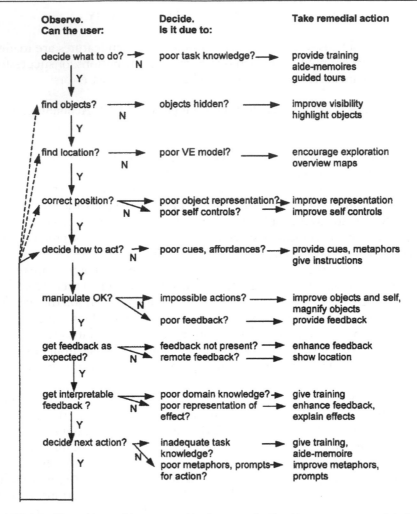

FIG. 3.11   User problems and their causes in the task-action cycle. The table suggests questions to help diagnose observed user problems by first locating where they are in the action cycle in column 1, then tracking to possible error causes in column 2, and finally indicating remedies in column 3.

selves, a consequence of not being aware of the "snap-to" auto-alignment mode. This error has three possible causes: lack of user device knowledge of the snap-to option, a working memory error in having forgotten the mode setting, or a design error in not giving mode status. These errors, and techniques to discover them from observation of users' problems, are dealt with in chapter 6.

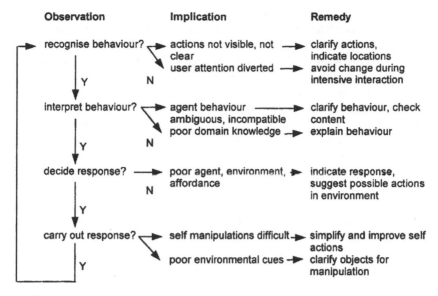

FIG. 3.12   User problems and their causes in the system initiative cycle.

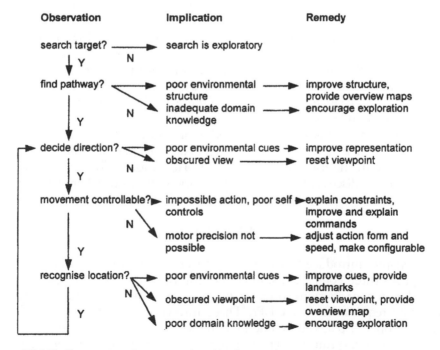

FIG. 3.13   User error types, their causes, and possible solutions in the navigation cycle.

Slips are more likely to occur at the *action execution* and recognize feedback stages. In contrast, mistakes are more probable in the *intention formation and action* specification stages, when faulty memory may result in the user applying the wrong rule to carry out a task, or applying a correct rule in the wrong circumstance. The latter is caused by a recognition error and failure to correctly analyze the current task context. Slip-errors are manifest in *action execution* and *feedback recognition* stages, when failure of attention may result in omitted or incomplete action, and failure to perceive feedback. Mistakes make their appearance again in *interpretation and evaluation of feedback*, where inadequate domain or device knowledge and reasoning failures may lead to users jumping to false conclusions.

The system initiative cycle is prone to mistakes when the original event is misinterpreted. This is common when the intentions of other agents are not clear, or false assumptions are drawn. Inadequate knowledge of the domain and status knowledge of the other party may be to blame, but inappropriate responses may also play a part. For instance, when we are unfamiliar with a system and it uses speech, we tend to attribute human-like qualities to computers and give apparently mistaken responses (Reeves & Nass, 1996). Mistakes may also be present in planning responses if domain and task knowledge are poor. Slips are more likely when the event first occurs and the response invokes an automated procedure. It may be missed or ignored if our attention is distracted.

In the navigation exploration cycle, mistakes are possible in *planning the search* and in *interpreting the change of location and feedback*. Goal-directed navigation will be more prone to mistake-errors because the user has to undertake more knowledge-based planning. Slips will happen during *navigation and feedback* perception, especially if there are distracting stimuli in the environment and features are missed.

In the *feedback* stages, design-induced errors will arise from inadequate or missing feedback, and presentation of feedback in a manner that does not make sense in the user's context (i.e., disorientation). These errors, and techniques to discover them from observation of user's problems when interacting with multisensory interfaces, are dealt with in chapter 6.

SUMMARY

This chapter introduced a theory of multisensory interaction. The theory comprises three components: models of interaction, cognitive resources, and design contributions to successful interaction that were expressed as usability requirements or GDPs. Three interacting submodels were described: one for planned task-action, one for reactive behavior to events, and one for opportunistic exploration and navigation. The models elaborate Norman's theory of action. The models describe generalized stages for action or reaction in a plan-specify action-interpret change cycle. The model stages provide the context in which user cognitive resources and system facilities are recruited to ensure usability for each stage in interaction. Cognitive resources are divided into general resource limitations of human information processing and knowledge sources which users need for successful interaction. Differences in complexity of domain, task, and device knowledge reflect novice and expert user profiles. GDPs were proposed for design requirements to support effective interaction at each model stage. Two rule sets, one for experts, the other for novices, link the contributions that the users should make with design requirements (GDPs) for successful interaction. Errors, mistakes, and slips are associated with human failings at each stage and design requirements are needed to counteract them.

4

Multimedia User Interface Design

This chapter deals with the multimedia subset of multisensory UIs. Multimedia raises special problems because most applications are information intensive, so design needs to focus on information presentation. That is not to say that multimedia systems are not interactive; indeed, the converse is the case. However, the dialogue design problems can be treated as an extension of standard GUI interaction. The more complex dialogue aspects of multimodal interaction are dealt with in chapter 5.

Multimedia applications have significant markets in education and training; however, many systems just use text and graphics with a restricted dialogue for drill and quiz interaction and simple navigation. This approach is oversimplified; for effective training and education, interactive simulations and microworlds are more effective. These necessitate more sophisticated approaches to dialogue design, which will be briefly introduced in this chapter. Multimedia has been used extensively in task-based applications in process control and safety critical systems (Hollan, Hutchins, & Weitzman, 1984; Alty, 1991); however, most transaction processing applications are currently treated as standard GUIs rather than using the potential of multimedia in design. With the advent of the Internet and e-commerce, this view may change.

Multimedia design involves several specialisms that are technical subjects in their own right. For instance, design of text is the science (or art) of calligraphy that has developed new fonts over many years; visualization design encompasses calligraphy but also considers design of images either drawn or captured as photographs. Design of moving images, cartoons, video, and film are further specializations, as are musical composition and design of sound effects. Many of these design specializations are taught in arts degree courses that teach skill by example, case study, and mentoring. This approach encourages creative and aesthetic design; in contrast, computer science encourages a systematic, engineering-based approach. Consequently, multimedia design lies on an interesting cultural boundary between the creative artistic community and science-based engineering. Although I do not intend to address the debate between these communities, I reflect on some of the tensions between them. One implication of this cultural collision (or rather, one hopes, synthesis) is that "within media" design, that is, guidelines for design of one particular medium such as animation and film, are not dealt with in depth. Successful multimedia design often requires teams of specialists who contribute from their own disciplines. Management of such teams and how they communicate is a vexed problem for further research.

The distinguishing characteristics of multimedia applications are that they are information intensive and have a complex design space for presenting information to people. Design, therefore, has to start by modeling information requirements, a topic that is not covered by most software engineering or HCI methods. This chapter starts with an information analysis then progresses to deal with issues of media selection and integration. The background to the design method presented in this chapter can be found in several publications (Faraday & Sutcliffe, 1997a, 1998b, 1999; Sutcliffe & Faraday, 1994). Other sources are the media taxonomies of Bernsen (1994) and Heller and Martin (1995), design principles (Johnson & Nemetz, 1998), user-centered design process for multimedia (Fisher, 1994), and studies of usability engineering for hypermedia (Costabile, 1999). Pragmatic graphical and multimedia design guidelines based on experience have also influenced some of the following recommendations, which have been incorporated in the ISO 14915 standard: *Multimedia User Interface Design: Part 3, Media Combination and Integration* (ISO, 2000). First an overview of the method and its stages is given, followed by more detailed description of each stage.

DESIGN METHOD OVERVIEW

The agenda which the method addresses is the creation of a task model incorporating specification of information requirements, followed by designing a coherent presentation that directs the user's attention to extract required information at the appropriate level of detail. In doing so, the design method makes designers aware of the cognitive issues underlying a multimedia presentation such as selective attention, persistence of information, concurrency, and limited cognitive resources such as working memory. Fig. 4.1 gives an overview of the method components.

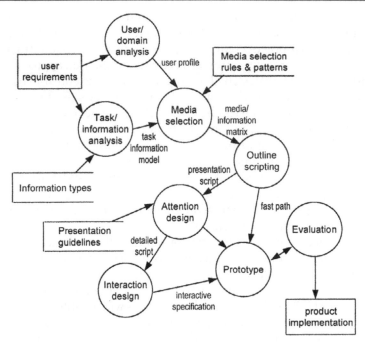

FIG. 4.1   Overview of the design method's stages expressed as a data flow diagram. Open rectangles represent method guidelines and circles represent method stages.

The method starts by requirements and task-information analysis to
establish the necessary content and communication goals of the application. It then progresses to domain and user characteristic analysis to establish a profile of the user and the system environment. The output from
these stages feeds into media selection and integration that match the
logical specification of the content to available media resources. Design
then progresses to thematic integration of the user's reading and viewing
sequence and dialogue design. The method can be tailored to fit different
development approaches. For instance, in rapid applications development, storyboards, prototypes, and iterative build and evaluate cycles
would be used. The guidelines in this case are applied both in design and
evaluation. On the other hand, in a more systematic, software engineering approach, more detailed specifications and scripts will be produced
before design commences. Notations such as UML for object-oriented

design can be adopted to fit within software engineering approaches. Although the method is described as a sequence, in practice the stages are interleaved and iterated; however, requirements, information modeling, and media selection should be carried out before the media and attentional design stages can commence.

Design approaches in multimedia tend to be interactive and user-centered. The time-to-market pressure gives little incentive for systematic design, so at first reading a complex method may seem to conflict with the commercial drivers of development. However, methods don't work by being followed as a rigorous cookbook. Maybe for the first few times the method steps and guidelines do have to be followed by referring to the manual (or this book), but thereafter the knowledge becomes internalized and the designer selects and integrates media without having to consciously think about a guideline. The background knowledge in chapter 2, models in chapter 3, and the procedural "how to do it" method in this chapter become part of the automatic design process. However, not all design is automatic. Many trade-offs have to be consciously evaluated during design, and the method's duty is to make these choices clear.

Design Approach and Technology

Design should always be user-centered as a cycle of requirements capture, prototyping, and evaluation. The important point is that users should be involved continuously. The prototype-evaluation cycle should be iterated several times, but only too often a design is tested once and then rushed to market. This approach just clutters the market with unusable products. Design needs to be based on the psychology of multimedia information processing. For example, we learn more effectively from interactive multimedia because active engagement encourages problem solving and this leads to the formation of richer memory schema (depth of encoding; see chap. 2). Consequently, tutorial multimedia should be designed where possible as interactive microworlds. Furthermore, we can apply the same principles to the design process. Requirements analysis and design refinement is an interactive process, hence interactive prototypes, simulations, and mock-ups all help. The method emphasizes specification for designers, especially software engineers; however, specifications should be developed in tandem with prototypes for user testing, because concrete examples of design stimulate reasoning.

Some variations on design realizations follow:

- *Storyboards* are a well-known means of informal modeling in multimedia design (Nielsen, 1995; Sutcliffe, 1999b). Originating from animation and cartoon design, storyboards are a set of images that represent key steps in a design. Translated to software, storyboards depict key stages in interaction with a product. Storyboards can be made semiinteractive by conducting walkthroughs to explain what happens at each stage, but this is still a passive representation. Allowing the users to edit storyboards and giving them a construction kit to build their own encourages active engagement. This is the essence of the PICTIVE method (Muller, Hanswanter, & Dayton, 1997). Other researchers are trying to extend the flexibility of storyboards toward "paper prototypes" (Wilson, Bekker, Johnson, & Johnson, 1997) that give a construction kit so that rough-and-ready sketches can be scanned into a computer and then linked in a script to create a limited animation. This approach converges with building concept demonstrators using standard multimedia or hypermedia authoring tools (e.g., Macromedia Director) to rapidly develop semi-interactive early prototypes (Sutcliffe, 1995b).

- *Wizard of Oz simulations*—One computer has a simulated interface of the application which is connected to another computer controlled by the human "wizard" who mimics more complex aspects of functionality that have not been implemented. This approach is useful for speech-based multimedia where the human mimics the intelligent agent. The user interacts with the simulation and should be unaware that part of it is still human.

- *Concept demonstrators* are active simulations that can be played or run. The simulation follows a script and exhibits behavior, but departure from the preset sequence is not allowed. The advantage of simulations is that they engage human reasoning more effectively, because we are challenged to interpret what we see. Also, several variations can be run to support comparison; however, the user experience is still mainly passive, as there is little opportunity to interact.

- *Interactive prototypes*—These are active and also interactive, so users can test them by running different commands or functions. The degree of interactivity depends on the implementation cost. At the low end, a set of scripts is provided which simulates a small number of commands. More expensive are narrow, in-depth prototypes in which functionality is fully implemented but only in a restricted subsystem, or broader, shallower prototypes that have functionality partially implemented throughout the system. Cost increases as prototypes converge with a fully functional product.

All these design realizations employ interactive media that engage our attention and thereby help requirements analysis.

REQUIREMENTS AND USER MODELING

First, the requirements for the application need to be established. It is not the purpose of this book to cover requirements analysis methods (although for details, see Sutcliffe, 1998 and 2002c); however, a brief introduction to multimedia-centric requirements analysis will be given. Requirements are expressed as goals that represent the users' intentions for the new system. These are elicited by a task analysis that develops requirements goals in task models of the user's current work and then translates this into a model of how the new system should work. However, requirements for multimedia also need to capture the designer's communication goals, as well as an outline of the necessary content. Three issues need to be analyzed:

- *The communication goals* of the application are specified in light of the domain, for example, to entertain users the communication goal might be to excite and stimulate, whereas for safety critical applications, the goals should be to warn the users and provide appropriate information for responsive planning. High-level application goals may be to educate or train; in this case, the learning outcomes need to be specified.
- *Nonfunctional requirements* (NFRs) are performance and quality of service parameters that will become benchmarks against which a design can be tested; hence, they need to be specified as measurable criteria. Some NFRs that have implications for multimedia are learnability, for which an example benchmark might be "Concepts x, y, z will be learned by 90% of the users so they can recall the information with < 5% errors after 5 hr instruction." Other NFRs are security, privacy, accuracy of information, response time, clarity of presentation, and reliability.
- *Users' information needs* may be related to their task or requirements in their own right, as in information retrieval systems, or the goal may be information provision in kiosk applications. Information may be required on different topics, levels of accuracy, at a certain cost, and so forth.

Requirements are listed and categorized into information, task-related, and nonfunctional classes. These will be expanded in subsequent analyzes.

User Characteristics

It is important to get a profile of the target user population to guide media selection. There are three motivations for user analysis:

- *Choice of modalities*—This is important for disabilities, but also for user preferences. Some people prefer verbal–linguistic material to image, and this may be linked to a gender difference (women are better with linguistic expression, and men at reasoning with spatial tasks and visual media; Richardson, 1977; Riding & Rayner, 1998).
- *Tuning the content* presented to the level of existing knowledge held by users. This is particularly important for training and educational applications.
- *Capturing the users' experience* with multimedia and other computer systems.

Acquiring information about the level of experience possessed by the potential user population is important for adaptation. Users start by being novices, but they rapidly become skilled. Unfortunately, the design has to accommodate a heterogeneous population of users, some of whom will be novices, others experts. The design solution is to provide individualization and adaptation facilities so that the user can tailor the sophistication of the interface and the information presented by preference files linked to their log-on ID. User profiles can be used to design training applications to ensure that the right level of tutorial support is provided, and to assess the users' domain knowledge so that appropriate media can be selected. This is particularly important when symbols, designed image, and diagrammatic notations may be involved.

The role and background of users will have an important bearing on design. For example, marketing applications will need simple focused content and more aesthetic design, whereas tutorial systems need to deliver detailed content. Analysis of user motivation also plays an important role. For marketing, the link to motivation is obvious; however, motivation is important for learning applications as well. A well-motivated participant will learn more effectively, so questions directed toward why users want to learn may lead to useful insights for design. A key question at this stage is whether the purpose of the system is to just deliver information or to ensure comprehension and learning. The difference may not be clear-cut. Information kiosk applications need to provide information as do task-based applications, but decision support and persuasive systems (Fogg, 1998) also need to ensure users comprehend messages. There may be several user groups or stakeholders in a population, so the role, background, and information requirements need to be recorded for each group. Design variants may then be targeted on each stakeholder group.

The following user characteristics are gathered by interviews or questionnaire:

- *General abilities*—May be captured from educational qualifications, job descriptions, or aptitude tests and used to assess the level of tutorial support in training applications.

- *Computer experience*—To determine if computer familiarization is necessary.
- *Domain knowledge*—Users may be novices or experts in the application area. Their knowledge of conventions, symbols, and terminology in the domain should be ascertained. Novices will require more complete information.
- *Preferences for media*—Some people prefer visual presentation, others are happier with language and text. This information may become part of a preference file that controls media selection.
- *User motivation*—People will have differing levels of curiosity, need for self esteem, power, and so on. Motivation is not easy to analyze because people may be unaware of their motivations or hide them. Questionnaire techniques that analyze motivations indirectly will be more effective than overt questions

More sophisticated data can be captured by use of psychological inventories that contain lists of questions to elicit personality characteristics. These inventories will be too complex for most design requirements; however, one scale that does have a direct bearing on multimedia is the visualizer–verbalizer preference (Riding & Rayner, 1998). This can be used to adjust media selection preferences for individual profiles.

Domain Modeling

The context and environment of a system can have an important bearing on design. For example, tourist information systems in outdoor public domains will experience a wide range of lighting conditions that make image and text hard to read. High levels of ambient noise in public places or factory floors can make audio and speech useless. Hence, it is important to gather information about the system environment and context of use. For example, see the following:

- *Location of use*—Office, factory floor, public or private space, hazardous locations.
- *Usage conditions*—Single user, shared use, broadcast, projected image for shared use.
- *Environmental variables* that are pertinent at the location: range of ambient light, noise levels, temperature.
- *Technology*—Distributed system, client-server architectures, and network support.
- *Expected change in location*—Change in environment, country, and culture; choice of language, icon conventions, interpretation of di-

agrams, and choice of content all have a bearing on design of international UIs.

As well as gathering general information about the system's context of
use, domain modeling can prove useful for creating the system metaphor. A
sketch of the user's workplace, recording spatial layout of artifacts, documents, and information, can be translated into a virtual world to help users
find the information and services they need. Structural metaphors for organizing information and operational metaphors for controls and devices have
their origins in domain analysis. Domain models are recorded as sketches of
the work environment showing the layout and location of significant objects
and artifacts, accompanied by lists of environmental factors (see Fig. 4.2).

Finally, the target technology needs to be analyzed. This can be difficult
in Web-based multimedia, so estimates based on surveys may have to suffice. The target technology imposes constraints on design. If most users have
low capacity PCs, there is no point in designing a sophisticated application
with video and high-resolution graphics. Technology analysis needs to establish the characteristics of the hardware and software platform that can be
expected, and network bandwidth for distributed multimedia. This part of
the domain model will constrain media selection and choice of interaction.

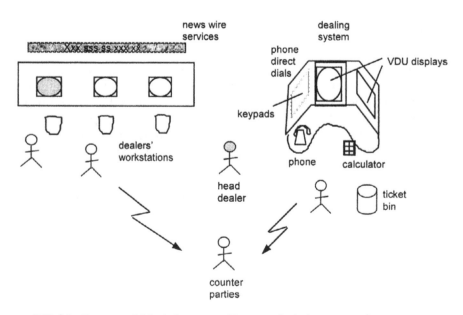

FIG. 4.2   Domain model for dealing system. Various media feeds are present for text news services, TV images for news, as well as computer screens. The system exists in a noisy environment, but there is considerable communication between the users by speech.

TASK AND INFORMATION MODELING

Task analysis focuses on the goals the user wants to achieve. However, user goals need to be supported by the design so requirements should describe how the system will help the users achieve their tasks. A typical task hierarchy diagram for an information retrieval task is shown in Fig. 4.3.

For the information-searching example, a user's requirements might be the following:

- The system shall show the user the available databases that might be searched (supports goal of *find resources*).
- The system shall indicate the relevance rating of retrieved documents (supports goal of *evaluate results*).

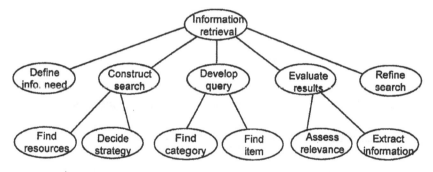

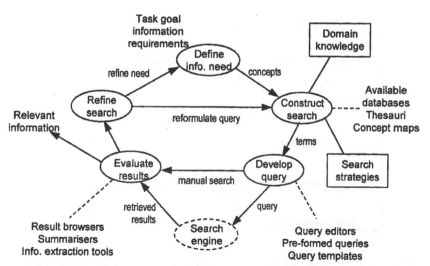

FIG. 4.3   Task knowledge structures (TKS) of information searching, showing goal hierarchy for an information retrieval task and a sequential view of the information searching process.

A useful alternative view of behavior is provided by use cases in object-oriented development (e.g., UML; Rational Corporation, 1999). Use cases focus on interaction between agents and describe the patterns of events or messages that flow between two or more agents. Use case sequence diagrams (see Fig. 4.4) model interaction and hence can complement task-oriented views. Requirements are also apparent in use cases, as each step in a sequence diagram implies the need for user support.

The circles in Fig. 4.4 identify information requirements as follows:

1. User information need or goal, available events or plays.
2. Articulate the need as search keywords.
3. Summarize search results (available plays) in a table or graph.
4. Prices of tickets, seats available.

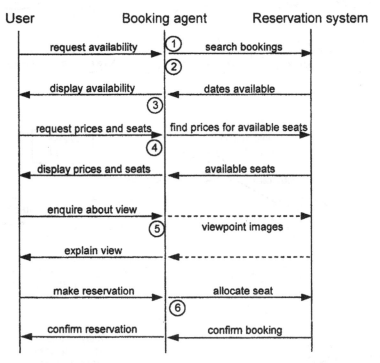

FIG. 4.4   Use case interaction diagram for a theater booking task. The system and human agents are represented by vertical bars, with events passing between them in sequence, reading down.

    5. Link views to seat position.
    6. Input and validate reservation.

Tasks and use cases are captured by a combination of interviewing and observing users' work in the real world. Interviews are suitable for gathering user requirements, and task descriptions of activity and domain knowledge for understanding how user activity is actually carried out and where it is located. Cross-checking interviews against observations frequently illuminates discrepancies between the way people say they carry out activities and the way they actually do things.

Scenarios of use are another effective way to gain information about the user's task. Asking the user to talk through "a typical day in the office" forms useful input to task analysis. This approach is also useful for discovering information needs by asking users about the documents and information they employ in the current system. Scenarios are a useful complement to task analysis because they give specific stories of use from which requirements can be extracted. Scenarios also provide concrete examples from which more generalized task models can be derived.

Space precludes a detailed description of requirements analysis techniques; for more detail, contextual inquiry (Beyer & Holtzblatt, 1998) gives plenty of advice.

Information Types

Unless design is based on the premise that the presentation content should be specified in logical terms before media are selected, *ad hoc* ineffective interfaces will be the result. Only when the "amodal" specification of content has been produced should media selection and design proceed. The approach is to carry out a task analysis and then augment the task model with the necessary information content. In tutorial multimedia, when the task is teaching or learning (for the user), task analysis is replaced with scripting the information content to achieve the user's learning goals.

To form the Task Information Model, the initial task–goal hierarchy is elaborated by attaching information types, which specify the content to be communicated to the user. The resulting model should allow the designer to answer the following question: "What information content does the user need for this task subgoal or input–output interaction?"

Information types are amodal, conceptual descriptions of information components that elaborate the content definition. The analyst progresses through the use case task model in a walkthrough, asking questions about information needs. This can be integrated with data modeling (or object-class modeling) so that the information in objects and attributes can be categorized by the following types, although one object will usually contain several different logical information types. Information typing extends data models to help the process of media selection. More complex ontologies are available (Arens, Hovy, & Van Mulken, 1993; Mann & Thompson, 1988; Sowa, 2000), so the taxonomy presented in Fig. 4.5 is a compromise between complexity and ease of use. A finer grained classification enables more finely tuned media selection decisions, but at a cost of more analysis effort. The following definitions are based on those in the Task-Based Information Analysis Method and ISO 14915, part 3 (ISO, 2000; Sutcliffe, 1997).

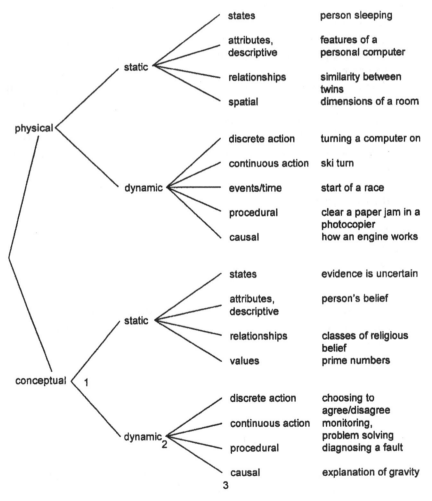

FIG. 4.5   Decision tree for classifying information types. The first decision point reflects abstraction from the real world, the second points to change in time, and the third categorizes content.

Components are classified using the decision tree and the following questions:

- Is the information contained in the component physical or conceptual?
- Is the information static or dynamic, that is, does it relate to change?
- Which type in the terminal branch of the tree does the information component belong to?

The first two questions guide the user toward subsets of the types; the third question identifies the individual type. The decision tree gives a set of ontological categories that expand on type definitions commonly found in software engineering specifications. It is important to note that one component may be classified with more than one type; for instance, instructions on how to get to the railway station may contain procedural information (the instructions "turn left, straight ahead," etc.), and spatial or descriptive information (the station is in the corner of the square, painted blue). The information types arc "tools for thought" which can be used either to classify specifications of content or be used to consider what content may be necessary. To illustrate, for the task "navigate to the railway station," the content may be minimally specified as "instructions how to get there," in which case the information types function as questions in the following form: "What sort of information does the user need to fulfill the task or user goal?" Content can be organized as a thematic outline or as a scenario, for instance directions, waymarks to recognize, and description of the target location. In the latter, case the information types may be used to segment the scenario into components. The granularity of components is a matter for the designer's choice and will depend on the level of detail demanded by the application. To illustrate the analysis, see the following:

> *Communication goal*—Explain how to assemble a bookshelf from ready-made parts.
>> Information Component 1:
>>> Parts of the bookshelf, sides, back, shelves, connecting screws
>>> Mapping to information types:
>>>> Physical-Static-Descriptive; parts of the bookshelf are tangible, don't change and need to be described
>>>> Physical-Static-Spatial; dimensions of the parts, how they are organized
>>>> Physical-Static-Relationship; to describe which parts fit together
>> Information Component 2:
>>> How to assemble parts instructions
>>> Mapping to information types:

Physical-Dynamic-Discrete action
Physical-Dynamic-Procedure
Physical-Static-State; to show final assembled bookshelf.

The information groupings and their respective types for the theater booking system are shown in Table 4.1.

INFORMATION ANALYSIS

At each step the level of the required information is assessed, although the quantity and quality of information may need to be modified in light of the user's domain knowledge. For instance, trained users will require little knowledge whereas novices may need considerable knowledge as prompts and instructions. The following questions help in eliciting information requirements in a walkthrough.

TABLE 4.1

Information Groups and Types for the Theater
Booking Application

Information Group	Information Type
1. Play schedule (dates, play title)	Descriptive, conceptual
2. Players (actors, director, company)	Descriptive, conceptual, physical
3. Seating plan	Spatial, descriptive, physical
4. Seat prices	Descriptive, conceptual, values
5. Seat reservation	Descriptive, conceptual, event, time
6. Play content (theme, synopsis)	Descriptive, conceptual
7. Actors' biographies	Descriptive, physical agents, conceptual
8. Director's biography	Descriptive, physical agents, conceptual
9. Company details	Descriptive, conceptual
10 Theater	Descriptive, physical, spatial
11. Customer changes	Descriptive, conceptual, event, time
12. Ticket	Descriptive, abstract, event, time

For each input from an external agent to the system and vice versa:

- What information does the user need to carry out the action manually?
- What information should the user supply to the computer as input?
- What supporting information should the computer supply to help the user complete an action?

For decision support and action steps:

- What information does the user require for decisions?
- What information is required to support execution of human activity and how should that be presented?

Other information may be required throughout the task; for instance, continuous monitoring of data, or knowledge about how to carry out the activity.

The information types are annotated on the task model to denote information required. If the application does not have a strong task model, the information content can be organized by other criteria, for example, see the following:

- *Historical or time sequence*—Where the content is structured by time or in the order of its development discovery. Access points are specified for time points or to address significant events in a history.
- *User preference*—Where the structure is arranged in the order which conforms to the user's model of the content, for example, by importance, frequency of use, or individual viewpoints.
- *Alphabetical order*—Where the content is alphabetically structured based on an index of meaningful descriptors.
- *Data model-based*—Where the content structure is determined by a data model, for example, in categories, entities, aggregation of attributes, objects, or classes.

Information structures are used to plan navigation and access dialogues as well as forming the basis for media selection. This analysis describes the information requirements of the task; however, if tutorial applications are being developed, task information will constitute the content that has to be taught. The teaching task has to be added as the pedagogical strategies to deliver the material and encourage students' learning. The task itself becomes the domain knowledge content and this necessitates further analysis of learning goals. Learning goals are established, then the delivery of knowledge is planned to incrementally develop the student's understanding. For instance, to teach students about the fresh water ecology of a pond, the learning goals (or outcomes) might be the following:

- Understand the roles of plants, herbivores, carnivores, and decomposers in an ecosystem.
- Be able to explain the concept of a food chain and dependencies between populations of plants and animals.
- Appreciate that pollution can upset the ecological balance and the reasons why.

The basic grounding knowledge that students will need before they can start will be facts about the objects, agents, and structures in the domain; for instance, fish, insects, pondweed, tadpoles, the pond, and its environment. Note that the quantity and quality of the grounding knowledge will be informed by the user profile analysis. The knowledge to be imparted is scripted in explanatory sequences; for example, the classification of pondweed as plants, tadpoles as herbivores, and so forth; the causal explanation that plants derive energy from the sun (photosynthesis) and are eaten by herbivores, which in turn are eaten by carnivores; with more advanced causal explanations for the effects of pollution either killing animals or encouraging excess growth of plants and so on.

Explanatory scripts, however, are a static presentation. As learning is encouraged by active engagement, specification of interactive microworlds should be considered, from domain analysis of content and causal explanation to encourage discovery-based learning (e.g., effects of adding pollutants, more herbivores to the ecosystem). A range of different pedagogical strategies should also be considered, such as teaching by examples, counter examples, and use of analogy. A good implementation based on the aforementioned domain is the Pondworld system (Rogers & Scaife, 1998). Further consideration of pedagogical strategies and specification of tutorial applications are beyond the scope of this book, but the reader can consult the following for advice: Boyle, 1997; Elsom-Cook, 2000; Laurillard, 1993.

MEDIA SELECTION AND COMBINATION

Media classifications have had many interpretations (Alty, 1997; Bernsen, 1994; Heller & Martin, 1995). Most have proposed commonsense definitions of categories such as text, image, animation, and speech. Bernsen's (1994) modality theory is more complex because it distinguishes among a modality of communication (vision, hearing, touch); an information encoding dimension, either realistic (analogue) or symbolic; and discrete or continuous media. The following classification focuses on the psychological properties of the representations rather than the physical nature of the medium (e.g., digital or analogue encoding in video). Note that these definitions are combined to describe any specific medium, so speech is classified as an audio, linguistic medium, whereas a cartoon is classified as a nonrealistic (designed) moving image. Media resources are classified using the decision tree illustrated in Fig. 4.6.

The approach to classifying media uses the decision tree with the following questions that reflect the facets of the classification:

- Is the medium perceived to be realistic? Media resources captured directly from the real world will usually be realistic, for example, photographs of landscapes, bird song sound recordings. However, the boundary case that challenges the category is a realistic painting of a landscape.
- Does the medium change over time? The boundary case here is the rate of change, particularly in animations where some people might judge 10 frames per sec to be still a video, whereas five slides shown in a 1-min Microsoft PowerPoint presentation is seen as a sequence of static images.
- Which modality does the resource belong to? In this case, the categories are orthogonal, although one resource may exhibit two mo-

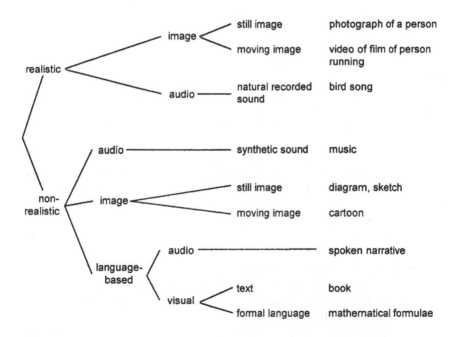

FIG. 4.6   Decision tree for classifying media resources.

dalities, for example, a film with a sound track communicates in both visual and audio modalities.

The classification may be used from different viewpoints; for example, a film of a professor illustrating a diagram may be classified as a realistic, moving image medium portraying a nonrealistic, still image medium. Classification of media resources facilitates mapping of information types to media resources; however, the process of selection may also guide the acquisition or creation of appropriate media resources. Thus, if the selection process indicates the need for a resource that is not in the media resource library, the classification guides the necessary acquisition or creation. Cost trade-offs will naturally be considered in this process. Finally, the classification provides a mechanism for indexing media resource libraries.

Media Selection Guidelines

Task and user characteristics influence media choice; for instance, verbal media are more appropriate to language-based and logical reasoning tasks; visual media are suitable for spatial tasks involving moving, positioning, and orienting objects. Some users may prefer visual media, whereas image is of little use for blind users. In some circumstances, the information model may specify content for which no existing media resource is available, so the costs of capturing or purchasing media resources have to be considered. If existing media can be edited and reused, this is usually preferable to creating new media from scratch. Graphical images can be particularly expensive to draw, whereas capture of images by scanning is usually quick and cheap. The information types described in Fig. 4.5 are used with the media selection guidelines

The mappings are used in multiple passes; for example, when a procedure for explaining a physical task is required, first realistic image media will be selected, then a series of images and text. The guidelines that differentiate physical from abstract information are used first followed by the other guidelines. The summary mappings in Table 4.2 are described in more detail in the following guidelines:

- *Physical information*—For physical information, visual media (e.g., realistic still or moving image) are preferred, unless user or task characteristics override this choice (Alty, 1997; Baggett, 1989; Faraday & Sutcliffe, 1997b), for example, a photograph is used to portray the landscape in a national park. When physical details need to be communicated precisely, such as the dimensions of a building, captions may be overlaid on an image. When a partial abstraction of physical information is desired, a nonrealistic image may be used (e.g., sketch or diagram).

- *Conceptual information*—Linguistic media, e.g. text or speech, are preferred for abstract or conceptual information (Booher, 1975; Faraday & Sutcliffe, 1997b), e.g. to convey sales objectives and commentary on the market strategy choose text bullet points or speech for the commentary. Abstract information with complex relationships may be shown by non-realistic images (graphs, sketches, diagrams) or by graphical images with embedded text; for instance, categories of animals can be placed in a tree diagram, or a flowchart used to portray the functions of a chemical process, with speech to describe the functions in detail.

- *Descriptive information*—Linguistic media (text, speech) are preferred for information describing the properties of objects, agents, or the domain (Booher, 1975), for example, narrative text describes the properties of a chemical compound such as salt. When describing objects and agents with physical attributes, language may be combined with an image (Baggett, 1989).

- *Visual–spatial information*—Still images are used for visual–spatial information (Bieger & Glock, 1984; May & Barnard, 1995), for example, the location of cargo on a ship is shown by a diagram; someone's face is portrayed in a photograph. Spatial, detailed information may be presented in a realistic image, for example, photographs. Spatial information that involves complex pathways may be conveyed by a moving image, for example, animating a pathway.

- *Value information*—Numeric text and tables represent numeric values and quantitative information (Booher, 1975; Tufte, 1997), for example, the height and weight of a person is given as 1.8 m, 75 kg. Graphs and charts can be combined with captions and tables to summarize trends, differences, and categories in quantitative data. Speech is not effective for values because they usually need to be inspected during a task, so a persistent medium is advised.

- *Relationships in value information*—A nonrealistic image (e.g., charts, graphs) represents relations within and between sets of values or conceptual relations between objects and agents (Bertin, 1983; Tufte, 1997), for example, the values for rainfall in London for each month are displayed using a histogram.

- *Discrete action information*—Simple or discrete actions map to still image media (Hegarty & Just, 1993; Park & Hannafin, 1993), for example, an image of the coffee machine showing a person performing the action illustrates filling a coffee percolator with water (André & Rist, 1993). Use of still image media for discrete actions allows the relation among the action, the object acted on, and the

TABLE 4.2

Summary of Media Combinations With Examples

Information Type / Media type	Causation	Conceptual	Continuous Action	Descriptive	Discrete Action	Event	Physical	Procedure	Relationship	Spatial Information	State	Value
Realistic audio	Sound of rain and storms		Sound of skiing		Click of ON switch	Sound of the starting gun	*Noise of a tornado*			Echoes in a cave	Sound of snoring	Musical note encodes a value
Nonrealistic audio		Rising tone illustrates increasing magnetic force	Continuous tone signals progress of action	Morse code describes a ship	Tones signal open and close door	Alarm siren			Tones associate two objects	Sonar and doppler effect	Continuous sound in a heart-beat monitor	
Speech	*Tell someone why El Nino happens*	Tell someone about Your religious beliefs	Tell someone what a ski turn looks like	Verbal description of a person	Tell someone how to turn computer on	*Tell someone a race has started*	Tell someone how it feels to be in a storm	Speak instructions on engine assembly	Tell someone Jack and Jill are related	Tell someone pathway to and location of railway station	Tell someone "Jane's asleep"	Verbal report of numbers, figures
Realistic still image	*Photograph of El Nino storms and ocean currents*	Statue of Liberty photograph represents "freedom"	Set of photographs showing snap shots of action	*Overview and detail photographs of a car*	*Photograph of computer ON switch*	*Photograph of the start of a race*	*Photograph of a person's face*	*Photographs showing engine assembly*		*Photograph of a landscape*	*Photograph of a person sleeping*	

Nonrealistic still image	*Diagrams of ocean currents and sea temperature to explain El Nino*	*Hierarchy diagram of plant taxonomy*	Histogram of ageing population	Diagram with arrow depicting ski turn motion	Diagram showing where and how to press ON switch	Event symbol in a race sequence diagram		Explode parts diagram of engine with assembly numbers	*Graphs, histograms, ER diagrams*	*Map of the landscape*	Waiting state symbol in race sequence diagram	*Charts, graphs, scatter plots*
Text	Describe reasons for El Nino storms	*Explain taxonomy of animals*	*Describe a person's appearance*	Describe ski turn action	Describe how to turn computer on	Report that the race has started	*Report of the storm's properties*	*Bullet point steps in assembling engine*	*Describe brother and sister relationship*	Describe dimensions of a room	*Report that the person is asleep*	*Written number 1, 2*
Realistic moving image	*Video of El Nino storms and ocean currents*		Aircraft flying	Movie of person turning while skiing		*Movie of the start of a race*	*Movie of a storm*	*Video of engine assembly sequence*		Fly through landscape	Video of a person sleeping	
Nonrealistic moving image	*Animation of ocean temperature change and current reversal*	*Animated diagram of force of gravity*		*Animated mannequin doing ski turn*	Animation showing operation of ON switch	Animation of start event symbol in diagram		Animation of parts diagram in assembly sequence	Animation of links on ER diagram			
Language-based—formal, numeric	*Equations, functions formalizing cause and effect*	*Symbols denoting concepts, for example, pi*			Finite state automata	Event-based notations		Procedural logics, process algebras	Functions, equations, grammars			State-based languages, for example, Z

Note. Italics denote the first preference selections.

agent performing the action to be inspected. Abstract actions, for example, mental processes, are described using speech or text.

- *Continuous action information*—Complex or continuous actions map to moving image media (Sutcliffe & Faraday, 1994), for example, turning while skiing is illustrated with a video. Complex physical action may be better illustrated with nonrealistic media (animation) so the coordination of motor actions can be inspected.
- *Event or temporal information*—For significant events and warnings, sound or speech help to alert the user (Pezdek & Maki, 1988), for example, the outbreak of a fire is conveyed by sounding an alarm followed by a red marker on a diagram of the building to show the fire's location. Abstract events may have to be explained in language (Bernsen, 1994). Temporal information may be illustrated in sequence as lists, text, or graphical images such as time lines (Ahlberg & Shneiderman, 1994).
- *State information*—For states, still image or linguistic media are preferred (Faraday & Sutcliffe, 1997a), for example, the state of the weather is shown by a photograph of a sunny day. Abstract states, such as a person's belief, may be explained in linguistic media or described in diagrams. If a sequence of discrete states is required, then an animation or a series of still images may be used as a slide show.
- *Causal information*—To explain causality, still and moving image media need to be combined with linguistic media (Narayanan & Hegarty, 1998), for example, the cause of a flood is explained by text describing excessive rainfall with an animation of the river level rising and overflowing its banks. Causal explanations of physical phenomena may be given by introducing the topic using linguistic media, showing the cause and effect by a combination of still image and linguistic media for commentary; integrate the message by moving image with voice commentary and providing a bullet point text summary.
- *Procedural information*—A series of images with text captions are preferred for procedural information (Hegarty & Just, 1993), for example, instructions for assembling a bookshelf from a kit are given as a set of images for each step, with text captions. To explain procedures, a richer combination of media may be necessary, such as a still image sequence with text, followed by an animation of the whole sequence. Nonphysical procedures may be displayed as formatted text, for example, bullet points or numbered steps.

The end point of media selection is media integration: one or more media will be selected for each information group to present complementary as-

pects of the topic or object. Some examples of media combination that amplify the basic selection guidelines are given in Table 4.2.

Allocation of media types to information types in the theater booking system is shown in Fig. 4.7. This illustrates media allocation for the browsing
task in which the customer inspects the forthcoming program and other
publicity material. Other information types are used in the reservation task
(not discussed here). Note that information may often have multiple types;
for instance, the players have descriptions in their biographies that are conceptual, but they also have physical identities.

Integration Heuristics.   The media combination and selection
guidelines are augmented with a set of heuristics that warn the designer
about undesirable consequences of media combination. The design principles described in chapter 2 can also be employed in this role:

- *Memorization of content* from dynamic media (animation, speech,
  sound) is generally worse than from static media. Key facts and important messages are conveyed more effectively by static media
  (text, still image) because users will generally acquire only
  high-level gist memory from dynamic media.

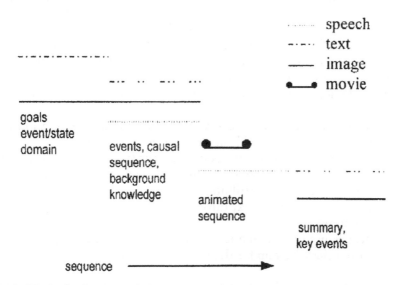

FIG. 4.7   Media allocation in the browse program task, using mapping from information to media types given in table 4.2. P=Physical; C=Conceptual information types.

- Dynamic media will attract the *user's attention* more than static media, so motion and stimuli which change, for example, animated captions, are hard to ignore. Beware distracting the user with superfluous animation. Dynamic media can be displayed concurrently with static media, although the user's attention will be diverted while the video or speech is playing. If dynamic media need to be integrated with other media, then provide controls to allow replay.
- Information presented in one medium can have a *priming effect* and help the user to understand following information in another medium. For example, text or speech can introduce an idea and should be presented before visual media to "set the scene" and direct the user's attention to information within the image.
- When *speech and text are combined*, the same wording should be used, unless speech is referring to a visual attribute of the text or preceding it as an instruction. Speech and text compete for language processing resources so they should not be used concurrently apart from language-learning applications.

Media Selection Patterns.   For larger chunks of information, such as causal explanations and procedures, single rules cannot specify the appropriate combination of media, so media selection is better expressed as templates or patterns. The following list is not exhaustive, but illustrates the concept.

Classification explains how instances of objects, agents, events, and so forth, belong to general categories. First the category is introduced, and then examples of well-formed members are given, followed by poor examples and members of related categories. The pattern concludes by summarizing the classification rules. Media selection will be different for conceptual and physical phenomena, and the following pattern is for the latter:

- Text introduces the category, its attributes, and its position in a large taxonomy (possibly augmented by a diagram).
- Image is used to explain a good member (text if conceptual), with captions and speech to point out the member's features that agree with the category's attributes.
- Image is used to explain a related category member or counterexample.
- Text is used to summarize the classification rules, supplemented with a class diagram for the large taxonomy.

The pattern of *composition* (whole or parts) explains the composition of a physical object in terms of its components and how they fit together. The pattern can be specialized to illustrate *decomposition* rather than composition.

- Image is used to introduce the whole object with speech and text to describe its role or function.
- Image then shows its parts in an exploded part diagram with captions to label the parts.
- A slide show sequence of still images is used to illustrate the composition or aggregation sequence from parts to substructures and the whole.
- The object and its parts are summarized using image and text captions to point out major subcomponents.

Regarding *task-based* (how to do it) presentation, the physical task sequence will be specialized for abstract cognitive tasks. The sequence should be organized to first provide the task goal (purpose), and then give details of its procedure, followed by a summary.

- Text is used to introduce the overall plan and explain the task goal. This may be accompanied by a diagram of the plan.
- Preconditions are described by text and image.
- Procedure steps are given with speech and a sequence of still images.
- A moving image of the procedure is used to reinforce the message and integrate the actions.
- Text bullet points summarize, with an image to show the postconditions for task completion.

Regarding *causal* (why or how it works) presentation, this starts with an explanation of the domain, important objects and concepts, then the causal model is explained, followed by background knowledge to back up why the events happen. A summary concludes with key events and their causal explanation (see Fig. 4.8).

- There is text to introduce the domain and important objects, illustrated with a diagram.
- The sequence of cause and effect is presented by diagrams and speech, using text captions to explain key facts and background knowledge.
- Animation of the sequence reinforces the message.
- There is summarization by a diagram and text captions for key events and causal explanation.

Each pattern has a generalized script describing the presentation sequence. Dialogue controls are added to make the presentation interactive, so a sequence can be replayed, paused at each step, played in reverse order, and so forth. Further development of a library of media combination pat-

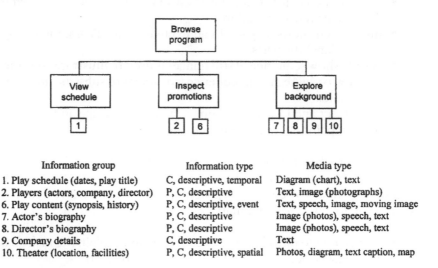

Information group	Information type	Media type
1. Play schedule (dates, play title)	C, descriptive, temporal	Diagram (chart), text
2. Players (actors, company, director)	P, C, descriptive	Text, image (photographs)
6. Play content (synopsis, history)	P, C, descriptive, event	Text, speech, image, moving image
7. Actor's biography	P, C, descriptive	Image (photos), speech, text
8. Director's biography	P, C, descriptive	Image (photos), speech, text
9. Company details	C, descriptive	Text
10. Theater (location, facilities)	P, C, descriptive, spatial	Photos, diagram, text caption, map

FIG. 4.8   Script pattern for presentation of causal information.

Aesthetic Motivations

terns to suit generalized information and task requirements may be developed in the patterns community which has started to address UI problems (Borchers, 2001).

Aesthetic Motivations

The aforementioned guidelines are oriented to a task-driven view of media. Media selection, however, can also be motivated by aesthetic choice, which is important in Web-based multimedia. These considerations may contradict some of the selection rules stated earlier because the design objective is to please the user and capture his or her attention rather than deliver information effectively. Guidelines for aesthetic design are not easy to find because this aspect of design is either acquired by experience or taught in the graphics arts design courses that emphasize example-based learning, rather than generalizing knowledge as guidelines. In spite of these limitations, some advice can be given. First, a health warning should be noted: the old saying, "beauty is in the eye of the beholder," has good foundation. Judgments of aesthetic quality suffer from considerable individual differences. A person's reaction to a design is a function of their motivation, individual preferences, knowledge of the domain, and exposure to similar examples, to say nothing of peer opinion and "fashion." Furthermore, aesthetic judgment is often more about content than the choice of media or presentation format. Hence, the following heuristics of media selection are rules of thumb that should be interpreted with care and their design manifestations tested with users:

- Dynamic media, especially video, have an arousing effect and attract attention (Reeves & Nass, 1996); hence, video and animation are useful in improving the attractiveness of presentations. However, animation must be used with care as gratuitous video that cannot be turned off quickly offends.
- Speech engages attention because we naturally listen to conversation. Choice of voice depends on the application: female voices for more restful and information effects; male voices to suggest authority and respect (Reeves & Nass, 1996).
- Image needs to be selected with careful consideration of content. Images may be selected with a background for aesthetic motivations, to provide a restful setting for more important foreground information (Mullet & Sano, 1995). Background in half shades and low saturation color provides more depth and interest in an image.
- Music has an important emotive appeal, but it needs to be used with care. Classical music may be counterproductive for a younger audience; older listeners will not find heavy metal or pop attractive.
- Natural sounds such as running water, wind in trees, bird song, and waves on the seashore have restful properties.

Media integration rules may also be broken for aesthetic reasons. If information transfer is not at a premium, use of two concurrent video streams might be arousing for a younger audience, as MTV (Music Television) and pop videos indicate. Multiple audio and speech tracks can give the impression of complex, busy, and interesting environments.

Image, Media Personality, and Identity.   Design of image for motivation is a complex area in its own right. Some effects are general, such as use of a faint background image to suggest depth and hold interest once the foreground image has been absorbed. The overlay of background and foreground image needs to avoid clashes in color and context between the layers. Content can have a more salient effect, especially through brands and logos. The image of the brand owner is projected first through the graphical icon that identifies the brand and then publicity that attaches attributes to the brand; for example, Sir Richard Branson's Virgin brand logo has become identified with an informal but modern company (see Fig. 4.9), from its origins in the music industry.

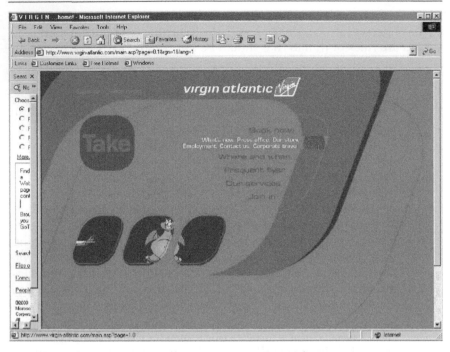

FIG. 4.9   Virgin Atlantic website (Virgin Atlantic Airways, 2000). Reprinted with permission
by Virgin Group PLC.

Human identity can have an important effect on user motivation. Simple photographs can personalize a Web site by indicating that real people
are present to help. Fig. 4.10 illustrates a powerful use of human image to
create an engaging Web site. The image works by gaze directed toward the
user and by choice of photograph of a young woman with an interesting appearance. More complex interactive animations (talking heads or full
body mannequins) also have an attractive effect. We appear to ascribe human properties to computers when interfaces portray human-like visual
cues (Reeves & Nass, 1996); however, the use of talking heads and human
mannequins in animations requires careful design to be effective. A list of
some of the problems follows:

- *Synchronization* of lips and speech generally has to be within 0.02 sec
  to avoid the dubbed film effect. This can be solved by predesigned
  canned presentations, but at the sacrifice of flexibility in responding
  to user actions and questions.
- *Facial expression* and other nonverbal communication—We use a
  variety of facial expressions to signal attention and reinforce

speech. For example, raised eyebrows show attention, head nods signal affirmatives, and eye contact is used in managing turn-taking. It is difficult to program these responses into virtual people, although research prototypes are becoming more natural (Cassel et al., 1999; Poggi & Pelachaud, 2000; Schiano, Ehrlich, Rahrjardja, & Sheridan, 2000). Talking agents without facial expressions distract attention because they look unnatural.

- Choice of the characters' *appearance and voice*—This is complex because we modify our reactions according to our knowledge, or assumptions about, the other agent's intention, role, group identification, and culture (Clark, 1996). For example, reactions to a military mannequin will be very different from those to the representation of a parson. Trust and power assumptions vary widely between different professional identities (Peters, Covello, & McCallum, 1997). People tend to trust scientists more than politicians and journalists. Male voices tend to be treated as having more authority than female voices.

Use of human-like forms is feasible with prerecorded video and photographs; however, the need depends on the application. Video representation of lecturers adds little to the content of their presentations, although video image does help in interactive question and answer dialogue.

Attention in conversations is governed by linguistic cues and by proximity, so when human image and speech are being used, designers have to bear in mind

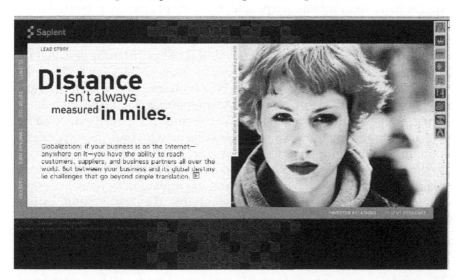

FIG. 4.10   Use of image to engage attention; the direct gaze is hard to avoid. Reprinted with permission by Sapient PLC.

the conversational context that is invoked. People manage personal space in meetings and pay attention to others who are close by and facing them. Images of virtual humans in multimedia need to be in a foreground shot for a normal size computer screen. In human–human conversation, we approach to within 0.5 m and look at the other person. This translates into a foreground face filling circa 50% of a 50 cm monitor at a normal viewing distance of 0.25 m. The size of a human image depends on projection technology and we react adversely to larger than life human forms with "big brother" connotations, so projecting a close-up of a face on an IMAX screen will not facilitate normal conversation.

Although it might seem to be gratuitous for a computer to say thank you and goodbye, politeness, in fact, does engender a more positive user attitude toward computer conversation. We all like to be flattered, and computers can fulfill this role, too. Praising the user has a positive effect on attitude, so in persuasive computing (Fogg, 1998), the application is obvious. Criticism is more difficult. We generally react badly to criticism that is unjustified and has no constructive content. Criticism from experts tends to be taken more seriously than from novices. These reactions can be embedded in a computer critic's conversations: start with some praise, then make the criticism constructive, justify the assertion, and sound confident to project an expert image.

We all attend to stimulating speakers. A good speaker holds our attention by a variety of tricks, such as maintaining eye contact, varying voice tone, using simple and concise language, as well as delivering an interesting message. These are still general effects, but they can be reinforced by the projected personality. We respect dominant personalities, leaders, and experts, more than submissive people. Friendly people are preferred over colder, more hostile individuals. TV announcers, who tend to be middle-aged, confident, but avuncular characters, have been selected to optimize the attention-drawing power of a dominant yet friendly personality. However, the preference has a gender effect. Men and women both prefer the dominant, friendly leader; and whereas both sexes pay attention to extrovert, young personalities, the male preference for beautiful young women is a particularly strong effect. These traits have been exploited by advertisers for a long time. There are lessons here for multimedia designs as the Internet and interactive TV converge.

Although the bounds of media selection are only set by the creative imagination of the designer, some fundamentals don't change: design still needs to be motivated by goals, even if it is to entertain; and testing with users is still essential.

PRESENTATION SCRIPTING

Once media resources have been selected, storyboards will be created and tested with users to gain further feedback on the design. In rapid application development, the design will proceed by developing concept demonstrators and early prototypes. In a software engineering approach, design will proceed with more detailed specification. Storyboards should illustrate the high-level dialogue design that is addressed in the next section, and show a set of snapshots of the application following a scenario of use. For instance, the theater booking system goes through a set of images that illustrate how the user selects a play, then makes a reservation (see Fig. 4.11).

Only a few dialogue controls are shown, in particular those relevant to the explanatory script. The story is walked through with the user to explain the choices and information available at each step. At this stage, it is also possible to develop concept demonstrators or early prototypes in authoring tools such as Director. Concept demonstrators follow a scripted scenario like a storyboard, but real media can be presented to provide a more realistic demonstration of the design. The task information model should give the approximate order for the presentation; however, decisions still have to be taken about concurrent versus sequential presentation and windows management.

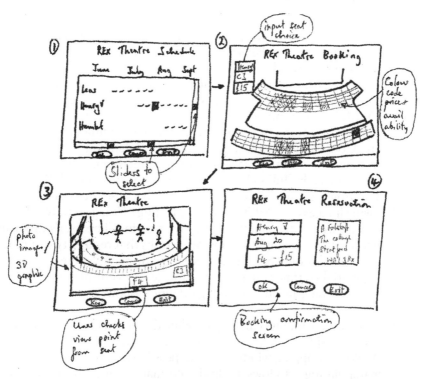

FIG. 4.11   Sketched storyboard screens for the theater booking application. In screen 1, the user selects a play using sliders to specify his or her choice; this leads to screen 2, where the available seats are displayed. The users can then inspect the view of the stage from their chosen seat in storyboard 3, followed by making a booking in screen 4.

Concurrent or Sequential Presentation

Generally, dynamic media enforce sequential presentation except when speech or sound and video share the same theme; in contrast, several static media can be presented concurrently. Maximizing concurrent presentation helps users by increasing visibility of information and reducing the burden on working memory. If users can scan a VDU for all the necessary information, this saves actions for manipulating windows and reduces the chance that the user will forget key facts. However, concurrent display should not be achieved at the expense of legibility. Reducing text font size or shrinking images to fit onto one screen can make detail difficult to perceive; furthermore, more detail increases the user's search time. Planning concurrent media presentations is therefore a trade-off between the available screen size, the demands of the task, and the user's preferences.

Window Management

Concurrent displays need to be planned for their spatial organization. For instance, each medium may be given equal screen area in a tiled display or placed in overlapping windows. If tiled windows are being used, the layout should be planned using a grid to allocate areas to each window and ensure windows do not depart from the golden mean of breadth: length (approximately 3:5; Mullet & Sano, 1995). Long thin or short fat windows look strange, disrupt attention unnecessarily, and hinder reading or viewing image content. Consideration of legibility and level of detail informs the decision about how much screen space to give each medium. For text media, density metrics given by Tullis (1988) can be used to assess readability; however, generalizing these to multimedia is difficult because the cognitive process of viewing images is very different. User testing of images is advisable to make sure they are not too small for effective viewing. The user's task can also be important. For example, comparative tasks that require two or more media to be viewed should be placed in adjacent displays, whereas tasks involving sequential or time series information (e.g., event histories, procedures) suggest a linear layout. Further guidelines follow:

- Juxtaposed windows can help to relate detail to a more general context with side-by-side display for comparison.
- Avoid overlapping windows where possible because of the effort in manipulating windows to find information and the burden on working memory if information has to be compared between windows, although the technique may be useful for multitasking when foreground or background displays are needed.

- Center-embedded displays can be used for foreground detail over-laid on background context for image media; however, center embedding of dynamic media in windows containing static media is nothing more than a gimmick.

When visual media need to be closely integrated, windows get in the way. Putting content in a window imposes a psychological isolation. The window boundary sets up an arbitrary dividing line between related information, which can be difficult to overcome, as illustrated in Fig. 4.12. Unfortunately, GUI operating systems encourage window proliferation and mapping single media resources to individual windows. The designer can counteract this effect but at the cost of doing more media design. Thus, if text and image need to be integrated, place them together within one document with captions pointing to image components. This overcomes the isolating effect of two windows: one with the image and one with the text.

Screen navigation maps, or draft site maps for Internet applications, can help to provide an overview of the major presentation components in a system, organized to reflect the hierarchy of content. This may be supplemented by a time line view of scripts illustrated by bar charts to show the

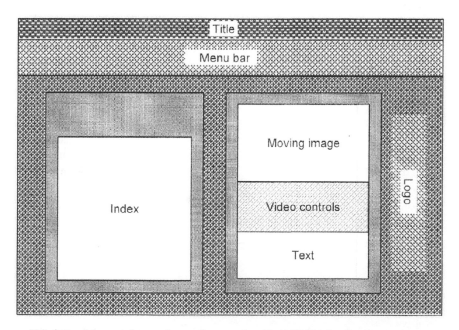

FIG. 4.12   Schematic layout of a page from a multimedia encyclopedia, illustrating poor use of windows. The text window under the video will not compete effectively for the user's attention; the index window takes up unnecessary space. No integration between the media has been attempted.

sequence, duration, and overlap of media segments. The presentation script in the theater booking system after allocation of media types to information types is shown in Fig. 4.13. This illustrates media presentation scripts for three option subgoals of the browsing task in which the customer may either inspect the forthcoming program, promotions, or other publicity material. The duration and order of presentation are indicated by the user's task. The bar chart illustrates which media should be presented when the user selects a task option. Decisions on timing also depend on the content of the media resource, for example, length of a video clip or frame display rate.

Scripting raises issues of synchronization between dynamic media. When speech and video are being played simultaneously and the speaker is visible, then close synchronization of 0.2 msec between the speaker's lips and the onset of speech is necessary. We are very sensitive to lip synchronization, as dubbing foreign language films demonstrates. A longer synchronization gap may be tolerated (circa 0.5 sec) for natural sound and action, for example, bird song and video of a bird singing; however, people find presentation unnatural when action is not associated with sound within a few seconds. When there is little expectation that sound and action should be linked (e.g., film of a whale swimming while vocalizing), then synchronization is less important.

One final point to bear in mind is that, generally, it helps to present linguistic media before image media to provide background information.

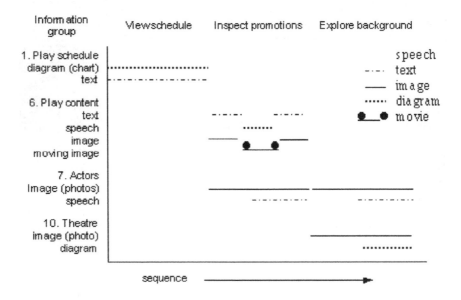

FIG. 4.13   Bar chart to illustrate media presentation script for the browse program task.

Giving language first activates relevant memories and cues the user to search for appropriate information in the following images, thereby providing a framework for building comprehension.

NAVIGATION AND CONTROL

Although discussion of the dialogue aspects of multimedia has been delayed until now, in practice, dialogue and presentation design proceed hand in hand. Task analysis provides the basis for dialogue design. Navigational and control dialogues enable flexible access to the multimedia content, and give users ability to control how media are played. Dialogue design may also involve specifying how users interact with tools, agents, and objects in interactive microworlds. These more complex aspects of dialogue are dealt with in chapter 5, so in this chapter, simpler dialogues are assumed that primarily provide users access to content rather than the ability to manipulate it in a sophisticated manner.

The first question to be resolved is whether the UI is to support a single dedicated task or a range of tasks. If the application supports many different tasks, then the interface design has to enable task switching. This implies an outer layer of dialogue that supports user access to appropriate task support functions with status indicators and aide-memoire displays to remind the user which system functions are active and where they are within a task sequence. If the application needs to support one or two well-structured tasks, the dialogue and screen sequence will follow the steps (goals or procedures) in the task model. Screen navigation diagrams are created from the task model sequence of subgoals and procedures, then storyboards are developed to illustrate key task steps, and they are validated with users. If multitasking is required with less well-structured tasks, then a high-level access dialogue will be necessary. Each task fragment (i.e., subgoal) is analyzed and storyboard minisequences planned as before. Commands are placed into task- or functionally-related groups and access dialogues specified. In simple cases, this will involve menu design; however, in more complex cases, commands may be organized by structural metaphors, for example, palettes in paint and drawing programs. Determining the requirements for multitask working and the user's need to cross-reference between tasks helps to plan how many dialogues and windows may need to be active at once.

Hypermedia Dialogues

In information intensive multimedia where access to content is the main design goal, hypermedia dialogues link content segments. Hypermedia enables browsing a network along all the possible pathways between segments that the user may need. Studies of user interaction (Bates, 1989;

Belkin, Cool, Stein, & Thiel, 1993) with hypertext systems have shown different user search strategies:

- *Random*—No particular order is observable.
- *Scanning*—Users sample different parts of the hypertext without systematically exploring any part in depth.
- *Spike exploration*—The user follows link pathways, although the search may not be directed to any specific goal, and sidetracks are evident in the trace of the user's search.
- *Searching*—Exploration follows pathways in a directed manner toward an information-seeking goal. Fewer diversions down sidetracks occur in searching.

Link structures and overview maps for scanning can be planned with these strategies in mind. Unfortunately, hypermedia systems assume a fixed database and link structure. This can be made more flexible by branch points in scripts, but the user is still ultimately limited to the pathways provided by the designer. More open-ended hypertext environments (e.g., Microcosm; Lowe & Hall, 1998) provide links with scripts and query facilities so users can access databases as well as browse the hypertext network. Preformed queries can be attached to hotspots in images or nodes in hypertext documents. These are more flexible because queries attached to links can provide access paths to a wider variety of data compared to static links. In this case, the division between hypertext links and database query languages becomes blurred.

Good hypertext design is a matter of sound information analysis to specify the pathways between related items, and use of cues to show the structure of the information space to the user. In document-based hypermedia (e.g., HTML and the Internet) links can only access the whole media resource rather than pointing to components within a document. Design advice on hypermedia Web interfaces is already swamping the bookshelves, so I will restrict myself to a synopsis drawn from Nielsen (1999) and Spool, Scanlon, Snyder, Schroeder, and De Angelo (1999). The design issues are to plan the overall structure, segment complex structures into a hierarchy of subnetworks, and then plan the connectivity in each subnetwork. The access structure of most hypermedia will be hierarchical, organized according to the information model and categorization of content, for example, information grouped by functional, organizational, task, or user preference. A template for Web site hypertext navigation structure is shown in Fig. 4.14. This shows a hierarchical access structure, with limited network links within content pages to view more information or to access related documents elsewhere. Restricting network links within the site and creating a page for network links outside the site help to preserve a clear navigation

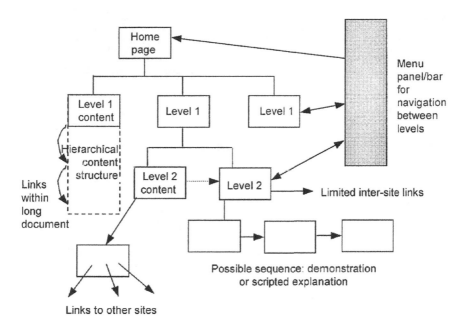

FIG 4.14   Website hypertext navigation structure. The dotted line between level 2 pages indicates cross-reference links.

structure. Return to home and exit pathways are always accessible. Navigation controls can be implemented as side bar menus, but it is also advisable to place these controls at the bottom of pages. Too many links within content pages can disrupt reading or viewing the medium, so a separate outlink or Web resources page containing links outside the site is preferable to embedding too many links within contents pages.

Overall, constructing good hypertext is based on translating the user's model of the information space into a hypertext graph. Unfortunately, individual users have different models, so this may not be an easy task. Too many links will make the system too complex and increase the chance of the user getting lost. Too few links will frustrate a user who cannot find what he or she wants.

One problem with large hypermedia systems is that users get lost in them. Navigation cues, waymarks, and minimap overviews can help to counter the effects of disorientation. Minimaps provide an overview of the hypertext area while another display shows the local part of the network (see Fig. 4.15). This gives the user a reference context for where he or she is in large networks. Filters or user views for part of the network can also help to reduce complexity by showing only a subset of nodes and links in which

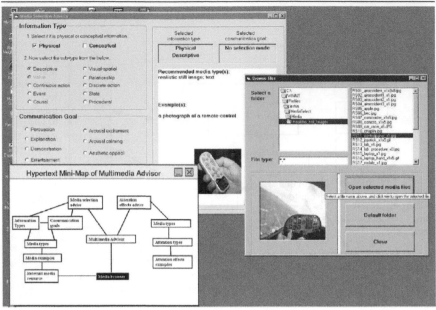

FIG. 4.15   Hypertext minimap.

the user is interested. Having typed links helps filtering views because the user can guess the information content from the link type, for example, reference, example, source, related work, and so forth. Other facilities for user navigation are visit lists containing a history of nodes traversed in a session. The user can backtrack using the visit list as a trace pathway. Nodes in visit lists can be tagged with the date they were accessed so that users can find out where they have been in a particular part of the hypertext and when, as illustrated in Fig. 4.16. Finally, bookmarks are a good means for users to tailor a hypertext with their own navigation mementoes. Bookmarks may be placed on hypertext nodes as iconic or text tags to remind the user about important nodes.

Another navigation problem is not knowing where to get started. Guided tours can help to solve this problem by taking the user on a preset exploration of the hypertext. However, guided tours do militate against the spirit of free exploration in hypertext because they enforce a particular pathway (Hammond & Allinson, 1989).

Once the structure has been designed, link cues need to be located within media resources, so the appropriateness of the cue needs to be considered within each medium. For example, see the following:

- *Text media*—The Web convention is to highlight and underline text in a consistent color, for example, blue or purple.

- *Images*—Link cues can be set as stand-alone icons or as active components in images. Icons need to be tested with users because the designer's assumed meaning might be ambiguous. Active components should signal the link by captions or pop-up "hover text" so the user can inspect a link before deciding whether to follow it.
- *Moving images*—Links from animation and film are difficult to design because the medium is dynamic; however, link buttons can be placed below the movie window. Active components within a moving image are technically more challenging although overlaid buttons can provide the answer. Buttons may also be timed to pop up at appropriate times during the video.
- *Sound and speech* make link origins difficult for the same reason as with moving images. Solutions are to use visual cues, possible synchronized with the sound or speech track. If speech recognition is available, then voice commands can act as links, but these commands need to be explained to the user. Automatic links can also be used, but if these are embedded within the speech or sound medium, then user controls to activate preset links before playing will be necessary.

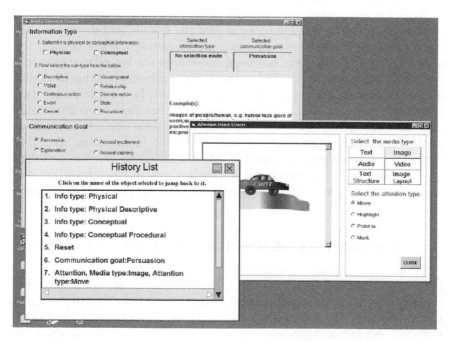

FIG. 4.16   Visit list.

Navigation Controls

The motivation of navigation controls is to give the user access to the logical content of multimedia resources. However, access to logical components may be constrained by limitations of physical media resources. For example, a movie may be logically composed of several scenes, but it can only be accessed by a timer set to the beginning of the whole film. Worse still, a video clip may only be playable as a single segment making implementation of navigation requirements impossible.

Specifying Media Controls

In many cases, controls will be provided by the media-rendering device, for example, the video player. If controls have to be implemented from scratch, then for static media there are size and scale controls to zoom and pan, page access if the medium has page segmentation as in text and diagrams, and the ability to change attributes such as color and display resolution, font type, and size in text. For dynamic media, the familiar video controls are stop, start, play, pause, fast forward, and rewind, along with the ability to address a particular point or event in the media stream by a time marker or an index, for example, "go to" component or marker.

As well as navigation controls, dialogue controls will be necessary for the information that the user has to input into the system, and the commands the user needs to give to invoke automated functions. These become the available command options; however, sometimes the boundary between a command and input data can be hard to define, for example, a dial metaphor used to set a temperature level on a thermostat may be considered as an input and a command, that is, system commands that implement automated or semiautomated actions in the task model. The final step is to select standard UI components (e.g., buttons, dialogue boxes, menus, icons, sliders) to implement user actions and controls. Most multimedia controls and data entry dialogues will employ standard UI techniques, that is, form filling, dialogue boxes, and selection menus (for more guidance, see ISO 9241, parts 12, 14, & 17; ISO, 1997).

DESIGNING THE READING OR VIEWING SEQUENCE

Having selected the media resources, the designer must now ensure that the user will extract the appropriate information. Visual media in particular may contain detailed information and, in the absence of specific directions, users will only extract high-level overview or gist. Presentation design is primarily concerned with visual media, as the user's viewing sequence is unpredictable; however, the design should also make important information salient in speech and sound. Another important consideration is to link the thread of a message across several different media. The need for focus shifts between information components are identified and attention-directing techniques are selected to implement the desired effect. This section addresses design to direct the user's attention across several media so the overall theme is delivered as a coherent whole.

Media Integration and Design for Attention

Recommendations on planning the user's reading or viewing sequence are specialized for presentation sequences, hypermedia dialogues, and navigation controls. The essential differences are timing and user control. In presentation design, the reading or viewing sequence and timing are set by the designer; whereas the reading or viewing sequence in hypertext and interactive dialogues is under user control.

Presentation techniques help to direct the user's attention to important information and specify the desired order of reading or viewing. Key information items are annotated onto presentation bar charts when planning the sequence and duration of media delivery (see Fig. 4.17).

The design issues follow:

- It is necessary to plan the overall thematic thread of the message through the presentation or dialogue.
- One must draw the user's attention to important information.
- One must establish a clear viewing or reading sequence.
- It is necessary to provide clear links when the theme crosses from one medium to another.

Design for attention is particularly important for images. User attention to time-varying media is determined by the medium itself, that is, we have little choice but to listen to speech or to view animations in the order in which they are presented. The reading sequence is directed by the layout of text, although this is culturally dependent; for example, Western languages read left to right, Arabic languages read in the opposite direction. However, viewing order in images is unpredictable unless the design specifically directs the user's attention.

Directing the user's reading or viewing sequence helps the thread of a message to be perceived more easily. In some cases, a common topic may be sufficient; however, when the thread is important or hard to follow, designed effects for attention are necessary to aid the user's perception. The term *contact point* refers to a reference from one medium to another and comes from the experimental work of Mary Hegarty (Hegarty & Just, 1993; Narayanan & Hegarty, 1998), who demonstrated that comprehension is improved by

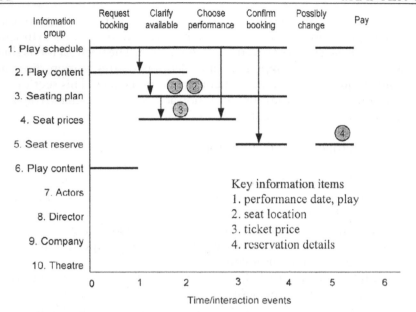

FIG. 4.17   Presentation bar chart, illustrating contact points which are represented by vertical arrows between the presented media, shown as horizontal bars. The duration of media presentation is cross-referenced to the task sequence and the key information items to be made salient are specified.

reinforcing the links between information in different media. Two types of contact point are distinguished:

- *Direct contact points*—Attention-directing effects implemented in both the source and destination medium; for example, in the text an instruction is given such as, "Look at the oblong component in Figure 1," while the component is highlighted. Direct contact points create a strong cross-reference between two media.
- *Indirect contact points*—Attention-directing effects implemented only in the source, or less frequently the destination, medium; for example, "In Figure 1, the assembly process is shown" is spoken, with no highlighting being used in the image. Indirect contact points have less attention-directing force and work by temporal sequencing or spatial juxtapositoning.

In most cases, the attentional effect in a direct contact point will be actuated in sequence, although occasionally both effects may be presented concurrently if the order of the association is not important. In hypermedia implementations, direct contact points become a link cue in the source medium and a highlight anchor in the destination medium. Contact points are specified in the presentation bar chart illustrated in Fig. 4.18.

A direct contact point should be used if the connection between information in two different media is important (Sutcliffe, 1999b). Implementation depends on the selected media; for instance, speech directs the user to the object in the image while highlighting the object that is being spoken about: "Look at the map; the road to London is … (highlight)"; or a text caption is revealed with an arrow pointing to the road. Direct contact points emphasize

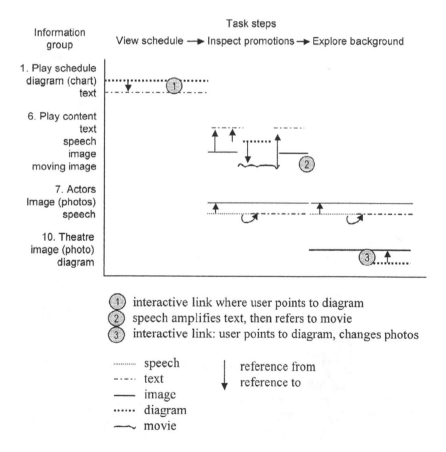

FIG. 4.18   Contact points for the browse program task. The information types have been substituted with media types and these are arranged in the first-cut script.

the links between media but can become intrusive if overused. An example of a direct contact point is shown in Fig. 4.19, where the speech track refers to an image component that is circled to draw the user's attention.

Indirect contact points are used when the connection between information in two media is necessary but perception of the destination components is less important (Faraday & Sutcliffe, 1997a), for example: "Look at figure 1," speaking about an object while displaying the image; freeze frame video while describing objects. Indirect contact points are less intrusive, so they may be used more frequently without becoming disruptive.

Multiple contact points can direct the user's attention to follow the theme and connect a thread of topics (Faraday & Sutcliffe, 1999). For instance, in a biology tutorial, explaining parts of a cell is organized with interleaved speech segments and a diagram describing the cell's components from top to bottom, left to right. Highlighting techniques locate each component in turn, following the order of the spoken explanation. A sequence of contact points is shown in Fig. 4.20; in this case, the contact points have been made explicit as buttons that jump to the start of a video segment that was related to the text. An alternative implementation would have been to highlight the text and pause the video clip at the start of the appropriate scene.

The attention-directing techniques described in the following section are used for implementing contact points.

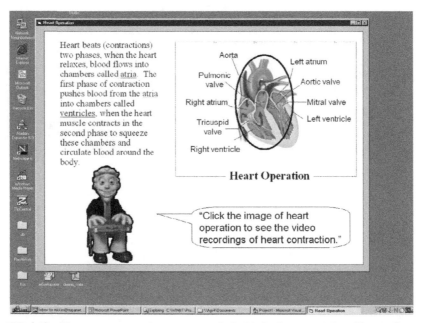

FIG. 4.19   Direct contact point between text and a highlighted image, reinforced by speech.

Salience Effects in Single Media

In larger development teams, within-media design is carried out by specialists, for example, video and animation designers, graphics and calligraphic specialists. However, in smaller teams, such experts may not be available; furthermore, novice designers still require advice. In this section, the principal design concern is making important parts of the content salient. Aesthetic and motivational issues are not addressed.

Still Image Media.   Extraction of information from images depends on domain knowledge, what people know about the components, the task, motivation (which govern how much they want to find information within an image), and design of the medium. The design problem is how to direct the user's attention to the appropriate information at the correct level of detail. Regular layout grids help design composite images (Mullet & Sano, 1995) and encourage a consistent layout in image sets. Users will tend initially to extract information from images at the scene level, that is, major objects will be identified but with very little descriptive detail (Treisman, 1988). A list of the key components that the user needs to focus on and an estimate of the facts that should be extracted from the image are prerequisites for this stage. The list is cross-checked against the design effects in Table 4.3 to see if the key components will attract sufficient attention.

Generally, users will focus on components that change or move, are brighter in color, set apart from other objects, larger in size, shown in more detail, sharper in focus, or nearer the front of the scene. If the key components have none of these properties, then a highlighting technique may be necessary. Alternatively, the window frame can be set to control which parts of an image are viewed. Larger window frames will be attended to before smaller areas. If a particular object needs to be located accurately, then mark it with a salient icon. This will act as a landmark, which will help to locate components more accurately and improve memorization of proximal objects.

A common highlighting technique will pick out spatially distributed objects, for example, change all the objects to the same color; co-located objects can be grouped by using a common color or texture for their background or drawing a box around them. The highlighted area will set the granularity of the user's attention. Captions linked to objects in an image are another useful means of drawing attention and providing supplementary information (e.g., identity). Dynamic revealing of captions is particularly effective and can be used to direct the user's viewing sequence. Sequential highlighting is also useful for showing the pathways or navigational instructions.

Highlighting techniques for designed and natural images, organized in approximate power of their effect, are summarized in Table 4.3.

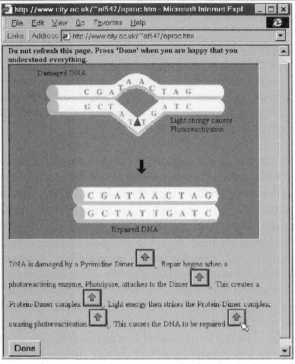

FIG. 4.20   Sequential contact points between text and video clips, implemented as buttons.

Moving Image Media.   Directing attention to components within moving images is difficult because of the dynamic nature of the medium. Design of film and video is an extensive subject in its own right, so treatment here is necessarily brief. The design advice is based on Hochberg (1986). First, the content needs to be structured into scenes that correspond to the information script. Scene boundaries structure animation sequences, and so a cut, wipe, or dissolve can be used to emphasize that a change in the content structure has taken place. Cuts, wipes, and dissolve effects will reset the user's attention and make the initial part of the following scene more salient. However, cuts should be used with care because continuity must be maintained between the two action sequences if they are to be integrated. Continuity maintains the same viewpoint and subject matter in the shot. Change in background or action, for example, a person walking left in one clip and walking right in the next, is quickly noticed as a discontinuity. The objects involved in the motion should be identifiable across the cut and the ground over which the action takes place should be stable. If the change in sequence required is large, then a wipe or dissolve can be used as an explicit signal. Cuts in general signal a smaller change in a theme.

TABLE 4.3

Attention-Directing Techniques for Different Media

	Highlight Techniques in Approximate Order of Power	Notes
Still image: designed and natural	Change of shape, size, and color of an object. Use of bold outline. Object marked with a symbol (e.g., arrow) or icon. Draw boundary, use color, shape, size, or texture to distinguish important objects from surrounding components.	Some effects may compromise natural images because they overlay the background image with new components (e.g., arrows, arcs, icons).
Moving image	Freeze frame followed by applying a still image highlight. Zoom, close-up shot of the object. Cuts, wipes, and dissolve effects.	Change in topographic motion, in which an object moves across the ground of an image, is more effective than internal movement of an object's components. Size and shape may be less effective for highlighting a moving object.
Text	Bold, font size, type, color, or underlining. To direct attention to larger segments of text use formatting.	Formatting techniques are paragraphs; headings and titles as entry points; indents to show hierarchical nesting, with bullet points and lists to guide attention.
Speech and Sound	Familiar voice. Silence followed by onset of sound. Different voices, or a change in voice prosody (tonality), amplitude (loudness), change and variations in pitch (frequency), voice rate, change source direction, alarm sounds (police sirens).	Voices familiar to the user (e.g., close relatives) are very effective in attracting attention over nonfamiliar speech. Male voices for commands, female voices for information.

An establishing shot which shows the whole scene should be used to start a new sequence and provide context. To provide detail of newly introduced object or context, the object is shown filling the frame with a small amount of surrounding scene; whereas to imply a relation or compare two objects a tight two-shot with both objects together in the same frame is advisable. If the start and end state of an action sequence are important, then a "slide show" image sequence may be better than animation, as recall of the details of action may be improved if shown in a set of stills or in slow motion. The onset or change in topographic motion, in which an object moves across the ground of an image, is more effective for attracting attention than internal movement of an object's components.

Linguistic Media (Text and Speech).   As with moving image, the literature on layout of text is extensive, so the following heuristics are a brief summary; see Levie & Lentz, 1982, for more detail. Two levels of linguistic media design are considered: first, structuring the text itself to make the segmenting of content clear, and second, design of markers within text to guide the user toward certain phrases and sentences.

Text may be structured to indicate subsections by indentation, formatting into paragraphs, columns, or use of background color. Bullet points or numbered sections indicate order more formally, for example, for procedures. If language is being used to set the context for accompanying media, it is important that the correct reference level is set. For instance, a higher-level concept or the whole scene is described at the beginning of a script. When detail or particular objects are important, then the level of detail is set by introducing single facts or individual objects.

Cue phrases and keyword markers can be used to make phrases and sentences more salient. For instance, when an action sequence or time is complex or unfamiliar, a cue phrase "in the following steps" can be used to explain the change. Sequence cues, for example, "at time x," "next," or "just after," locate an important time point or event, such as the start or end of a sequence, whereas "next," "until," "while," or "if … then … otherwise" indicate order in sequences. Causal relations can be suggested by markers such as "because," "in order to," "consequently," or "resulting-in"; whereas comparisons may be signaled by "in contrast," "as opposed to," "on the other hand," or "either … or." Finally, voice change (active to passive, first person to third) in text or spoken language can be used to segment text and emphasize different sections. The effects, ordered according to their power in attracting attention in text and speech, are summarized in Table 4.3. These effects are used to draw attention to important information within each medium as well as making clear thematic links between media.

This concludes the method stages, which have now produced a detailed and thematically integrated presentation design. The guidelines will have been applied either to the specification bar chart before implementation or iteratively during a cycle of prototype implementation, evaluations, and critiquing.

Case Study Example

To illustrate the guidelines, an example of a commercial CD-ROM, "The etiology of cancer," is used. This application was designed for undergraduate training of medical students. The content is directed toward causal explanation and conceptual learning, and the following segment explains how an enzyme repairs a mutation in a DNA sequence. The important facts that should be conveyed follow:

- The identity and attributes of the objects—DNA, with the mutation to be repaired, the photolyase enzyme, the dimer (enzyme bound to damaged DNA), and light energy.
- The actions organized in the sequence of repair—DNA is damaged by mutation, enzyme attaches to damaged DNA, forms dimer complex, light energy activates enzyme, DNA is repaired, enzyme detaches from DNA.
- Causal explanation—That DNA is repaired by the photolyase enzyme which forms a dimer complex with the DNA and requires light energy to activate it.

The information types for this explanation task are shown in Table 4.4. In the original product, no bullet points were used, and there were only a limited number of text captions to augment the image and speech soundtrack. Part of the presentation used a sequence of revealed captions, with limited animation in the light energy sequence; however, the design did not follow the causal explanation media pattern. The goal was not introduced and no summary of key concepts was given, although the causal sequence was portrayed as a series of still images with minianimations. The whole sequence was not repeated with an animation to integrate the causal explanation.

Several contact points should link the speech and between-image and text components. However, few contacts were implemented in the initial version of the product (see Fig. 4.21). Furthermore, no attempt was made to highlight key components, such as the enzyme or the dimer complex.

TABLE 4.4

Information Analysis for the DNA Photolyase Sequence

Information Topic	Information Type	Appropriate Media
DNA, enzyme, dimer light, energy objects	Conceptual and physical, descriptive, visio-spatial.	Still image: captions.
Attach, activate, repair, and detach actions	Discrete actions, conceptual and physical.	Still image, text captions.
Damaged and repaired DNA	States, also events, on physical objects.	Still image.
DNA repair	Causal explanation.	Text, still image, animation, speech.

The redesign to improve contact points between media is shown in Fig. 4.22. These strengthen coordination between the speech track and image components as well as making key objects more salient. Comprehension tests were carried out on this product before and after improvements using the contact point guidelines (Faraday & Sutcliffe, 1997b). Comprehension was significantly improved for novices after redesign; experts showed some improvement. This experimental evidence demonstrated the value of directing the user's attention with image-based media as well as showing the importance of integration in multimedia.

SUMMARY

This chapter described a method for designing interactive multimedia, including modeling techniques and guidelines. The method starts with requirements analysis to capture the users' goals. This is followed by analysis of the users' characteristics; domain analysis to create a profile of the users' knowledge, roles, and abilities; and a description of the system domain, environmental variables, available technology, and domain layout. This information influences media selection and choice of metaphors. Analysis proceeds by task analysis to decompose requirements goals, possibly supplemented by use case description of user-system interaction. The next step is information analysis, which establishes the content for education multimedia and the information needed to support users' tasks. Information units and groupings are classified with a set

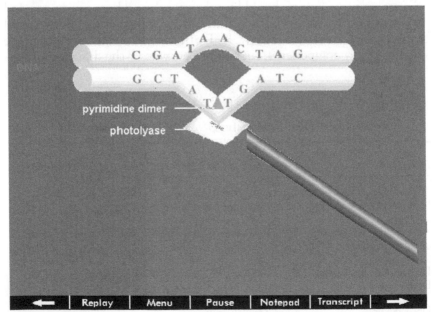

FIG. 4.21   DNA photolyase sequence before the application of contact point guidelines.

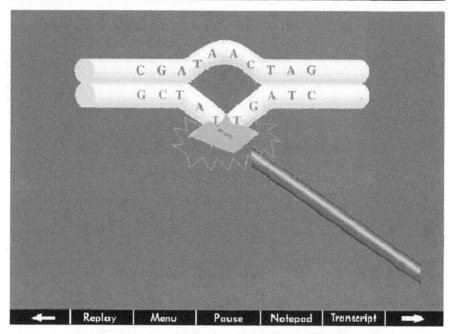

FIG. 4.22   DNA photolyase sequence after the application of contact point guidelines.

of amodal information types that facilitate mapping to appropriate media. Media resources are selected for the information types using a set of mapping rules and the presentation is organized in a first-cut script. These are used to create storyboards and mock-ups of the system, which are tested with users to get early feedback on the design. Aesthetic effects modify selection rules and focus on choice of media for attractiveness and arousal. Use of human image can project personality and develop persuasive dialogues.

More detailed design focuses on presentation layout and specification of the user-system dialogue. Dialogues are based on the users' tasks, with additional controls for navigation and manipulation of media. Presentations are specified in screen maps and bar charts, which show the order and layout of windows and playing audio media. Navigation is based on the logical model of information with search and access facilities. The second aspect of detailed design is highlighting information to draw the users' attention to key facts and establish contact points between related information in different media. Design effects for making information salient in each media type are used to add contact points to the presentation.

5

Designing Virtual
Environments

VR has been primarily driven by technology. Design of VR systems does need considerable improvement (Bolas, 1994); furthermore, the support for the user's perception, navigation, exploration, and engagement is often inadequate (Wann & Mon-Williams, 1996). Significant usability problems with current VEs have been reported by Miller (1994); Kaur, Maiden, and Sutcliffe (1996), in a field study of design practice, found that designers lacked a coherent approach to interaction design, were not aware of usability concepts underlying VEs, and did not use conventional HCI methods or guidelines. VE applications have radically different interaction styles from standard GUIs, as illustrated in the work of Bowman, Koller, and Hodges (1997), and Poupyrev and Ichikawa (1999); and this means that standard HCI design guidelines (e.g., ISO, 1997) are unlikely to be applicable. Very little HCI design advice for VR has been produced, apart from the research of Debbie Hix (Hix et al., 1999), who collated guidelines from the available experimental evidence (Gabbard, Hix, & Swan, 1999). The problem with most new technologies is that they outpace the experimentalists' ability to test them. Hence there is little experimental psychological evidence on which guidelines can be based. However, several studies have been conducted on topics ranging from navigation (Darken & Sibert, 1996) to the effectiveness of different interaction techniques and the sense of presence (Slater, Usoh, & Steed, 1995).

Although some guidelines have been produced, designers need a method to provide an agenda to organize the design process and contextualize design advice. This chapter describes such a method and inter alia provides guidelines that are appropriate to each stage. It owes its origins to Kulwinder

Kaur's thesis (Kaur, 1998) that produced guidelines and a method that were tested in industry with VR designers. Her work has been expanded and refined since in the EPSRC ISRE (Immersive Scenario-based Requirements Engineering) project to produce the advice in this chapter.

INTRODUCTION

VR has been accused of being a technology looking for a real application. In spite of the inevitable hype that accompanies most innovative technology, VR has survived and found use in several domains; for example, see the following:

- *Education and training*—The task in these applications is to learn (from the student's point of view) or to instruct or teach (from the teacher's viewpoint). There may also be an embedded task that is being taught, for example, a VR world for training surgical tasks.
- *Requirements analysis and virtual prototyping*—In these applications, a prototype product is represented in the virtual world for user testing. The main task is requirements validation, checking that the prototype does what the user wants, but this implies a secondary task which is whatever the product is designed to do, for example, a virtual scalpel for dissection. Virtual prototyping can take many forms such as walkthroughs of virtual buildings to validate architects' designs.
- *Entertainment and fun*—The games market predated VR but is now starting to assimilate VEs. In this case, the user has just one high-level goal: enjoyment. Once again there may be a secondary goal, which is the objective of the game, for example, exploring a mythical world, destroying various monsters, and so forth.
- *Teleoperation*—Telesensory or telerobotic environments enable us to see and interact in remote, inaccessible, and otherwise inhospitable environments, such as controlling robots in nuclear reactors, microsurgery, and exploring deep-sea locations. User tasks are exploring, navigating, and controlling a remote device. There may also be a secondary task with telerobotic applications such as digging for samples on the seabed in marine exploration.
- *Marketing*—VR has been employed to market products either before they are designed or to give prospective customers a feel of interaction by virtual operation. The main task is to convince the user of the value and quality of the product.

VR has been used in many other applications, including domains where there is little real world to model, for example, virtual representations of information categories for browsing and retrieval. However, most VR applications have a close correspondence with the real world. Many applications are not suitable for VR. There is little point in VR sales order processing or accounting, although the convergence of marketing with sales does have VR potential, for example, in future home banking applications a VE interface might be more attractive for users if they can fly through a virtual bank and interact with virtual (but realistic) people for enquiries rather than typing requests in an anonymous form-filling dialogue. As with multimedia, VR is just one point on the continuum of design possibilities for interaction. UIs in the future will increasingly blend traditional menus and form-filling dialogues with multisensory interaction in graphical 3D worlds.

It should be apparent from the brief survey of applications that tasks in VR come in layers. The main task frequently can only be expressed in terms of high-level goals, whereas the secondary task is often a property of the environment itself, such as operating a product or simulation. In virtual worlds, interaction is often unconstrained and exploratory, so we need to revise conventional analytic approaches. That is not to say we should ignore task analysis or use cases completely, rather that we need to complement them with a domain analysis.

DEVELOPMENT APPROACH

Designing virtual worlds is in many ways similar to designing any human computer interface. The job of the designer is to make the UI as predictable and observable as possible, so that interaction is intuitive. However, in other ways the design problem is very different. In many applications, virtual worlds are intended to mimic the real world, so design is constrained by the appearance and function of the modeled (real) world. Sometimes we find the real world very confusing and unusable, so transforming it into a virtual world just transfers the confusion. This may be acceptable when the application is intended for training or for prototyping designs when usability problems need to be uncovered. However, when usability is a key quality, for example, telesensory operation, the virtual world and its controls have to be predictable.

If anything distinguishes VR from other UIs (including multimedia), it is the 3D graphical world and interactive devices that represent part of the user (the presence or self) in the virtual world. The designer therefore has to create a complex graphical representation and choose (or create) interaction devices that are appropriate for the users and their task. Both devices and computer graphics are at the cutting edge of technology, which changes rapidly. This means that VR design has to be carried out within the constraints of available technology. Technology will improve, so many constraints will go away; however, others may persist for some time to come.

This chapter reviews the process of VR design and describes a method that starts with the conventional HCI view of task analysis and then proposes techniques and guidelines for designing VEs and interaction. The method has five stages, which are summarized in Fig. 5.1. Analysis commences with requirements and system scoping. This is accompanied by task and domain analysis, which capture aspects of the real world that will be represented in the VE. Although this also occurs in design of multimedia and GUIs, it assumes more importance in VR. The third stage is design of the

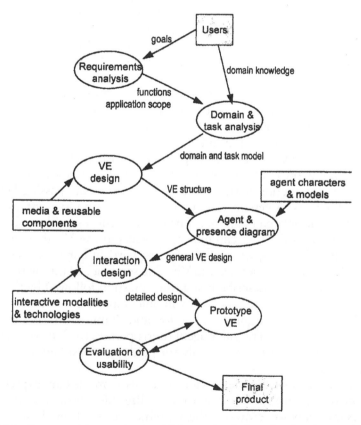

FIG. 5.1   Overview of the virtual reality development method as a data flow diagram showing method stages and resources.

VE, interaction, and the user presence, which is followed by design of user support and navigation. The final stage is evaluation, which leads into iterations of design until the prototype is improved and released as the final product. The method advocates a user-centered approach; hence, involvement of users in the requirements analysis and evaluation are essential for achieving a usable product.

TASK AND REQUIREMENTS ANALYSIS FOR
VIRTUAL ENVIRONMENTS

Tasks describe user activity. Conventional methods (see Annett, 1996, Hierarchical Task Analysis; Johnson, 1992, Task Knowledge Structures and KAT) carry out a top-down functional decomposition of user activity as goals, as described in chapter 4. For VR design, we supplement the task analysis approach with use case modeling. Use cases were invented by Jacobson, Christerson, Jonsson, and Overgaard (1992) as the requirements analysis phase of object-oriented system engineering method, and have since become incorporated into the Unified Modeling Language (UML; Rational Corporation, 1999). They have the advantage of representing interaction explicitly and lend themselves to agent-based specification. However, use cases do not readily represent cognitive and noninteractive tasks, so a combination of goal-oriented task analysis and use cases is advisable. A use case of an interaction with a possible simulated world is illustrated in Fig. 5.2.

Behavior of agents in VEs can be specified by task models; however, task models do not express interaction, so a better alterative is use cases, which capture how interaction is structured as a set of events passing between agents and objects. A general description of interaction in a system with a guide agent is illustrated in Fig. 5.2. The guide agent responds to the user's queries directly, or the user can indicate objects in the VE that the guide then explains. Three agents are specified as vertical bars: the user, guide agent, and interactive objects in the VE. The sequence of interaction reads from top to bottom to describe first a user question followed by the guide agent's answer, then the user points to an object in the environment which responds by notifying the guide of its action and giving a visual indication of its response to the user. The guide agent then operates the VE object, which carries out appropriate actions. Finally, the guide agent explains the demonstration to the user.

This is an abstract high-level view. Use cases are usually expressed in more concrete terms; for instance, to specialize this interaction, the guide agent operates a power switch in the VE which responds by showing it has changed state to "on" with a red light. This illustrates one of the problems with use case specification: we want to specify behavior in abstract terms,

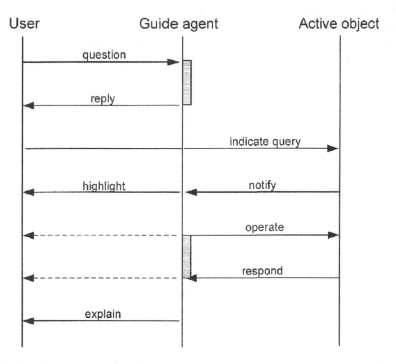

FIG. 5.2   Generic use case describing interaction between an explainer agent, an active object, and the user in a virtual environment.

but unfortunately, use cases tend to include physical detail which rapidly becomes overpowering in VEs. In the requirements phase we want to avoid premature commitment to design, so more abstract use cases can provide the answer. For example, in the initial exchange between the user and the agent, questions and answers could be implemented by a menu dialogue or by speech understanding with sophisticated answer generation. The use case states the requirements rather than the implementation. Use cases can be refined by adding more detail of interaction, but the specification of low-level physical interaction is rarely worthwhile. In Fig. 5.2, visual feedback from the active object and the guide to the user could be indicated, although this could be taken as an implicit property of the VE, that is, that all actions are inspectable.

The whole system will be composed of several use cases allowing the complexity to be broken down into manageable parts, with each use case describing a task or service carried out by one of the interacting agents. Use cases share a goal orientation with tasks, so each use case should achieve one particular goal (Graham, 1998). Use cases are decomposed to describe interaction in increasing detail. In the guide example, two use cases for explaining and demonstrating goals could be developed for the guide. Specific use cases could describe demonstrations of specific equipment in the domain such as electrical switch gear, moving floor partitions, and so forth. Use case descriptions contribute specifications of agents' behavior. In some applications, a physical reality may not exist to be modeled (e.g., chemical molecules for protein analysis), so the use case has to be created as an initial design vision. Use cases give an initial scope for the application by describing the agents and their activity in a context. The software engineering aspects of specification can then proceed to analyze classes of objects and agents; activity is described in more detail in activity sequence diagrams, following UML notation.

Another approach to initial specification is to use scenarios. These are simple narrative descriptions that either state a usage scenario as the user would interact with the system, or a problem that needs to be solved by the design (Carroll, 1995). In VEs, scenarios might describe the interaction between the user and virtual agents; so for the business park application, if we name our guide agent Jim and the user Mary, the scenario narrative will be as follows:

> Jim greets Mary and introduces himself as the guide for the tour around the business park. Before Jim starts the guided tour, he informs Mary that she can stop and ask a question at any time. He then starts the tour, going to the first large facility after the entrance to the park. He enters the building and gives basic statistics about the floor area and facilities. After asking if Mary has any questions, he continues to explain the electrical system. Jim opens the switch panel and demonstrates the voltage phase control system by changing the level on circuit 1. When the switch is moved down a red light indicates that the 512 voltage circuit is live …

The merits of scenarios are that they provide concrete, realistic examples, which are easily identifiable with users, hence they help the process of requirements elicitation and validation. By anchoring the specification with an example, points of detail become clear. Scenarios can be transformed into use cases and specifications as activity sequence diagrams or used to motivate development of early prototypes. Note that in the previous example, details of how Mary and Jim communicate are not specified. This refinement by speech or simple menu controls for fixed questions is added later in design.

TASK AND DOMAIN MODELS

Domains are the part of the real world that is to be represented in the VE. Many VR systems are used to investigate designed or real worlds, for example, simulations of buildings for fire safety training, operational testing of virtual aircraft. In these applications, faithful simulation of the real world in the VE is important. Usability criteria have to be sensitive to the system objectives; for instance, giving help and guidance may not be advisable in safety assessment when the aim is to see how people evacuate a building, and diagnose flaws in evacuation routes. On the other hand, when the system exists to help the user achieve a task goal, support for the user's task should be explicit. Taking a virtual library as an example, the user's goal is to retrieve specific information and to browse through the library. The application should help the user navigate and locate information, even if this means that the correspondence between the real-world library and its virtual counterpart is violated.

Accordingly, the application domain and user tasks need to be classified for the degree of desired naturalness. Some examples of natural VEs are design simulations (aircraft), applications for exploring spatial information (geography), and training for action in the real world (operating machinery). These applications are characterized by a high degree of correspondence between the VE and the real world that it models. Ideally, interaction would be totally immersive and the user should be unaware that the virtual world is artificial. Hybrid natural environments correspond to the real world but allow basic laws of physics to be broken in some way, for example, in tutorial applications for physics, the laws of gravity can be reset to experiment with different effects. The departure from the real world gives designers a greater degree of freedom to specify the look and interactive feel of the VE. Included in this group are virtual worlds which are not directly observable by people; for example, molecular chemistry and imagined worlds of games and virtual MUDs and MOOs (multiuser dungeons and object-oriented variants thereof) that are models loosely based on observable reality, although there is no corresponding real world. Artificial environments bear little or no correspondence to any real world. Examples are virtual libraries where the visualization is based on abstract shapes for information categories (Mackinlay, Rao, & Card, 1995). The designer has complete freedom to create the topology and interaction in the VE.

The representation of environments and the naturalness of objects' behavior have a strong bearing on how users' tasks will be carried out. For example, in a physics tutorial application, the user's task may be to explore and try out simulations of gravity, whereas the system's tasks are to test the user's understanding and explain the laws of physics. For exploration and information provision, the user's tasks may simply be to explore and navigate. In simulations, the user may have a more directed task; for instance, to vacate a building via escape routes in a safety assessment application. The task domain environment is investigated by questions that focus on the naturalness of interaction:

- How close should the correspondence be between the real world and the virtual world?
- How important is it that interaction with objects directly mimics the real world?
- Should natural modalities (haptic kinaesthetic feedback) for interaction be provided?
- Should the user's action be constrained by laws of physics?

The answers are used to set objectives for what the system should achieve in terms of natural engagement and user support. An illustration of the naturalness trade-off is provided in Fig. 5.3.

The leg in Fig. 5.3 is represented in a seminatural manner as a compromise between full photo realistic images for students to learn about the leg's appearance, and exploring the internal structure of the leg, which is facilitated by a semitransparent display. Where reality is at a premium, the design may create an "augmented reality" in which some artifacts and controls are tangible real objects contained within the virtual world. The need for accurate haptic feedback in manipulation tasks may point toward augmented rather than full VR.

Tasks in VR applications tend to be a collection of services rather than having the well-formed sequential structure more common in transaction processing applications. Consequently, task analysis has to locate activity in particular parts of the environment, and describe the artifacts and tools involved as well as the agents and their location. Task or use case descriptions document the physical actions undertaken by the user and the perceptual demands for sensory–motor coordination. These will have an important bearing on the design of the user presence and controls. Considerations about the properties of interaction that should accompany a task (or behavior) analysis follow:

- The *complexity of manipulations* undertaken, in terms of precision required and sensory–motor coordination—Action complexity may be recorded as inspectable video footage; or users can be asked to rate the complexity of tasks on scales of 1 to 10. A more sophisticated categorization of complexity can be captured using the NASA task complexity questionnaire (Hart & Staveland, 1988).
- *Haptic feedback*—Some tasks depend heavily on the sense of touch and judging the feel, weight, or temperature of the object. As haptic

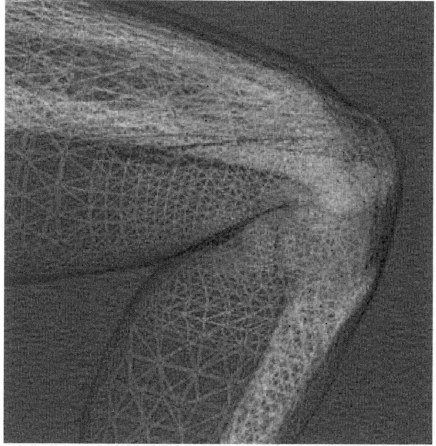

FIG. 5.3   Anatomy in a virtual reality medical application, showing leg bones in semi-transparent mode. Reprinted with permission by Ming Lin.

feedback technology is still in the prototype stage; cross-modal feedback may have to be considered.

- *Perceptual feedback*—If the task requires accurate visual feedback to show incremental effects of action, close coupling between user actions and effects will be necessary, with implications for rapid updating of the graphical display.
- *Cognitive feedback*—In tasks where mental activity and decision making predominate, the quality of the information presented in the VE may be vital, so it needs to be visible and comprehensible.
- *Navigation requirements*—Some tasks require the user to navigate around the environment, for example, exploring a virtual planet or

browsing in virtual libraries. Navigation facilities need to support movement and wayfinding.
- *Limbs and body parts involved*—Some tasks require two-handed input; or parts of the body may be used in the real world, and this will influence design of the user's presence. The extent and type of movement of the user's hands, limbs, body, and viewpoint should be noted.

Users may carry out tasks sequentially or concurrently. From the psychology of skill acquisition (see chap. 2), we know that people can only multitask effectively if they have been trained, for example, driving a car while navigating. In VEs, the same principles apply. Don't ask users to carry out two unfamiliar tasks at the same time. At the interaction level, design will have to address navigation, that is, movement of self about the world for exploration and wayfinding; object selection and movement, involving pick, drag, drop-type interaction, sufficient for simple composition or assembly-type tasks; and object manipulation, that changes the state of objects rather than their location or orientation.

In VEs, users often need to navigate and manipulate concurrently. This may cause learning and usability problems when users are unfamiliar with navigation and manipulation controls. The designer should strive to make navigation and interaction match the user's experience as far as possible. As with any UI, task design should follow the HCI mantras which should be common sense:

- Include interaction to take account of the user's knowledge and experience.
- Take user aptitudes into account, for example, spatial manipulation and orientation abilities. Motor coordination and visual acuity decrease with age.
- Take user ergonomics into account: shape, height, size, and arm reach are all-important in virtual worlds and most show gender and age differences.

Task analysis is complemented by domain analysis. The objectives of domain analysis are to capture facts about the real world that will be transformed into the virtual world. This leads to description of the objects, agents, spatial structures, and physical areas that will constitute the virtual world. Description is necessary because some objects, agents, and surfaces may become active or respond to manipulations, so we need to specify their form. The (usually visual) representation of the real world has to be captured so it can be translated into a graphical VE. Here, technology intersects with the method. We may want to sketch the domain roughly and then create graphical components to build the virtual world; alternatively, to save time on painstakingly painting shapes with a graphics package, video or digital photographs can be taken and pasted directly into the VE. However, pasted texture map images (e.g., PICT, JPEG, and GIF formats) have no depth, so some of the 3D illusion may be lost. Nevertheless, 2D images are useful for rapid implementation of VE background.

There is a trade-off in domain model capture. Digital imagery is cheaper and quicker, but it raises problems in interaction. If we have constructed a VE room from digital photographs, the computer will only be aware of each photograph as an object. To make a door handle an active object that the user can turn, the photograph has to be segmented so that the computer can identify the door handle, door, and surrounding wall. This means either that the photograph is manually edited into objects and then reassembled in the virtual world, or that an image processing system is used that can automatically segment a raster (pixel) image into meaningful shapes. Identity and meaning have to be attached to shapes to make them into interactive objects, hence domain descriptions are important.

Domain analysis can be carried out by sketching the domain taking digital (or analogue) photographs, and observing people interacting. The latter is especially important because we need to record who does what, with what, and where to produce lists of active agents (who), the tasks they carry out (does what), the location of activity (where), and the objects they interact with (with what). Agents in the virtual world will be people, animals, machines, or natural phenomena that take action on their own initiative. It is important to subdivide agents according to whether they will be facades to be controlled by users in virtual conversations and collaborative action, agents that are scripted to act in a certain way, or agents with embedded intelligence that react according to the stimuli they perceive. Objects that can be interacted with are differentiated from the background VE by the property of changing in response to interaction or external events. The dividing line between active objects and agents becomes hard to distinguish, but the judgment revolves around initiative. Objects react in response to events (a door handle turns when manipulated) whereas agents take the initiative. Description of spatial or physical structures is only necessary for components which may become objects or agents in future designs or for aspects of the VE where particular attention is necessary for design of navigation (e.g., waymarks) or affordances for manipulation (e.g., to make sure an object is accessible).

The output from domain and task analysis follows:

- Domain models captured as photographs, video, and sketches of the environment to be modeled.
- Lists of significant agents and objects in the modeled world.

- Task descriptions as services linked to agents and possible locations in the virtual world. Use case descriptions may provide an alternative representation.
- Description of visual objects and other sensory properties, for example, audible sounds produced, smells, and tastes.
- Artifacts and objects involved in tasks.

The lists of domain components form the input to stage 2, environment design.

Business Park Exploration: Case Study Example

The application (see Fig. 5.4) is a VE of Business Park buildings produced by VR Solutions, Manchester, UK, for the Welsh Development Agency. The application's purpose is to promote the Business Park to potential customers and explain its facilities.

The user tasks are to explore the building layout, to find facilities and equipment provided in the building, and gather information about these facilities. The system task is simply to simulate the building and its facilities. The system provides boxes linked to equipment objects with information texts that explain the advantages of the Business Park and its features.

The system requirements were assessed using the following walk-through questions:

- *Correspondence with natural world*—A realistic image of the building layout and facilities should be provided.
- *Interaction mimics real world*—Moderately important. Some interaction may be necessary to test equipment in the buildings but no detailed operation is necessary.
- *Interaction modalities*—Limited modalities could suffice, as visual exploration is the main application focus. Audio and sound play a minor role and haptic feedback is not vital. Speech is not required unless a conversational mannequin is used to give an interactive guided tour.
- *User's actions constrained*—Helping navigation on 2D planes is advisable, as the application should give a realistic look and feel.

> Main structures: Buildings, roadways, background, roadsides (noninteractive).
> Passive objects: Buildings, rooms, doors, windows, furniture, equipment, electrical switches, drawing boards, desks, PCs, power points.
> Active objects: Equipment, door handles, windows.
> Agents: Office workers.

"Welcome to Rural Wales Newtown site.
There now follows an automated drive
to introduce you to the site." *ongoing speech track
at start*

FIG. 5.4   Business Park virtual environment during the early phase of the guided tour. Image courtesy of VP Group.

VIRTUAL ENVIRONMENT DESIGN

VE design is inevitably a trade-off with technology. Although technical constraints will become less critical as graphical processing power increases, in practice such constraints will be with us for several years to come. This first high-level decision is choosing between immersive or desktop worlds. There are four options with increasing costs:

- *Desktop VR*—This does not give true 3D depth perception, and the sense of presence is low because the user's peripheral vision is still in the real world; however, it is cheap because only a standard PC is required.

- *Head mounted displays for immersion*—The user's movement of body and head is tracked and his or her field of view updated accordingly. Separate images are projected into the left- and right-hand side mini-VDUs so the user sees true stereo images (Fig. 5.5).
- *Immersive workbenches* (illustrated in Fig. 5.6)—Several users can view a virtual world with shutter glasses that coordinate stereo left and right eye images projected in the VE. Users see true 3D depth but can also see each other in the real world.
- *CAVE technology* (illustrated in Fig. 5.7)—Shutter glasses are used as with immersive workbenches. Several users are present in a room that forms the screen for the projected 3D world. One user is head and motion tracked to control the view. Other users have a less than perfect 3D view because the stereopsis is not calculated from their viewpoint, so coordinated movement is difficult because depth perception is misleading. Dome technology is similar but the curved projection space allows the difference in stereo viewpoints to be reduced.

The naturalness principle and task or domain analysis will indicate the choice of VR technology. Immersive worlds are advisable when the user's task involves continuous motion, complex spatial coordination, depth of field interpretation, and egocentric views. The appeal of desktop VR is low cost. Immersive VR encounters scalability problems because immersing several users in their own virtual worlds soon makes excessive demands on processing power because each user's world has to be updated according to their field of view. Furthermore, users bump into each other in the real world, so immersive head mounted displays are only suitable for single user interaction when the application requirements are for naturalness and exploration.

Multiuser worlds can be achieved by fish-task VR (Ware, 2000) and immersive workbenches in which several users can view and share interaction within a virtual space. Immersive workbenches are suitable for design and groupworking tasks where models or artifacts are manipulated in a restricted space. In applications with more extensive worlds, multiple users are represented as avatars, but each viewpoint has to be computed. Distributed worlds make the problem worse because network bandwidth constraints and transmission delays give uneven update rates. Multiuser immersive VR is more commonly achieved by CAVE environments in which one user is the master and controls movement and field of view through the world while other users are passive viewers within the master's world. They can, of course, physically move to explore different viewing angles. CAVE environments are very expensive because of the hardware installation necessary to project a room-size 3D world on three walls, floor, and ceiling.

(a)  (b)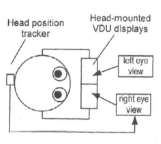

FIG. 5.5 (a) Head mounted display for immersive virtual reality with (b) a schematic diagram showing the relationship among the left-and-right-eye images and head tracking. As the user moves her head, the virtual reality graphics system calculates a new field of view for each eye.

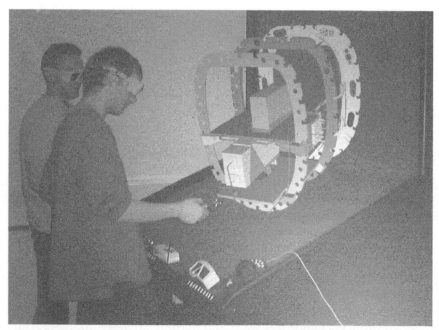

FIG 5.6 Immersive workbench in which the virtual world is projected on the desktop. Users wear shutter glasses to receive interleaved left-and-right-eye images. Reprinted with permission by Terrence Fernando.

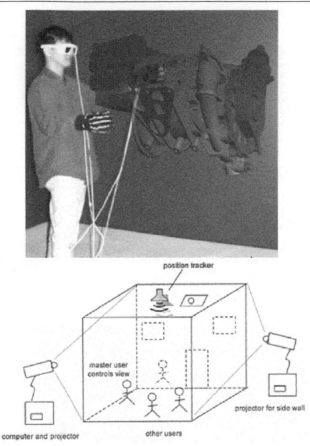

FIG. 5.7   CAVE (Computer Automated Virtual Environment) technology, in which several users are immersed in a virtual world projected on to walls, floor, and ceiling of a room. Users wear shutter glasses. Reprinted with permission by Terrence Fernando.

Once the immersion versus desktop decision has been taken, VE design is composed of three subactivities: designing the virtual world's graphical representation and the objects and agents therein, selecting the interactive devices and user presence, and design of interaction and manipulation in the virtual world.

Ideally, VR systems should be multisensory and multimodal. Such an ideal is not currently achievable and systems are likely to remain constrained for some time in the future. For example, complex force feedback, texture sensing via haptic feedback, and natural language interaction, are three technically difficult problems to solve, as well as being expensive design features. Usability therefore has to be achieved within the constraints of a technology baseline, which in turn reflects the cost constraints on a design. A review of VR technology is beyond the scope of this book; more-over, the technology is changing rapidly. However, performance is a key aspect of usability in virtual worlds, so a major consideration for the developer is to choose a tool kit that renders polygons in the virtual world efficiently. The issue is updating: if the software environment renders all the polygons each time the view is refreshed, 20 to 30 times a sec, then the graphics processor will struggle to keep up and visual judder could appear. However, tool kits that render only the objects which change position are more efficient (e.g., MAVERIK; Hubbold et al., 1999). Other VR tool kits allow distributed environments to be developed and populated with agents, with support for updating different views and components of the world (Frécon & Stenius, 1998).

VEs are rarely designed from scratch. The cost of constructing all the graphical components is enormous so most designers reuse shapes and components. VR construction tools such as Division's dVise and Superscape's VRT provide shape-component libraries for generalized environments such as buildings, rooms, streets, landscapes of fields, roads, trees, and so forth. Design teams build up their own more domain-specific shape libraries with exchangeable components.

The design steps follow:

- *Create the background* for the virtual world. Ideally the whole virtual world would be represented in detail. Detailed graphical design costs time and money, so the level of detail may have to be restricted to optimize graphical refresh rates. Very detailed representation is not vital for effective performance in VEs (Wickens & Baker, 1995), so detailed background should be included only when aesthetic considerations are important (i.e., marketing applications). The VE background will include areas and shapes that provide the visio–spatial structure. Noninteractive boundaries in the world, for example, walls and landscapes, may be implemented by photographed images; however, this will create a detail clash with other parts of the VE that are hand drawn with graphical tools.
- *Design interactive objects, agents, and structures.* The first step is to decide which objects, agents and structures should be active. Active areas of the system have to be segmented from the background. If realistic media (photographs) are being used to create the virtual world, the original bit map image will have to be edited in a drawing tool, such as Photoshop, to create separate interactive objects.
- *Add navigation waymarks and pathways.* The extent and intrusiveness of navigation features will depend on the demands of naturalness. In applications where being faithful to the natural world is less vital, landmarks can be introduced to help users remember

certain locations (e.g., placing a pub at a corner in a virtual city); portals can be cued so users can find access to different worlds; and other features can be added as graphical indications for navigation pathways.

• *Plan integration of the VE* with the whole UI. In desktop VR, the virtual world may be placed in one window surrounded by a GUI desktop. Other GUI components may be planned as pop-up features within the VE, for example, menus, dialogue boxes, and so forth.

Part of the VE design also involves selection of devices and communication modalities. Because interaction influences representation, this step in practice is interleaved with the next.

SELECTING MODALITIES AND INTERACTIVE DEVICES

Choice of devices and design of the user presence need to consider inbound and outbound interaction. Inbound interaction can be divided into control or command action and data entry, although the boundary between them is blurred, for example, operating a virtual power plant using a virtual slider to set the power generation level acts both as a command and inputs a value.

The prime objective is to make multimodal dialogues natural to use in terms of the user's characteristics and task. Mapping inputs to devices depends on the type of input, for example, discrete or analogue, language or value, or whether manipulation is suggested by the need for natural interaction. A limited set of heuristics is provided in this chapter; however, further advice can be found in Buxton (1995) or the modality theory of Bernsen (1994).

Modalities for computer–human communication are vision (desktop, immersive head mounted, immersive environment), audio (speech, sound), haptic (force feedback, texture), motor (various devices, pressure sensors), and olfaction. Audio is necessary when speech interaction is planned, for warnings, supplementary information to avoid overloading the visual channel, or when the user is mobile. Speech may be necessary for command input and audio output from human avatars. Most VEs will provide visual and audio feedback; however, haptic communication is desirable for fully natural object manipulation, for example, in virtual surgery the feel of pressure, elasticity, viscosity of flesh and other organs are important. Devices for implementing force feedback and surface texture perception are still limited. Other sensory feedback, for example, smell and taste, may be desirable if applications demand a high degree of naturalness, for example, smells and taste of fruit in a virtual jungle exploration, although current technology makes this difficult to implement.

The choice between real devices or software surrogates (i.e., augmented reality) in the virtual world depends on the cost of creating devices, how dedicated the application is, the need for haptic feedback, and cost. Devices may be implemented either in hardware or software; for instance, in the surgery application, the doctor could be provided with real tools to manipulate in virtual space or a software tool held in a dataglove. Systems devoted to one goal, for example, games, may justify investment in real racing car controls for interaction in a virtual racetrack, but most applications will not. For other applications, the choice may not be so obvious. For example, in a scientific analysis VE, a calculator could be designed as a separate pop-up interface with a traditional GUI look and feel; alternatively, the calculator could be part of the environment. The choice will be influenced by the naturalness trade-off and modality choice. In immersive VR, GUI components in the virtual world will be difficult to interact with via a dataglove, whereas in desktop VR the user can switch to the keyboard with ease. The use of real devices changes the application from virtual toward augmented reality. At this stage, the key issues for the designer follow:

- The importance of haptic feedback—If precise feel and proprioceptive feedback is important for the task, then tangible devices are preferable.
- If naturalness is an important concern, GUI widgets should be avoided.
- If applications will be dedicated to one domain or world and haptic interaction is important, then augmented reality becomes more cost effective.

Control and representation of motor actions depend on the motor action and body movements required by the user's task, and the level of precision for manipulations. If the user has to operate a device and the physical detail is important for learning a task, then the representation should be sophisticated and as natural as possible. Datagloves can suffice for simple gesture, but if the task requires arm or body positioning, then a more complete representation of the user's self may be necessary with a body suit. Speech may be necessary for command input and audio output from human avatars.

This analysis creates a list of modalities for each task or high-level requirements goal. In many current applications, achieving a full realistic graphical representation is not possible because of the limited processing power and consequent poor response times. Poor response time leads to usability problems at the perceptual level when users experience motion sickness caused by uneven update of virtual world images. Another trade-off is between "low gain" devices for precise manipulations and "high gain" devices for longer-range movement. Devices can map users' real-world actions to their virtual counterparts either faithfully with low gain (i.e., 0.5 m movement in the real world is represented as 0.5 m movement in the virtual world), or they can be high gain (or rate controlled). In high gain devices, a small movement is amplified to empower the user's movement for navigation. In most VEs, a combination will be necessary: high gain devices that allow users to move long distances for relatively small actual movements, and low gain devices that render action faithfully when interacting with objects.

Isotonic devices do not provide a direct mapping between the degree of force exerted by the user and the movement of the control, whereas isometric devices do. Most VR devices are isotonic because they offer near-zero resistance; for instance, a dataglove can be moved easily and is only subject to the resistance of gravity while the virtual hand moves through the virtual world. Where haptic feedback is required, isometric devices, such as a joystick or space ball (see Fig. 5.8), should be employed. In this case, the force exerted by the user is proportional to the deflection in the joystick, giving a more realistic interactive feel.

Pointing and Selecting

Object selection is usually effected by a pinch metaphor. The user's action is detected by dataglove sensors so a pinch contact of fingers when the virtual hand is proximal to the object is interpreted as a select. Ray casting can activate objects for selection when the ray intersects with the object boundary, or the ray can terminate when it intersects with the first plane. This enables exploration of depth within VEs (Fukumoto, Mase, & Suenaga, 1995). Cone spotlights require less precise movement to locate objects, but suffer from more occlusion than ray casting.

(a)   (b)

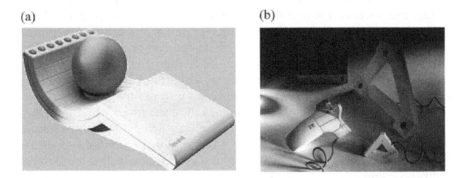

FIG. 5.8   (a) Space ball; the ball can be moved forwards, backwards and sideways, as well as being twisted for rotation. Six infrared senors detect motion of the ball. (b) Space mouse; ultrasound is used for tracking movement and location. Both devices are isometric.

Selection may be integrated with querying. This is necessary when users want to explore the properties, behavior, or state of objects. Pop-up text, animation, or speech can provide the explanation. In augmented reality, querying is more important, because applications are frequently designed to provide information about real objects in the user's view. Speech is efficient for querying, but the user may have to learn a restricted sublanguage of question types. Alternatively, GUI dialogue boxes can be popped up for query formation.

Speech in Virtual Worlds

In immersive environments, speech presents the problem of whom to speak to. Placing an avatar or agent presence in the virtual world provides a focus for speech. Speech increases naturalness of interaction, but it comes with the penalty of complex natural language processing. As speech and natural language understanding is not 100% reliable, error repair dialogues are necessary when machine understanding breaks down. Repair dialogue should be part of spoken interaction for another reason. Speech is powerful when combined with deictic (pointing and gesture) interaction. Unfortunately, we often refer to objects in the world by elliptic reference, for example, "you can see it now, just by the corner over the page." People are good at solving such elliptical references by using general knowledge and context cues from the other person's direction of gaze, and so on. Computers rarely have access to additional information, so they will often have to ask the user where is "there." Speech dialogues therefore have to be planned with the limitations of machine-based natural language in mind.

Audio has the advantage of increasing naturalness of interaction and increasing the sense of presence. Audio may be stereo in headphones for head mounted displays or quadraphonic for CAVE environments. The location of sound sources provides a strong sense of naturalness.

Haptic Interaction

Tactile devices generally use vibration as the means of communicating properties of a surface, whereas kinaesthetic devices use hydraulic or pneumatically generated pressure to convey force feedback that would normally come from muscle tone and gravity. Vibration can be used to communicate properties associated with contact in several ways; for instance, the feel of a loose key in a lock, or the sliding of an object over a rough or smooth surface. Vibrations can be used to signal proximity or the angle of approach, as well as contact with a surface. In some cases vibration can be used to convey kinaesthetic feedback such as grip pressure, but generally it is advisable to separate the devices for rendering touch and grip. Haptic devices are either worn as gloves with vibrator actuators in the fingers, or on the desktop, such as the Phantom thimble style interaction, which communicates force feedback very accurately but is limited to one finger.

Selection of haptic devices depends on the cost and reliability of the technology. Force feedback is necessary to increase the naturalness of a wide variety of physical tasks; in fact, it is necessary whenever handgrip, lifting, press down, pull, push, and twist actions are encountered. Devices can be divided into point feedback, which gives force feedback to a single finger as in the Phantom (see Fig. 5.9a), or exoskeleton devices (see Fig. 5.9b) that give feedback over a larger area of the user's hand or arm. The problem with exoskeletons is that they rapidly become heavy and cumbersome to wear.

Accurate representation of grip and kinaesthetic feedback is necessary for tasks that need to correspond to the real physical world. Vibration can communicate a wide variety of different surfaces. We learn to associate vibration with the visual rendering of the texture, but this substitution has to be used sparingly. Trying to encode different textures on to different vibration frequencies will encounter the human limitation of poor frequency discrimination. Communicating complex texture is therefore best left to the real object in augmented reality.

Interacting in virtual worlds is usually constrained by inadequate haptic and proprioceptive feedback, so dialogue design has to provide additional facilities to counteract the limitations of technology. Although the lack of haptic feedback is not critical for movement, it does become more important in complex manipulation.

Substituting feedback with other modalities can ameliorate the absence of haptic feedback in most VR applications that cause user errors and im-

(a)   (b)

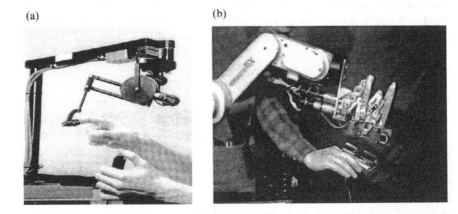

FIG. 5.9   Force feedback devices. (a) Phantom finger point device, and (b) exoskeleton for hand and arm force feedback.

pair the sense of naturalness. Haptic and kinaesthetic feedback are necessary for the following:

- Grip, touch and manipulation—making simple manipulations easier to avoid reaching through virtual objects.
- Communicating physical properties of objects: plasticity, elasticity, sense of deformation, and grip or pressure interaction—so interaction obeys the laws of physics that constrain real-world interaction.
- Giving a sense of the surface texture of objects: roughness, smoothness, stickiness, and so forth.

The substitutable modalities are visual encoding by use of color and surface textures, for shape deformation and grip pressure; and audio encoding by use of amplitude, frequency, and more complex tones, music scales, and possibly speech feedback, for surface properties or grip pressure.

The requirements for haptic feedback are implicit in tasks, for example, maintenance that involves disassembly, cleaning, adjusting, repairing objects, grip, manipulation with pressure sensitive feedback, and surface texture plasticity. Object manipulation should result in haptic feedback about the object's surface, its deformation in response to grip, and mass when lifted. If haptic devices are not available, modal substitutions can be provided visually or aurally. Changes to object properties that are scalar can be mapped to audio scales or color spectrum changes, for example, grip pressure is communicated by a rising pitch. Visual feedback can interfere with the object's appearance, so audio is the better modality for mapping mass or lifting exertion, or grip pressure or deformation, to the dimension of sound frequency, for example, increasing pitch maps to more force being applied. In simple cases, color change is used to signal proximity and grasp of objects in a similar manner to the "handles-select" metaphor used in graphics packages. The object changes color when the user's presence is near; the user then selects the object by a grip gesture or simple control; the object color is changed to signify the selected state and it moves following the user's actions. Visual cues can substitute for the sense of touch, for example, highlighting the object when it is approached, changing the highlight when it is touched, and possibly making automatic contact by a snap-to feature. The disadvantage of visual cue substitution is that the interaction hardly appears, let alone feels, natural.

Unfortunately, modal substitutions are not easy to interpret. Textures have many properties which can be mapped to the large variety of audible tones, but the suggestibility of tones for surface properties is weak. Color and visible texture give a very limited experience of roughness and other textures. However, mapping pressure and grip force to color spectra or audio scales does give reasonably comprehensive feedback. Object mass and deformation are normally perceived through the proprioceptive sense, so trying to signal these properties requires the user's presence to be monitored and then interpreted in light of the object's properties. A further trade-off is to examine when it may be more effective to implement haptic interaction via augmented reality compared to virtual reality.

Selecting Communication Modalities

Communication modalities often involve a design trade-off to optimize choices for a particular user population. For example, for professional users, devices with a higher learning and memory cost might be acceptable to achieve lower interaction costs; whereas for general public use, lower learning costs might be traded for higher interaction costs. The former design would employ shortcuts, modes, and power commands, whereas the latter will have longer but simpler dialogues.

These choices can be helped by using a cost trade-off model as a "tool for thought." The costs of interaction are stated as follows:

- *Cost of interaction*—Each dialogue action costs time, so a dialogue should aim to fulfill the task with the minimum number of steps, following the economy principle (Sutcliffe, 1995a).
- *Cost of memory*—If information or commands are not directly visible, the user has to remember how to obtain them. This may be remembering the status (mode) of the system or maintaining a conceptual map of an information space. The less information is visible, the more work the user has to do to remember where it is.
- *Modality cost*—Speech and natural language are the most natural way for us to communicate commands and alphanumeric data. If we have to translate language into another modality, this will impose a cost. Similarly, gesture and manipulations are the most natural modality for constructing drawings, and manipulation with haptic feedback is optimal for natural action. The more direct the transformation of our intent into action, the lower the modality cost.
- *Learning costs*—Interaction costs can be reduced by shortcuts and power commands, but at a penalty of increasing learning.

The cost metrics can be used to discriminate between different hardware input devices according to the nature of the information and commands that are to be input. The volume of data to be entered and the approximate number of commands expected per task are estimated. This provides an interaction volume that is used to estimate operational and error time. The analysis steps follow:

- Estimate the operational time per task and multiply it by the estimated interaction transaction volume. GOMS–KLM metrics (John & Kieras, 1995) may be used to estimate unit task times in detail.
- Estimate the error correction time per task, based on an expected error rate and correction time.
- Assess the naturalness of the chosen modality-device combination for the user's task. Rate naturalness on a 1 to 7 scale (1 = *unnatural, hard to use*; 7 = *very natural, very easy to use*).
- Assess the cost of learning either as an estimated learning time to train users to an adequate performance level or assign a difficulty rating on a 7-point scale (easy … hard to learn).

The first two steps provide an overall operational time for each modality choice, to which learning time may be added. Naturalness will have an impact on learning time and error rates but it may not be so amenable to direct measurement. Ideally, timing values should be gathered from experiments with device mock-ups and prototypes. The values instantiated in the following formula can be judged from typical times to complete an operation using speech, pen input, and so forth; error costs can be estimated from the average time it takes to correct errors and observed error frequencies.

$$Cost^{mod} = Cost^{oper(x)} + Cost^{error\ corr} + Cost^{learn}$$

The modality of the device should be appropriate for the user's task and context (e.g., mobile use, use in noisy environments, etc.) to achieve the lowest possible modality cost. So, for example, if the input is primarily commands, speech input may suffice even with the penalty of a 5% error rate; however, for high volume data entry, speech may not be appropriate because the error rate negates any advantages gained from the natural mode of communication. The output from this stage is specification of interactive tools linked to system tasks, with desired modalities, and notes about the match between the two, taking cost and available technology into account.

DESIGNING THE USER PRESENCE

The starting point is taken from the domain and task description of the range of physical movements and manipulations that the user needs to execute. In applications where little interaction is required and the user simply has to explore the virtual world, traditional indications of the user's location can be used, for example, the cursor arrow controlled by GUI style devices such as 3D mouse, tracker ball, and so forth. However, simple representations do not give much sense of presence or immersion; moreover, interaction is limited to movement and selection, with drag and drop being familiar from direct manipulation UIs.

Whole body representations may be displayed, although they are controlled by simple interactive devices (e.g., joystick, 3D space mouse). User representations or avatars can be operated by a command language for movement and change of facial expression, but the need to control the avatar by keyboard or menu commands makes interaction complex and impairs the sense of immersion, so most collaborative VE Web spaces use simple controls for a full presence representation with typed text or speech communication. Interaction by manipulation is strictly limited. Alternative representation is to show the user's hand, which corresponds to an instrumented glove device. In this case, the movement of the user's hand and fingers is detected and rendered on screen (see Fig. 5.10).

Movement of the user's hand is tracked by position sensors as well as changes in finger position. Navigation is controlled by gestures to fly the user's presence through the VE. Two-handed interaction can be supported, but motor coordination in two-handed interaction can be difficult. When using two hands, one hand tends to be dominant and the other subordinate. We use the dominant hand for precise manipulations while the subordinate is used for holding or gripping. Thus, we anchor a piece of paper with one hand, while

(a)   (b)

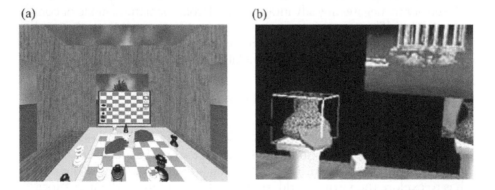

FIG. 5.10   Illustration of the user's presence implemented (a) as a virtual hand, and (b) as a virtual hand with the go-go extension for selecting distant objects—the actual position of the hand is represented as the foreground cube. Reprinted with permission by Ivan Poupyrev.

writing with the dominant (for most people, right) hand. However, with training we can achieve more equitable two-handed interaction; typing is a good example. Design of two-handed interaction needs to take the task and user preference (left- or right-handed) into consideration. When both hands have to be coordinated, this works fine when we have practiced the skill, but in an unfamiliar task without haptic feedback it can be very difficult. The reason is not hard to see. Consider what is going on in terms of the ICS cognitive model. There are two input streams, one from each hand (Somatic→Obj→Prop), but two further streams are input from the visual image of each hand (Vis→Obj→Prop). As soon as the two hands touch, but the user doesn't feel the touch, the cognitive processes have to do extra work to coordinate interaction with inaccurate information (Prop→Implic mismatch).

Design of the user representation is influenced by the viewpoint selected; this may be either of the following:

- *Endogenous*, in which the user is immersed in the VE and sees the whole world through his or her own eyes. In this case, the self can only be part of the body that would normally be visible, for example, hand, arm, front of the body, legs, and feet.
- *Exogenous*, where the users can see themselves embodied as a virtual human, because they view themselves from an external point. The self in this case is represented as an avatar or mannequin. Views may be switched between the two, although this can cause disorientation.

Movement differs in each condition. In endogenous mode, the user moves the view with the self, but in exogenous implementation, the user can move himself or herself around the VE while holding the external view constant. Movement controls guide the mannequin, which responds to simple movement such as flexing the body, arms, and manipulations by the hand.

A further issue is whether the user needs to communicate with other people. In collaborative VEs, the user's presence will need some representation of facial expression and embodiment in a human form. Human facial expressions in the real world are subtle and capable of a large number of different signals (approximately 40 different expressions can be discriminated; Russel & Fernandez-Dols, 1997). However, communication can be effective with a small subset of facial expressions, represented in stereotyped form, as cartoon designers have demonstrated for many years. Faces for expressing pleasure, displeasure, surprise, and fear can be implemented with simple combinations of mouth and eye or eyebrow shapes. Facial expressions need to be coordinated with speech, as in laughter, greetings, head nods when agreeing, and so forth, unless they are being used for simple stereotypic feedback, for example, smiling or disappointed face to signal agreement or disagreement (Ibster, Nakanishi, Ishida, & Nass, 2000; Poggi & Pelachaud, 2000).

To summarize, the design issues for the user's presence follow:

- The requirements for the user's body presence are set by the physical nature of the task. More complex manipulations indicate a whole hand presence; representation of the whole body may be necessary for maneuvers involving the user's torso and lower limbs.
- Navigation and movement controls may not require a realistic user presence, depending on the viewpoint. When exogenous views are being implemented, the user's head should be rendered in detail so that the direction of gaze can be observed.
- When communication with others is necessary, the user's presence should be lifelike and equipped with a range of facial expressions. The ability to turn the head to face the other party is also important.
- In simple exploratory applications when the user's only task is navigation, detailed representation of self may not be necessary.

DESIGNING THE PRESENCE OF OTHERS

In collaborative VEs, other users may need to be represented in the virtual world, and intelligent agents may have human-like manifestation. User presences for computer-mediated communication need to depict the intent of the other person as faithfully as possible. To an extent, computer-mediated communication is a media selection problem. Two-way video connections with a speech channel provide the most effective way of delivering verbal and nonverbal communication; however, in some circumstances, video connections may not be possible, or people may want to disguise their appearance. In these circumstances, multiple virtual presences are necessary. Internet VR meeting places have simple presences without facial expressions although individual users design bizarre images to represent their real or imagined personas. Simple scripted interaction allows walking or lip movement synchronized to speech. For more realistic communication, a range of facial expressions is necessary; for example, eyebrows raised for interest and attention, smiles, frowns, head nods, and so forth (Cassell et al., 1999). Unfortunately, nonverbal communication is automatic human behavior, so even if controls can be provided for "smile," "frown," and so forth, it is difficult for us to consciously articulate these acts. More complex agents embed planners that represent the intent and emotion of characters based on cognitive theory (Ortony et al., 1988). Thus, happy agents will smile and greet the user (André & Müller, 1998). Control of verbal and nonverbal communication can be achieved by planners and complex scripting languages; however, users' control of their own presence is defeated by the complexity of gaze operations and facial expressions. A set of high-level abstract controls are needed to express emotional effects.

Nonverbal acts can be programmed into intelligent agents (André & Rist, 2000; Oviatt & Cohen, 2000), equipped with human-like speech and appropriate nonverbal communication. Designing agents can become complex if the range of speech and natural language understanding increases, so most applications restrict speech interaction to a limited domain where a sublanguage can be specified, such as the language involved with questions and answers about train timetables, flight bookings, and so forth (Smith & Cohen, 1996). Sublanguages restricted speech generation or understanding to 500- to 1000-word vocabularies with simpler parsing and semantic analysis than full natural language. Nonverbal acts can be specified as rules to trigger appropriate facial expression for specific discourse acts, such as the following:

- Initial greeting—Face forward, eye contact.
- Question—Face forward, eye contact, eyebrow raise.
- Attending to task—Face away.
- Indifference—Shrug shoulders.

Attending to the user is important because we signal our attention by looking at the other person and adding small utterances (e.g., "aha," "yep," "em," "ok") to signal that we wish the conversation to continue. Artificial agents can do the same by facing the user when speaking. People exchange conversational turns by looking away, voice tone, small gaps in speech, and explicit discourse acts to elicit a response. Speech, and glancing away, can be effective initiative exchange signals from agents.

Attention to agents can be affected by the screen size of the agent's face. People look at and pay more attention to others who are close by and look at them when they speak. The computer equivalent in desktop VR is to have the agent facing the user and half filling the screen. In immersive VR with an endogenous viewpoint, an agent will be considered to be in close proximity at approximately 0.5 to 1 m virtual distance, the usual interpersonal distance we prefer in reality. We all like to have personal space surrounding us, generally about 0.5 m, although this is culturally dependent. Research has demonstrated that personal space gets projected onto artificial personas and we don't like having our personal virtual space invaded (Höök & Dahlback, 1992). Consequently, agents should not appear to approach the user too closely or rapidly because these movements will be interpreted as a threat. Also, the size of an agent has to be adjusted to the projection technology. Filling an IMAX large-projection screen with an agent's head will intimidate users with a "big brother" image.

Design issues with human-like presence that are frequently neglected are character and personality. We tend to think of software agents as being impersonal, so character is irrelevant; however, even simple representations of faces and language (text or speech) evoke responses to computer agents that mimic our human–human reactions (Reeves & Nass, 1996). Hence, design of appearance and behavior of virtual agents needs to be approached with care. The key design issues are politeness and using personality to improve the quality of interaction. Reeves and Nass's (1996) experimental work on people's reactions to human-like multimedia representation indicates that agents should be polite. Requests from agents should be courteous and users should be thanked for responses; however, overdoing politeness can become transparently contrived, so the key is to make the agent's language courteous yet not effusive. Conversations should start with a greeting and end with a farewell, literal "hellos" and "goodbyes."

Agents frequently need to persuade people to take a course of action or volunteer information. This concerns design of conversational strategies. Strange although it may seem, people are susceptible to fairly naive manipulation by computerized agents. We respond to praise by liking the other person, even if we are aware that the praise is in fact unwarranted flattery. Use of praise helps to engender a favorable predisposition toward the agent (Fogg, 1998; Nass & Gong, 2000). As with many facets of interaction, both human–human and human–computer, the effect can be misjudged. The tone of praise has to achieve a subtle balance between insincerity (damned by faint praise) and overdoing the effect and appearing to be a fawning sycophant. Criticism, in contrast, has a very different reaction. We reject adverse criticism that we feel is unfounded, but if is it reasoned and justified, we are more likely to accept it. Unwarranted critics are looked down on, but critics who do give valid suggestions are valued and are seen to be more intelligent. Once again human reactions generalize to computerized agents. The design implications are to be careful with computer-based criticism because it can frequently be wrong. If the computer is criticizing users, for example to persuade them to change their behavior, then a little praise first helps sugar the pill; the criticism should be justified and delivered politely yet with confidence.

The principal dimensions of human personality are introversion or extroversion, friendliness, conscientiousness, openness, and mental stability. The problem with personality is trying to match the computer's attributes with the user's. People tend to like similar characters to their own, and studies of more public "media personalities" show a liking for friendly dominants. Computer-based personality modeling can only be achieved by intrusive questionnaire-based dialogues based on psychological personality tests, hardly an acceptable dialogue technique. One immediately implementable dimension is dominance or submissiveness that can be reflected in four aspects of dialogue:

- Use of language—Dominant personalities use more commands and assertions whereas submissive characters make more suggestions and tentative proposals, and qualify assertions.
- Turn-taking initiative—Dominant personalities take the first turn; submissive personalities wait for the other party to speak.
- Dominants interrupt, submissive characters don't.
- Dominants are more confident than submissive personalities. This can be expressed in language or by simpler means such as giving a confidence rating scale (1–7) after assertions and proposals.

Dominant personality can also be indicated nonverbally. Submissive characters can be signaled by openness, gestures of raised hands with palms upwards, with hunched shoulders; in contrast, confident dominants smile and keep eye contact with the user. Dominant characters can be more persuasive (Fogg, 1998), but the design of believable and acceptable computer personalities is still in its infancy, so these design effects may not be reliable. Moreover, like the illusion of theater, they may be very susceptible to error. Once something goes wrong in the user's experience of an agent-based dialogue (or an actor forgets his lines), we change our reactions rapidly.

If no model of the user's personality is available, then computer agents should tend to be dominant but friendly and polite. If a user model can be captured beforehand from a questionnaire, then the computer agent's character can be matched with the user's: dominant with dominant, submissive with submissive. If no model is available, it may still be possible to infer something about the user's character from his or her response. When natural language is being used, this can be checked for discourse markers and phrases that signal assertiveness or otherwise, for example, use of first person, commands, modal verbs (should, must). The computer agent's character can then be adjusted accordingly.

To control agents' characters and responses requires scripted interaction or complex AI-based inference. Agents' movements may be controlled by rules and scripts of body movements to extend reactive behavior. The representation of agents in virtual worlds has improved as graphics rendering devices have become more powerful. Early implementations depicted multiple users as blocks with stereotype facial features (DIVE; Benford, Greenhalgh, Bowers, Snowdon, & Fahlen, 1995); however, more recent implementations have cartoon-quality images with more complex facial expressions and a full range of limb movements (André, Rist, & Müller, 1998); see Fig. 5.11.

FIG. 5.11   Illustration of an avatar presence in an inhabited Internet world. Reprinted with permission by the Swedish Institute for Computer Science (The DIVE Project).

Business Park Example

The application's inbound devices are keyboard, mouse, and 3D space mouse. The user tasks do not require complex manipulation of objects, so these modalities should be sufficient. The outbound device is a desktop VE simulation, although it could be run in immersive mode using stereoscopic glasses. However, use of immersive VR makes some of the text explanations difficult to read, and this highlights a clash between the demands of naturalness and artificiality in VEs. Graphical images are semirealistic and full texture detail is only partially implemented. These compromises are due to cost and platform constraints of implementing the system on standard PC workstations. Speech output is used to a limited extent, although this could be used more extensively by implementing a "human guide" mannequin to explain the Business Park facilities in an interactive dialogue. The agent should be confident and have a slightly dominant, yet friendly, personality because many different users will interact with the application. The text and speech generated by the agent should be polite, make proposals, and state facts in a confident manner. Dominance will be signaled by initiative, although the user should have the ability to interrupt at any time. This is a clear limitation that is accepted because speech technology, especially input, will not be available on many customer machines. Sound (speech) output, however, is becoming a common feature, so the specification is conservative in using prerecorded speech to explain set pieces in the VE. Recorded speech sounds more natural than its synthetic counterpart.

DIALOGUE AND CONTROLS

This stage takes the VE design and high-level specification of user presence and interactive agents, and completes the detailed design. VR dialogues differ from conventional GUI style interaction because there are many interactive objects and agents. VR dialogues are not really dialogues at all, but the integration of action, movement, and interaction, as well as conversations with other agents. Design of controls is partly a matter of providing functions to improve usability and partly constraining the users within the requirements of naturalness. For instance, ergonomic testing of building designs might indicate that the user should only move along surfaces at a height that corresponds to reality. In contrast, for exploratory or games applications, users might be given the freedom to move through walls and fly wherever they please. Hence, the first step in dialogue design is to specify the constraints on user movement. These will be implemented as appropriate affordances for control of the user's viewpoint and presence and by interactions in the VE, for example, moving the view through a wall is either permitted or inhibited.

Design of Interactive Agents

VR applications may be composed of several cooperating agents. Many of these will have been specified from the task and domain analysis; however, other agents may be added at design time to help users. In addition, the overall system design has to consider the partitioning of interaction and automated functionality. Agents may fall into four categories:

- *Interactive conversational agents* that carry out tasks, possibly in collaboration with the user. These agents will undertake physical actions in the virtual world and respond to user interaction.
- *Automated agents* that are algorithms and other processes which are triggered by the interface and system but do not have a manifestation at the interface. For instance, an algorithm for finite element analysis carries out calculations that it communicates to a VE simulation of stress in concrete in building designs.
- The *user agent* or presence that is a subclass of interactive agents but also supports user controls to move and navigate. Movement and

navigation are assumed in many tasks; however, manipulations and physical tasks may need to be specified in more detail.
- *Objects that respond* to the user's actions and change state to record the effect of actions. Objects in the VE may need to communicate state change to databases; for example, a book in a virtual library may need to signal its status as on-loan when it is handed to the user.

The system design, therefore, is composed of many interacting agents; some will be manifest in the interface, and others will implement back-end functionality. The proportion of back-end to interactive agents will depend on the application, as will the patterns of cooperation. A generic view of VE collaborating agents is illustrated in Fig. 5.12.

VR dialogues have four components:

- Movement and navigation of the users around the VE, which involves design of controls for the user's presence, supported by feedback from the environment. Controls may be manifest as non-VR features such as overview maps, pop-up menus, and dialogue boxes.
- Manipulation and interaction of objects in the VE by the user, with the reactive behaviors of those objects. This may involve specification of behavior of virtual tools in response to user manipulation.
- Conversation with other agents; this is closer to the true sense of dialogue, although in design terms it may be scripted responses to events.
- Design of non-VR features to support data entry and GUI style interaction, if necessary.

Dialogue design in software terms is the specification of multiple interactive coroutines, or in HCI terms, event-driven interaction with a population of reactive and proactive agents. The dialogue can be either scripted or generated by an interference mechanism in intelligent agents. The trade-off depends on costs and requirements. Scripted dialogues are cheaper but less flexible. The designer's problem is to specify the scripts and their triggering conditions. In simple dialogues, the agent will run through the scripted behavior until the endpoint. Initiating triggers may be under user control or automatic when certain parts of the environment are entered, for example, guided tour wizards are invoked. More flexibility can be built into the script by parameterization so the script can branch at certain points and the agent can change its behavior in response to user's feedback. For example, a guided tour agent can ask the user for route preferences and act accordingly. However, full flexibility necessitates design of intelligent agents.

The architecture of generalized intelligent agents is composed of a monitor, inference engine, and an action mechanism. First, triggers are detected by a module

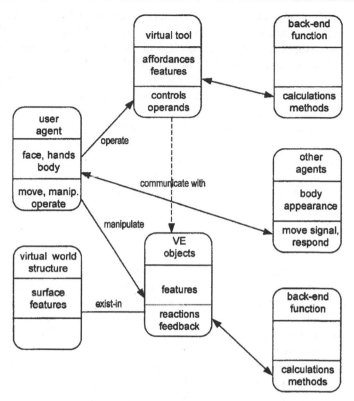

FIG. 5.12   Interactive and non-interactive agents illustrated as an object class diagram.

that monitors the environment for spoken requests or events in the VE that the agent should respond to. The monitor has to interpret the request or event. This may involve complex natural language understanding, interpreting events in the virtual world with reference to a model, or interpreting the user's action and updating a user model. Once the stimulus has been interpreted, the agent has to plan a response following the initiative cycle model described in chapter 3. Detailed description of AI planning is beyond the remit of this book, so this description will remain at the architectural level. The agent's plans are usually predesigned as a goal tree with procedures attached to subgoal leaves of the tree. Task models lend themselves to specification of planners' goal hierarchies. Rules search the tree for the appropriate response and then run the procedure as a script. More complex planners can compose a response from several goals, and this involves integrating different procedures. Planned responses can be flexible but they are still constrained by the knowledge that the designers originally captured. To escape from this limitation, agents can have a learning component that analyzes the history of interaction and then adjusts their future behavior; for example, a learning agent might adjust its personality to become less dominant if it detected from a pattern of nonassertive language and no initiative-taking that the user was submissive.

The final components of agents, both intelligent and otherwise, are the actor devices. These control movement of the self, manipulation of objects, and generation of speech, text, and other output.

Viewpoint Controls

In multiperson environments, viewpoints are not shared. In CAVEs, the world view is changed by one user whose movement and gaze is tracked. Because other users receive the same view, they experience the unnatural experience of a changing view over which they have no control. Other users can change their viewpoint by physically moving in the CAVE, but the correspondence between their view and the master user's view is not good. This may not be important for passive viewing, but when interaction is attempted, for example, passing an object from one person to another, the problem of different perspectives becomes apparent. The master user's depth perspective is very different from other users' depth perspectives.

When there are multiple immersed users, the problem of shared views becomes worse. Each user can see the other users (more than 2–3 is stretching the limits of current processing power), but all the users have no idea where the others are looking, so conversing about a common object or working together with shared objects is very difficult. One improvement is to signal the user's viewpoint by direction of their face and gaze, or more explicitly by a spotlight showing the zone in the VE at which they are looking. This allows users to coordinate their attention to shared objects. In collaborative design applications, the shared gaze problem can be partially solved by the immersive workbench approach. This uses "fishtank" VR (Ware, 2000), where users gaze from a position above the shared world; hence, two or more users have viewpoints that originate from a similar perspective.

Viewpoint controls for single user interaction are simpler to design. The first consideration is the viewpoint height. Depending on the naturalness demands of the task or domain, the user may be constrained to his or her normal head height view; alternatively, he or she may need to reset his or her view from above or below a surface. Vertical displacement of the view may be integrated with navigation controls either by a gesture (raise hand) or a mode switch for vertical viewpoint change. Other viewpoint controls that may be generally useful follow:

- Bird's-eye overview from above the virtual world.
- World in miniature viewpoints, so the whole VE model can be inspected and manipulated, rotated, and so forth, to help orientation.
- Viewpoint trace facilities, so the user can replay a sequence of movements and hence views; this can be useful for prototyping, testing-type applications.
- Controls to move to set viewpoints, rather like setting remote cameras or viewpoint bookmarks. Illustrating the change of view on an overview diagram of the VE world helps to reduce disorientation.
- Switch to viewpoints of other avatars; this control is more specialized in multiagent applications where different views may need to be inspected.

Viewpoints change when the user moves, so viewpoint controls are designed in tandem with navigation.

Navigation and Movement

The user presence will require controls for movement in three dimensions. These controls may be implemented with software supplied with the interactive device, for example, 3D space mouse, or an interpreter may have to be specified to map gestures to movements. The design issues are how to specify the direction of movement, and change direction once in motion; control of movement velocity and acceleration; and design of power controls to circumvent the limitations of human locomotion.

There are four options for tracking user movement:

- *Head-based trackers* that signal the direction of gaze as well as movement of the user's body. Head-based tracking is commonly used with head mounted displays.
- *Hand-based tracking*, where the user holds a joystick that is tracked; movement of the hand is translated into motion in the virtual world.
- *Body position sensing*—Leaning in different directions is translated as a navigation gesture.
- *Device mediated movement* with bikes or treadmill—Pedaling or movement on the treadmill controls motion.

The last two mechanisms leave the hands free for task-based interaction, although the bike implementation may require handlebars for changing direction. Specification of motion control is inevitably constrained by the technology. Simple devices such as joysticks give direction settings with velocity either being preset with an on and off switch, or by a trigger grip to control speed. Another simple control is to move a hand-held position sensor, so forward, back and lateral movement is controlled by hand movement, with velocity controlled by the rate of movement. Vertical movement is enabled by an invisible mode switch when the hand is held close to be body. Unfortunately, this design has the artificial constraint of forcing the user to stop before changing the viewpoint height. Hand or dataglove gesture interpreters provide movement control with six degrees of freedom (lateral left or right; vertical up or down; planar forward or back), with rotation in each dimension to give pitch and yaw control. Some tasks may not require all the degrees of freedom; for instance, if the naturalness principle demands that the user is constrained to walk along a plane, then the movement degrees of freedom are limited.

In two-handed implementation, the distance between two hands can be used as velocity control. Direction can be set by direction of gaze or by pointing. Gaze is less effective than pointing because it interferes with inspection, so when the user wants to turn his or her head to look at an object in the VE, it is difficult to untangle this from gaze-directed navigation commands; likewise for glancing sideways while in motion. Pointing, although it occupies hands for controls, is more effective (Bowman et al., 1997).

Velocity control is more difficult as it has to be overlaid on the direction controls. Walking movement can be controlled by a joystick for movement on a plane, although this alters the user's sense of presence, as he or she is consciously controlling his or her own representation within the VE rather than acting and having his or her action automatically transformed into the virtual world. A separate velocity control may be designed, but this increases the user's cognitive load for coordination. Natural metaphors, such as treadmills, modified bikes, or pedal accelerators and brakes from automobiles, necessitate nonstandard hardware and more expense, but give intuitive mapping (Slater et al., 1995). Velocity may also be controlled from gestures by a duration response or detecting the rate of change; for example, rapid forward movement of a dataglove is interpreted as fast forward movement, but this is difficult to tune to individual users. More reliable is duration detection of move forward and hold, with the duration of hold forward being interpreted as increasing velocity until the hand is moved backwards to slow and stop. Jump-to-a-location is not effective for task-oriented movement because of the disorientation it produces, although long-range "magic" movement effects may be necessary because of the limitations of human movement. An example is power facilities such as the go–go function (Poupyrev & Ichikawa, 1999) that uses a nonlinear mapping between the user's physical and virtual hands. When the user's physical hand is close to the user's body, so is the virtual hand, but as the arm is extended, the virtual hand moves a proportionately greater distance than reality, thus providing a long virtual reach. The degree of augmented motion should be under user control. Magic portals transport the user via a shortcut into another world, and virtual magic carpets move to preset locations or are under user control for rapid transit. Rapid change of viewpoint can cause conceptual disorientation, although this can be reduced by designing a fade-out to close the first view before opening the second. Helicopter metaphors can be useful for showing users a bird's-eye view for long distance navigation, so as the user moves forward faster, the system automatically helicopters the viewpoint upward; when forward motion decreases, the viewpoint gently floats downward for local detail (Tan, Robertson, & Czerwinski, 2001).

Adding Interaction Support

As well as controlling movement via interactive devices and the user's presence, facilities may be necessary to improve interaction within the constraints of interactive technology. In group environments, proximity to other agents can be signaled by highlighting effects which represent a surrounding zone that enables communication or interaction. For instance, when the zones of two avatars or user presences intersect, speech communication or interaction is enabled (Benford et al., 1995). Support for selecting and querying objects may be needed to facilitate interaction. In most VEs, single user select and manipulate is the norm. Multiple object selection support can use metaphors such as lassoes (as objects in the virtual world if you really want to push naturalness), bounding boxes, or multiple select mode controls. Querying objects may be supported by either automatic pop-up text (VR tool tips) or an explicit control. Selection can be helped by providing the user with collision detection when approaching an object, for example, by low-level highlighting to signal proximity, and then detecting touch by increasing the highlighting. The object then has to be explicitly de-selected. Support may be necessary for proximity and cueing interactive objects, because judging relative position in a VE can be difficult, especially in desktop environments where 3D depth cues are poor. Active objects can be designed to snap to the user's hand either automatically or in response to an explicit command. Once objects have been selected, they are stuck to the user's hand for transport until being explicitly de-selected. Selection support becomes tricky in two-handed interaction because one hand has to de-select an object before the second hand can select it. Two-handed interaction can be facilitated by making objects manipulable but not explicitly selected; unfortunately, this makes the interpretation problem difficult, deciding the order in which each hand altered the object's state.

This is a rerun of the CSCW shared artifact control problem. Selection support has to solve the problem of signaling the mode and state of the object, for example, see the following:

- An object is active and therefore the user can interact with it. Another command or manipulation is required to execute the state change. The GUI equivalent is shape handles in a drawing package.
- An object is selected and is treated as being unified with the user's presence until de-selected. This is equivalent of the GUI mouse down, drag icon state.
- An object is active and shared by two users. In this case, two hands (or users) could deform an object in different directions.

The choice of adding interaction support depends on naturalness requirements for the application. In simulations, interaction should be driven by movement of the body alone, with additional facilities to help when users become lost or disoriented. When naturalness is less important, interaction can be improved by support facilities and magic effects.

SUMMARY

Design starts with a task and requirements analysis to establish the high-level goals for VR. Simulation, education support, and validating prototypes are common applications. Task models are complemented by domain models that record the structures, spatial layout, agents, and significant objects for the VE. Tasks are modeled as services attached to agents. Interaction can be specified with use cases. VE design commences with general structural layout, then planning agents' behavior and representation. The requirements for naturalness are considered in design representation of background structure, agents, and interactive objects. The user presence requires particular attention to determine the immersion of the user in the VE as an avatar (exogenous) or presence as a body or hand (endogenous). Controls have to be designed for navigating, orientation, and movement velocity as well as manipulations to select and change objects. In exogenous collaborative VEs, design of other presences' personalities has to be considered. Speech, facial expression, and gesture can signal dominant or subordinate and other characteristics. Dialogues are specified as conversations between agents and interaction with significant objects. Responses may be either scripted or planned using AI mechanisms for intelligent user agents. The user's controls, navigation, and interaction need to be integrated with planned or scripted responses by other agents and back-end automated functionality.

Interaction support is necessary to help user navigation, control of viewpoint, and object selection. Navigation can be augmented by magic effects or controlled by flying gestures from dataglove presences. Viewpoints help overcome disorientation with VE overviews, pathway tracking, and preset views. Object selection counters the lack of haptic feedback by lasso, ray-casting, and snap-to effects. Alternatively, cross-modal substitution of color and audio can convey haptic properties and kinaesthetic feedback.

6

Evaluating Multisensory
User Interfaces

Standard evaluation methods (e.g., Nielsen, 1993) may be able to discover some usability problems for multisensory interfaces but, as Höök and Dahlback (1992) noted, no current evaluation methods fit the specific problem of VR applications. The need for VR evaluation was highlighted by Gabbard and Hix (1997). An adaptation of standard formative usability evaluation methods following a guidelines or checklist approach has been described (Tromp, Sandos, Steed, & Thie, 1998); Mills and Noyes (1999) presented generic design issues for VEs. Kalawsky (1999) developed a questionnaire based on standard GUI principles for VE use (VRUSE), although this focused on device-level issues with a small number of general usability heuristics drawn from Nielsen (1993).

Few methods for multimedia evaluation have been proposed apart from general frameworks (Crozat, Hu, & Trigano, 1999). VR design principles for evaluation have been proposed by Johnson (1998), who pointed out the need for task fit, natural representation, and ease of navigation, whereas Kalawsky (1998) described an evaluation framework based on Nielsen's (1993) heuristics. Guidelines for VR design may also be used for evaluation; however, this does not guide the evaluator to understand why a user experiences a problem, and diagnose the cause of a usability error. This chapter provides methods for evaluating multisensory interfaces that can be used for expert style evaluations as well as usability testing with users. It also addresses a more fundamental point for all HCI evaluation methods: how evaluators can link observation of users' problems to diagnosis of their cause. Few methods attempt to bridge that gap although Cockton and Lavery (1999) proposed templates that aid interpretation of usability errors,

and Keenan (1996) described a taxonomy of usability problems for diagnostic purposes. In this chapter, a more complex taxonomy is linked to the interaction models described in chapter 3 with decision tree techniques for
diagnostic guidance.

INTRODUCTION

Usability evaluation is an integral part of design. Evaluation is usually classified as formative (during the process of design) or summative (when a design is complete). Formative or diagnostic evaluation focuses on debugging
the design, and summative or benchmark evaluation establishes whether
the product achieves an acceptable level of performance. Diagnostic evaluation takes place during the design process to improve the UI, whereas
benchmark evaluation takes place when a product is nearly complete as
part of a quality assessment exercise. Evaluation methods are covered in
most HCI textbooks (e.g., Shneiderman, 1998), so only a brief overview will
be given here; however, multimedia and VR do require slightly different
techniques, so these will be described in more depth.

BENCHMARK EVALUATION

The following five sections apply to multimedia and desktop VR applications as well as standard GUI interfaces. More detailed techniques for VR
evaluation are described later.

First, the usability goals need to be set. These will be determined by the
task and requirements analysis that set the initial product goals. For
task-based applications, the goals are typically task completion times and error rates; for example, see the following:

> Finding information in a multimedia kiosk with five representative
> searches is completed by 90% of users in 20 min; or a multimedia presenta-
> tion achieves memory performance of 75% recall of appropriate informa-
> tion with less than 5% errors by all users.

In tutorial multimedia, the situation is more complex because learning
outcomes can have several meanings; for example, see the following:

- Initial recall of information within a short time of presentation
  (1–2 hr).
- Long-term recall of information after several weeks.
- Ability to use information to solve a problem or carry out a task.

Both memorization and performance tests are necessary to check that
the information was conveyed to the user and the concepts were understood

so they could be used. Poor performance needs to be investigated by memory tests to discover which facts were not understood. Learning goals will set the benchmark and these are particularly important to assess depth of encoding, that is, that the information was learned as a rich schema rather than a shallow set of disconnected facts, the desired learning outcome. This may be expressed as a "gold standard" of expert knowledge that an ideal student may be expected to learn, composed of basic facts and more complex propositions, implications, and explanations.

The user is asked to carry out a set task and performance is measured as task completion times and errors. Posttest measures consist of memory tests: either free recall, when the user is asked to note down as many facts as he or she can remember from the presentation; or cued recall, when he or she is shown a cue from the presentation and asked to write down any relevant facts. Problem-solving performance may also be measured to demonstrate that information has been learned effectively. These are particularly important to assess depth of encoding. Other variations are posttest quizzes which assess how well the user has understood the information content. A questionnaire can be added to capture user attitude on 1 to 7 scales. This can provide more quantitative feedback on the users' reactions to particular design features and give a population level view of the users' responses to the prototype.

DIAGNOSTIC EVALUATION

These sessions test the application with a representative set of tasks, observe users' problems, and then try to diagnose problem causes as the responsible design features. Evaluation sessions are organized as follows:

1. *Specify scenarios*—These will be drawn from task analysis or learning goals. The number and range of scenarios are not easy to judge. More scenarios give better test coverage, but at more expense. Generally, the number of scenarios should be judged by how many can be completed within 60 min of testing, and chosen to cover key user tasks.
2. *Select a representative set of users*—This is not as easy as it sounds because getting hold of potential users who are willing to give their time can be difficult; moreover, selecting an appropriate range of people from a potential user population may require many individuals. The issues to beware of follow:
   - *The age and abilities range* of the user population—The sample should be balanced for age and gender considering the application. Testing for a range of abilities and disabilities is becoming increasingly important for many products. Color vision (i.e., color blindness) needs to be assessed for multimedia.

- The *nationality and culture* of the potential user population—In international user interfaces, including many Internet applications, a range of linguistic abilities and cultural differences will need to be considered.
- The *level of computer experience* and knowledge of the operating system—Younger users will tend to be more familiar with computer operation than older users.

Some organizations have user panels that provide a ready-made sample for testing their products; however, there is a danger of using "captive" users too often. Tailoring the user sample to the expected population of the product is better. Generally, more users give better results, but there is a law of diminishing returns, and testing 8 to 10 users will usually uncover most of the important usability defects. The sophistication of the test environment depends on the quality of data required. Usability laboratories evaluate products in special rooms equipped with video recorders and one-way mirrors to make observation as unobtrusive as possible. However, this approach can still be criticized because it places the user in an artificial setting. Testing in the user's workplace, in contrast, is more natural and helps put the user at ease (Beyer & Holtzblatt, 1998). Whatever the approach adopted, the location and recording equipment for the session need to be prepared.

Once the session has been prepared, evaluation can commence. Users can be tested individually or in pairs. Testing pairs of users has the advantage that their conversation often reveals many problems without the need for follow-up questioning. Within each session the steps are as follows:

- Subjects are asked to complete a *presession questionnaire* about their computer experience (e.g., Microsoft Windows). This establishes a baseline of experience that is useful in judging individual differences in user reactions. In tutorial multimedia, this will capture the user's prior knowledge.
- Users are *trained* with the product. The training should ensure that the user can operate the system sufficiently well so that most users can complete the set tasks. The amount of training depends on the type of product. For general public "walk up and use" CD-ROMs or kiosk applications, little training should be given because it is important that people can use them without support. In contrast, a more complex office product intended for skilled users may require more training.
- Users are *briefed* about the tasks and reassured that it is the system that is being tested and not the user. Users are asked to complete the test using the system and to provide a commentary when they experience difficulty with the system. Some users are better at verbaliz-

ing their opinions than others, so it helps to give examples of the feedback required during the training session. The analyst observes the users; if difficulties are apparent but the user does not give any reason, then a miniinterview is conducted to elicit the reasons for the problem (for details, see Monk & Wright, 1993). Users work at their own pace and their behavior and commentary may be video recorded if necessary. Problems encountered need to be noted by the analyst, with task completion times. In the benchmark mode, no commentary on problems is elicited and the user's performance is measured against a gold standard for expert achievement.

- A *de-briefing session* is carried out after the test to follow up on the reasons for problems, missing requirements, and to elicit suggestions for improvements.

Comprehension walkthroughs are a useful additional forensic tool, to test information delivery. These investigate the adequacy of media integration and design for attention. The starting point is to create a script of information content that the user should acquire from a presentation, similar to the information gold standard used in performance testing. The user is shown the presentation and asked to give a running commentary on the facts he or she noticed and understood. This is carried out by playing short segments of interaction, allowing the users to report on what they saw and heard, and then playing the next segment. The motivation is to assess contact points and media integration to see if the user does perceive and comprehend the information as the designer intended. This can be combined with eyetracking analysis for more detailed assessment of attention in visual media. The duration of the hands-on test session needs to be limited to about 45 min, as user concentration fades in longer sessions, so the test tasks have to be selected with care.

Data Analysis and Classification of Usability Errors

The objective of the evaluation is to link observed problems with the responsible design features and suggestions for improvement. Critical incidents and breakdowns, when the user was puzzled or could not proceed, are analyzed in miniinterviews by asking questions to identify the responsible design features. In many cases, the problem is obvious from the user reports; however, some problems have deeper-seated causes that are not immediately apparent. In multimedia, the first distinction is between interaction and comprehension problems:

- Is the difficulty associated with not being able to find the desired information, or control, or not being able to navigate to the desired location?

- Is the feedback from interaction clear and does it make sense?
- Is the information content difficult to understand?

Answers to the first two questions point toward requirements and interaction errors; the third question indicates content and media selection problems. The interaction cycle models described in chapter 3 can help to walk through recordings of sessions to identify usability problems with the following taxonomy that indicate possible causes (three sections follow: requirement defects, information delivery problems, and interaction problems):

- Task fit (*missing functionality*)—The system does not contain a function for the user's goal, indicating missing requirements. Missing requirements are usually reported directly but may be indicated by the user searching unsuccessfully for a command or icon.
- *Missing information*—The information content necessary for the user's task, decision, or learning objectives is not provided. In tutorial applications, this will only become apparent by comparing performance data, whereas missing information is more likely to be reported directly for task and decision support systems.
- Task fit (*inadequate information or functionality*)—Users can partially achieve their goals but they find it difficult to do so because the information provided is incomplete, ambiguous, or inappropriate, or the function does not exactly match their expectations.

- *Recognition failure*—The information is present but the user fails to see or hear it. This can be apparent from observations when signals and warnings are missed, but it may only be discovered in debriefing interviews.
- *Comprehension failure*—The user did perceive the information but could not make sense of it. Poor integration with existing knowledge is the usual cause but comprehension failure may also be a consequence of inappropriate media selection. User-related causes need to be explored, such as poor motivation or lack of domain knowledge.

- Cue, prompt, or metaphor (*poor location*): the user interface does not guide the user to find the appropriate information, object or command even though it exists. Possible causes are poor hypermedia links, misleading metaphors and ambiguous menu names.
- Cue, prompt, or metaphor (*predictivity*)—The interface does not help the user guess how to operate the system, or how to find information. This problem is related to poor task fit, ambiguous metaphors, or poor hypermedia link design.
- *Disorientation*—The user is lost in an information space and cannot find the items he or she requires; possible causes are poor navigation controls and misleading navigation structures.

- *Manipulation or operation*—Cursor movement or other manipulations are difficult because the target is too small or hard to operate, or carrying out the action exceeds the normal physical coordination abilities of the user.
- *Missing feedback*—No message or effect is visible or audible. Media content cannot be recognized.
- *Inadequate feedback*—Feedback is present but is either ambiguous or not sufficiently salient, so the user overlooks it. Media content cannot be understood.
- *Hidden effects*—Modes or parameter settings are not apparent or have been forgotten by the user, leading to unexpected effects.
- *User error*—The system functions correctly but is used suboptimally for the task. This may be a training problem, but task fit problems should also be considered.

The available data to derive these categories will be either user verbal reports or problem observations. If video recordings have been made, these can be replayed by first eyeballing the session to spot potential problems, which are then investigated in more depth. Errors are identified by design feature and rated for severity. If an error is encountered by all users, then it is severe; however, if a problem occurs for one or two users, then it may be solved by training. If performance data has been captured, then comprehension and usability errors can be compared with user performance. Care should be exercised when interpreting performance taken from diagnostic evaluation sessions, as the users' explanations of problems will interfere with task completion times and error rates.

Errors should also be categorized according to their origins as application system errors, subtyped by cause (e.g., prompts, affordance, VE visual design, feedback, functionality, task fit, manipulation, etc.); operating system errors; or user errors caused by lack of task knowledge. Operating system errors cannot be immediately changed, so training is the only remedial treatment. This policy may also be adopted for errors that are difficult to cure, for example, backward compatibility with previous versions. The usability problems are analyzed to create a matrix of problem categories by design feature. The frequency of the problems is used to prioritize their severity and allocate resources to fixing them in the next prototype version. Design features which give frequent errors for all users are serious and must be fixed; however, features which cause all user problems, but infrequently, could have easily-learned cures and probably require no modification. The prototype is modified to take account of the problems discovered in the first round of testing and then evaluated for a second time. The observed problems should decrease fairly dramatically. If this is not the case, then the homogeneity of the user population and initial requirements are suspect.

Postsession comprehension tests against gold standard solutions also help to identify problem areas of multimedia products, in particular failings in information presentation and attention. The problem areas where content has not been assimilated can be investigated further by walkthroughs (see chap. 3) or eyetracking studies.

EYETRACKING ANALYSES

This is a specialized and resource intensive analysis but it can prove useful to diagnose problems with user attention in complex visual media. Its main use is to assess attention to still images. Although eye tracking can be used on moving image, interpreting results is more difficult. Eyetrackers produces a trace of the eye movement by shining an infrared beam into the user's fovea (central vision) and detecting the reflection. A track of all eye movements, including the very rapid and unconscious saccades, is produced. Because sample rates in the order of 50 per sec are produced, the data has to be condensed and overlaid on the test image for further assessment. A raw eyetracking trace is shown in Fig. 6.1 (Faraday & Sutcliffe, 1996).

As can be seen in Fig. 6.1, the trace shows busy clusters of small rapid eye movements (called fixations) in particular areas, followed by longer-range

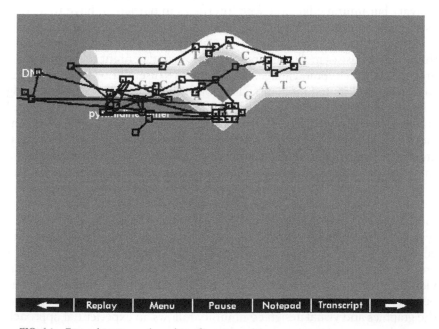

FIG. 6.1   Eyetracking trace of a multimedia presentation.

movements (called saccades). The eye tracks over the image, focusing on selected objects. The next step is to reduce the data by dividing the image into squares and grouping all the eye movements that fall within each square. This gives a density analysis of eye movements that can be refined by counting the source and destination of movements within and between each grid square. By converting movement into a grid density analysis and overlaying this on top of the stimulus image, the sequence of attention to objects becomes clear (see Fig. 6.2).

The summarized eyetrack can then be compared with design expectations, to investigate which image components were looked at and how effective contact points were in directing attention. Attention and eye movement densities do not always correlate so not all the objects that were looked at will have been comprehended, although eye movements are a reasonable guide. Eyetracks are often more valuable for revealing what was not attended to. If a key component of an image received few fixations then it won't have been held in central vision, so little information will have been extracted from this area of the image.

ASSESSING ATTRACTIVENESS

In multisensory UIs, operational usability is only part of the assessment process. So far we have dealt with usability and effectiveness for information delivery but multimedia, and Web interfaces in particular, have to attract users. This section presents an expert evaluation method for that issue.

Attractiveness can be divided into generic qualities of a UI such as aesthetic design, use of media to direct attention, and content related issues of linking visual style, brand image, and messages to users' knowledge of the organization and its requirements. The following heuristics extend existing advice on Web site design (e.g., IBM, 2000; Nielsen, 1999) and can be used either as design principles or evaluation criteria. Nielsen (1993) recommended using four to six evaluators in a double pass process. First, the evaluators familiarize themselves with the user's task and the product, and then, they critique the product using a task scenario as a test sequence, before conducting an overall review of the usability characteristics. More evaluators can be used, but there is a law of diminishing returns as approximately four evaluators can pick up around 80% of the errors in conventional GUI systems. Human factors experts perform a little better than novices. More general attraction can be fostered by aesthetic design and use of media for arousal. Aesthetic attractiveness is a complex variable that is subject to individual differences, as summarized in the saying "beauty lies in the eye of the beholder." Proposing principles for aesthetic design is contentious because the graphics and visual design community follows an experiential approach rather than an engineering design philosophy, so articulating design princi-

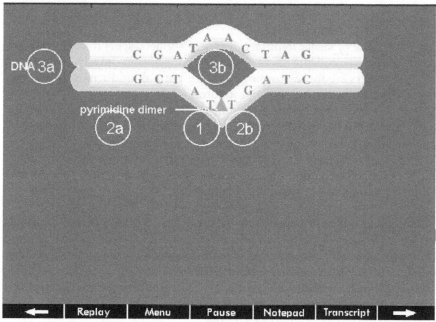

FIG. 6.2   Summarized eye trace after grid density analysis. The numbers refer to the sequence of fixations made by the user's eye.

ples is not encouraged. Nevertheless, some researchers have partially formalized good design qualities and the following heuristics are based on their recommendations (Kristof & Satran, 1995; Mullet & Sano, 1995).

The generic heuristics for attractiveness and aesthetic design are as follows:

- *Judicious use of color*—Color use should be balanced and low saturation pastel colors should be used for backgrounds. Designs should not use more than 2 to 3 fully saturated intense colors.
- *Symmetry*—Visual layout which is symmetrical helps attractiveness, for example, bilateral, radial organization that can be folded over to show the symmetrical match.
- *Shape and style*—Use of closure (complete circles, ellipses, and other areas) and of curved shapes conveys an attractive visual style in contrast to rectangles and square shapes.
- *Structured and consistent layout*—Use of grids to structure image components and portray a consistent order; grids need to be composed of rectangles which do not exceed a 5:3 height to width ratio.
- *Depth of field*—Use of layers in an image stimulates interest and can be attractive by promoting a peaceful effect. Use of back-

ground image with low saturated color provides depth for foreground components.

- *Choice of media to attract attention*—Video, speech, and audio all
  have an arousing effect and increase attention. Images of designed
  objects are more arousing than are natural landscapes. Music can
  attract by setting the appropriate mood.
- *Use of personality in media to attract and persuade*—Use of human image
  and speech can help to attract users and persuade them to buy goods by
  being polite and praising their choices (Reeves & Nass, 1996).
- *Design of unusual or challenging images* that stimulate the users' imagination and increase attraction—Unusual images often disobey
  normal laws of form and perspective.

Describing rules for recognizing each of these qualities is more difficult
for some (unusual design) than others (structured layout). As with general
HCI heuristics, a greater number of evaluators will provide a more reliable
opinion; however, experts may be unreliable in judging aesthetic qualities.
Graphical design experts are prone to disagree about aesthetic qualities
more than are ordinary users.

The content related heuristics follow:

- *Consistent visual style*—This heuristic is on the borderline between
  the two sets. Visual style is generic in the sense that a multimedia presentation or Web site needs to be consistent in terms of layout that reflects the organization's identity or designer's objectives.
- *Visibility of identity and brand*—The effectiveness of this heuristic
  depends on the strength of the brand image and corporate identity.
  The design principle just recommends making the identity visible in
  a consistent manner.
- *Matching arousal to user's mood and motivation*—This heuristic focuses on the match between the user model and multimedia content. Hence, a Web site targeted at the youth market should use
  arousing material, whereas a site targeted at older users may use
  more restful, natural images. For tranquility, choosing natural world
  content is advisable; conversely the image of a modern, dynamic organization is reinforced by technological subject matter (e.g., racing
  cars, jet aircraft, spacecraft; Reeves & Nass, 1996). Ultimately, this
  is a complex topic dealt with in many books on marketing research.
- *Selecting content to suit users' requirements*—This should result from a
  sound requirements analysis, but poor content display may con-
  found a thorough analysis. Content related to users' requirements
  should be clearly stated, in unambiguous language, with clear cues
  on how to find it.

- *Stimulating users' interest by secondary motivation*—Attractiveness can be increased by adding functionality that is not geared to the application's primary purpose, but may attract for another motivation. Some examples are placing games and simulations on e-commerce sites for users' amusement.

When being used for evaluation, the heuristics are combined with existing usability principles to give an overall usability or attractiveness assessment.

ASSESSING MULTIMEDIA WEB SITES

In this section, the heuristics are put to use for evaluating multimedia Web sites with an emphasis on e-commerce applications. The initial stage of attraction involves gaining the user's attention, and use of appropriate media is important (see Fig. 6.3). For instance, dynamic media (video and speech) are more attention-directing than static media (text, still image; Sutcliffe, 1999b). However, the effect can be overdone; for instance, too many animated banners compete with each other and rapidly become annoying, as many of us have experienced with commercial Web sites. Video, audio, and change in image by highlighting all focus attention (Sutcliffe, 1999a). Once the user's eye has been drawn to the Web page, content-based attraction takes over. Projection of brand and organizational identity that promote trust (Kollok, 1999; Lohse, 2000), and information that conveys the potential utility of the Web site, will also contribute to holding the user's attention. User models need to specify knowledge of brands as well as requirements.

Once the user has been attracted to the home page and has been persuaded to stay, the next phase begins. In most cases, finding the goods, service, or information necessitates navigation. In exploration and navigation, the conventional quality of usability is paramount. Clear prompts, consistent layout, and controls and observable effects all promote ease of use, which can be assessed by standard evaluation methods (Monk & Wright, 1993). However, on Web sites, information plays a key role that goes beyond conventional usability. Early hints on directions to follow toward the search target are important.

Usability problems can terminate interaction as this stage, so careful design is vital. Critical incidents in which users are confused but can eventually guess what to do may be survivable if their motivation is high; however, misleading cues for information searching will have a deleterious effect on users' patience and motivation. Web sites with a close match between the product offering and users' requirements may be able to get away with poor usability, but most sites will not.

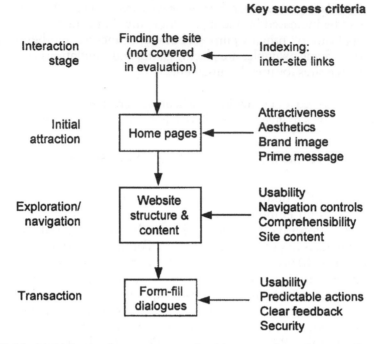

FIG. 6.3   Model showing the attractiveness and usability criteria during the stages of interaction with e-commerce websites.

The final stage is the transaction when the user purchases the goods or service. Operational usability will be important as well as motivation to counteract any difficulties. In information intensive applications, presentation in appropriate media with a well-structured layout will be a key usability requirement (ISO, 1997).

Design of successful Web sites has to provide different features to fulfill users' needs at each stage. Initial attention is replaced by arousal and content related attraction. This raises users' motivation by the promise of the reward to come. The motivational capital has to be maintained during the exploration and navigation stage to counteract any difficulties and disappointments when searches result in dead ends. Once the search target has been reached, user motivation needs to be encouraged and usability errors eliminated to engender successful interaction. Each interaction step is a user cost. Long-winded multiple step dialogues incur more cost, a lesson not lost on amazon.com, which implemented one-click shopping. The other element of cost is errors, caused by usability problems, misleading cues, and failed searches. The phases of interaction can be evaluated by the following measures and techniques:

1. *Finding the Web site*—Tests with different search engines using a selection of keywords; percentage of searches that correctly identify the Web site, with a relevance ranking.
2. *Initial attraction*—Dwell-time measured from user interaction logs; debriefing interviews to investigate which features users noticed and what attracted or repelled them. Free recall memory tests to establish the topics and features users remember about a site.
3. *Exploration and navigation*—Usability measures such as errors (percentage of searches correct) and task completion times. Expert judgment about conformance to design guidelines and heuristics. Cognitive walkthroughs of interaction to identify design flaws (Sutcliffe & Kaur, 2000).
4. *Transaction*—Usability measures as previously discussed, plus debriefing interviews to discover users' rating of the Web site's utility.

The generic heuristics apply more strongly to the initial attraction phase of Web site interaction, and both sets apply to initial attraction, exploration, and transaction stages. If the site is rated well on the heuristics, user motivation will be maintained. Use of the heuristics for evaluation of attractiveness and usability are illustrated in the following case study of three Web sites.

Case Study: Web Site Evaluation

Three airline Web sites were assessed: EasyJet (EJ), Virgin Atlantic (VA), and British Airways (BA). The study is reported in more depth in Sutcliffe, 2001 and 2002a. Evaluators rated each site on a 1 to 5 scale for each heuristic and were asked to report the rationale for their decision and the ease with which each heuristic could be interpreted. The rating scores were converted into Net Positive Values (NPV) to reflect the range of the evaluators' assessments. A worked example of this analysis is provided in Table 6.1. The frequency of the evaluators' ratings is multiplied by the +2 to −2 scale and the products summed to give a value for the heuristic.

All three sites aim to provide information about the airline as well as online sales of flight tickets. The companies concerned have different corporate images that to a lay observer may be characterized as blue chip reliability and quality (BA), modern and exciting (VA), and cheap and

TABLE 6.1

Worked Example of the Net Positive Value for the Rating of Web
Site Persuasiveness by the Nine Subjects

Rating	1	2	3	4	5
Scale	−2	−1	0	+1	+2
Rating frequency (subjects)	2	0	4	3	0
Product	−4	0	0	3	0
Total Net Positive Value (NPV) = −1					

cheerful (EJ). The ratings of each site are given following a walkthrough
with a common scenario of buying a flight ticket.

Assessment on the design quality heuristics (see Table 6.2) tells a complex story. Two used color for projecting corporate identity (red for VA, orange for EJ); however, this led to a low rating for VA. Both organizations'
colors are part of the corporate image, so judgment on this heuristic indi-

TABLE 6.2

Net Positive Value Scores for Aesthetic Design Qualities of the
Web Sites Judged From Front Pages

	EJ	VA	BA
Use of color	3	−4	6
Symmetry and aesthetic style	−3	−5	−6
Structured layout	3	2	−2
Depth of field	−4	3	−3
Choice of media	−9	3	−11
People and personality	−8	−11	−10
Unusual images	−11	7	−14
Totals	−29	−5	−40

Note. EJ = EasyJet; VA = Virgin Atlantic; BA = British Airways.

cates a possible clash of aesthetic appeal and brand projection. Symmetry and style were judged to be below average in all sites; however, several evaluators commented that this heuristic was the most difficult one to interpret.

VA and EJ were rated more favorably than BA on well-structured and consistent pages, which seems to conflict with irregular appearance of the EJ's pages (see Fig. 6.4).

EJ and BA scored poorly on depth of field and choice of media to attract interest. None of the sites scored well on use of personality and people to engage users. VA scored well on use of media to attract attention, and overall created more exciting content by use of animation and design layout, as illustrated in Fig. 6.5.

The conclusions from the stage 1 analysis rated VA highest in terms of aesthetic design, reflected in the evaluators' comments that its appearance was clearly different from the more traditional block structure layout of the other two Web sites. However, the aesthetic qualities of all three sites were judged to be below average, with BA being particularly poor.

The content assessment shows a less clear-cut picture, as summarized in Table 6.3. In this case, judgment is made by browsing throughout the Web site to assess visual style and brand visibility; primary and secondary motiva-

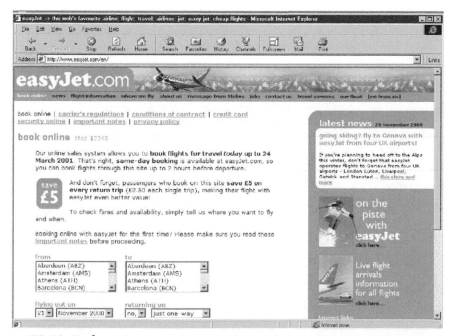

FIG. 6.4   EasyJet web front page. It has a somewhat irregular layout but is good at presenting its basic message: cheap flights and the economic incentive for booking on the Web (EasyJet Airline Company Ltd, 2001).

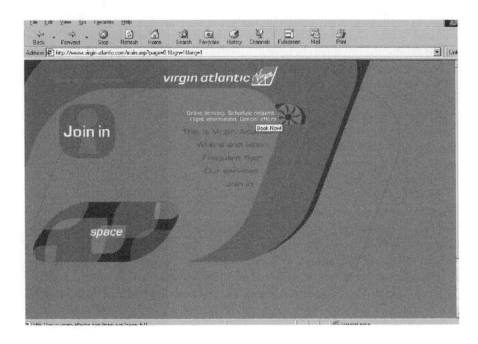

FIG. 6.5 Virgin web site, illustrating the contrast in graphic design with figure 6.4. The jet windows and keyhole metaphors contain animations to attract attention (Virgin Atlantic Airways, 2001). Reprinted with permission by Virgin Group PLC.

TABLE 6.3

Net Positive Value Scores for the Content and Attractiveness Heuristics

		EJ	VA	BA
Visual style		11	8	−2
Brand visibility		12	9	6
Mood and first motivation		0	2	0
Secondary motivation		−3	2	−9
Content and requirements		5	2	5
	Totals	25	23	0

Note. EJ = EasyJet; VA = Virgin Atlantic; BA = British Airways.

tion, and contents and requirements match, were judged on the first 2 to 3 Web pages encountered when following the flight-booking scenario.

Both EJ and VA were rated well on a consistent visual style and good brand visibility. In contrast, BA was noted to be more discreet about its corporate identity (see Fig. 6.6).

There was little to choose between the three sites in primary motivation, because all provided services for searching flight availability and booking, although EJ did make this functionality easier to access on the home page. VA scored slightly higher than BA and EJ for secondary motivation, although the services offered were similar (e.g., car rental, frequent flyer, etc.). The match of content and requirements for flight information and booking was similar for all three sites. In content attractiveness, BA came off worst, whereas the clear brand image and corporate visual style paid off for EJ and VA. Three evaluators commented that the chromatic identity of VA was

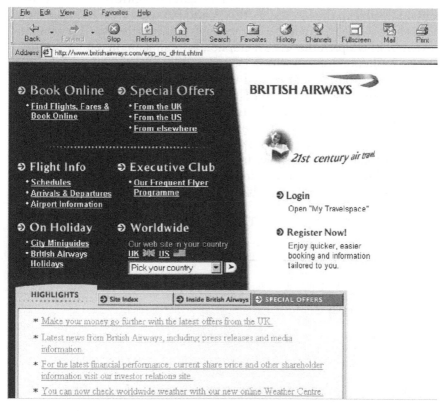

FIG. 6.6   British Airways front page, with a low-key corporate identity (compared with figure 6.5); however, the structure is well laid out and the content meets with users' requirements for flight browsing/booking (British Airways 2001).

striking even if they didn't like it (see color rating in aesthetic heuristics). The final part of the assessment for stage 2 (navigation) and stage 3 (transaction) was judged by browsing extensively through the site and following a flight-booking transaction. Nielsen's (1993) heuristic evaluation criteria were used to judge the usability of navigation and transaction support. A summary of the usability assessment for each site is provided in Table 6.4.

In the latter phases of interaction, EJ does not compare so favorably. The navigation controls and support are weak because no site map is provided; navigation bars have overlapping content; the side bar animations contain link cues but the layout changes unpredictably, making navigation confusing; and no back-to-top commands are given on the bottom of long pages. Transaction controls also suffer from similar defects, for example, no exit, long and cumbersome scroll boxes. VA and BA do better by supplying the essentials of good navigation (site maps, consistent navigation menus, back-to-top, exit and home), although navigation controls are more consistent and visible in the VA site. Both VA and BA use a clear task step metaphor (1–2–3–4–5) to guide the user through flight reservation, booking, and payment. EJ adopted the same metaphor, but implemented it less clearly.

The evaluators' scores with Nielsen's (1993) heuristics (see Table 6.5) showed less variation and tended to neutral assessments, apart from the high consistency score given to EJ. EJ and BA came out more favorably on these heuristics; however, the high EJ rating on consistency did not agree well with the structured layout heuristic in the aesthetic set, demonstrating some inconsistency in evaluator judgment.

The summary picture is shown in Table 6.6. Overall, VA appears to be the best placed site with a first rank in the overall attractiveness and aesthetic heuristics, and joint first on usability and navigation. However, EJ ranked

TABLE 6.4

Usability Assessment of the Navigation and Transaction Phases

Usability Criterion	EJ	VA	BA
Navigation commands	1	3	2
Navigation support	2	3	2
Transaction prompts	3	4	5
Form fill layout	2	4	4
Transaction controls	1	4	5
Totals	9	18	18

Note. EJ = EasyJet; VA = Virgin Atlantic; BA = British Airways.

TABLE 6.5

Evaluators' Net Positive Value Ratings Using Nielsen's
(1993) Heuristics

	EJ	VA	BA
Visibility of system status	2	1	−1
System Realworld (RW) match	6	6	6
Control and freedom	−1	0	3
Consistency and standards	15	6	6
Error prevention	2	0	−4
Recognition opposed to recall	8	−4	3
Flexibility and efficiency	1	−3	0
Aesthetic and minimalist design	3	6	4
Error handling	7	2	0
Help and documentation	−7	−8	4
Totals	36	6	21

Note. EJ = EasyJet; VA = Virgin Atlantic; BA = British Airways.

first on Nielsen's (1993) heuristics and content-related attractiveness. Although BA came in third in most assessments, it does have the consolation prize of being first on persuasiveness, although its advantage was not great.

The evaluation shows clear strengths and weaknesses of each site at each stage. Overall, VA wins on attractiveness and aesthetic design as well as having a well-designed transaction and navigation interface. EJ is strong on initial content-driven attraction but suffers from basic usability defects in the exploration and transaction phases, for example, no escape route. Overall, the VA site is likely to be more effective because it combines reasonable motivation with aesthetic attractiveness and sound usability engineering.

EVALUATING VIRTUAL REALITY APPLICATIONS

This section describes an evaluation method for multisensory UIs that does offer explicit diagnostic procedures and extends the cognitive walkthrough

TABLE 6.6

Summary of Net Positive Value Totals of all the Evaluation
Heuristics and Phases

	EJ	VA	BA
Overall appeal	3	**11**	4
Aesthetic attraction	−29	**−5**	−40
Content attraction	**25**	23	0
Usability and navigation	9	**18**	18
Persuade to buy	1	0	1
Nielsen heuristic	**36**	6	21

Note. Bold typeface denotes first ranked site. EJ = EasyJet; VA = Virgin Atlantic; BA = British Airways.

approach (Wharton et al., 1994). The method had its origins in evaluation of display-based interfaces (Sutcliffe et al., 2000) that was subsequently extended to VE evaluation (Sutcliffe & Kaur, 2000). The method builds on the Interaction Theory described in chapter 3 and puts the extended Norman models to work as evaluation tools. The models provide an agenda to organize evaluative questions in a cognitive walkthrough. This approach has proved successful for evaluation of standard UIs and is widely practiced (Wharton et al., 1994). First, a heuristic evaluation for VR is described, that follows in Nielsen's (1993) footsteps; and then a walkthrough method for diagnosing observed user problems is explained.

Expert Evaluation for Virtual Reality

Many VEs are used to investigate designed or real worlds, for example, simulations of buildings for fire safety training, and operational testing of virtual aircraft. In these applications, faithful simulation of the real world is important. The user's task is to explore, critique, and learn about the virtual world. In these applications, usability criteria have to be sensitive to the system objectives; for instance, giving comprehensive tutorial support may not be advisable in safety assessment of how people evacuate a building, and discovering flaws in design of evacuation routes. On the other hand, in applications where the system exists to help the user achieve a task goal, support for the user's task should be explicit. Accordingly, the application and its tasks need to be classified for the degree of desired naturalness.

The VE required is assessed by questions that focus on the naturalness of interaction:

- How close should the correspondence be between the real world and the virtual world? Design simulations and tutoring applications may need more faithful representation.
- Is it important that interaction with objects directly mimics the real world? If detailed physical tasks are being taught or a virtual prototype design is being assessed, then realistic manipulations will be necessary.

The answers are used to set objectives for what the system should achieve in terms of natural engagement and user support.

Ideally, VR systems should be multisensory and multimodal. Such an ideal is not currently achievable and interaction is likely to remain constrained for some time in the future. Usability therefore has to be measured against a technology baseline of the system design, which in turn reflects the cost constraints.

Assessment has to establish a trade-off between these demands, cost, and current technology. In many current applications, achieving a full realistic graphical representation is not possible because of the limited processing power. This necessitates a trade-off between natural representation and response time. Poor response time may lead to usability problems when users experience motion sickness with uneven update of virtual world images. The baseline of requirements that may be implemented under ideal conditions with unlimited budgets is used to inform judgment of design quality in heuristic evaluation.

Heuristic Evaluation

Heuristics are a means of rapid evaluation that produce approximate results. Heuristics are similar to general design principles in that they require considerable interpretation in the context of a design. Their merits lie in simplicity and being easy to assimilate. The following heuristics develop Nielsen's (1993) approach:

1. *Natural engagement*—Interaction should approach the user's expectation of interaction in the real world as far as possible. Ideally, the user should be unaware that the reality is virtual. Interpreting this heuristic will depend on the naturalness requirement and the users' sense of presence and engagement.

2. *Compatibility with the user's task and domain*—The VE and behavior of objects should correspond as closely as possible to the user's expectation of real world objects, his or her behavior, and affordances for task action.

3. *Natural expression of action*—The representation of the self or presence in the VE should allow the user to act and explore in a natural manner and not restrict normal physical actions. This design quality may be limited by the available devices. If haptic feedback is absent, natural expression inevitably suffers.

4. *Close coordination of action and representation*—The representation of the self-presence and behavior manifest in the VE should be faithful to the user's actions. Response time between user movement and update of the VE display should be less than 200 msec to avoid motion sickness problems.

5. *Realistic feedback*—The effect of the user's actions on virtual world objects should be immediately visible and conform to the laws of physics and the user's perceptual expectations.

6. *Faithful viewpoints*—The visual representation of the virtual world should map to the user's normal perception, and viewpoint change by head movement should be rendered without delay.

7. *Navigation and orientation support*—The users should always be able to find where they are in the VE and return to known, preset positions. Unnatural actions such as fly-through surfaces may help but these have to be judged in a trade-off with naturalness (see heuristics 1 and 2).

8. *Clear entry and exit points*—How to enter and exit from a virtual world should be clearly communicated.

9. *Consistent departures*—When design compromises are used they should be consistent and clearly marked, for example, cross-modal substitution and power actions for navigation.

10. *Support for learning*—Active objects should be cued and if necessary explain themselves to promote learning of VEs.

11. *Clear turn-taking*—Where system initiative is used it should be clearly signaled and conventions established for turn-taking.

12. *Sense of presence*—The user should be engaged and perceive being in a "real" world as being natural.

The evaluator assesses the application by running through a representative set of scenarios and noting any problems. The usability problems may be classified with the heuristics to create a score; alternatively, observed problems are analyzed by considering each heuristic in turn and posing questions of conformance, for example, does the system support clear turn taking? Notes on severity of the problems may also be helpful in this assessment.

Once several tasks have been completed, problems are scored using the heuristics to arrive at the final rating. The system is scored on a 1 to 7 scale where 1 = *poor fit with the heuristic* and 7 represents a *good design*, and any parts of the design which offend the heuristic are noted. Interpretation of the heuristics has to take the task or domain model into account, especially the need to maintain naturalness in the VE. Some heuristics may not apply to some applications; for example, entry and exit points in a CAVE are obvious: take off the glasses and step outside. This produces a score for the application against each heuristic and a list of problem features that indicate areas where design improvement is necessary. Carrying out a heuristic evaluation with several independent evaluators helps to trap more usability problems. As with evaluation of GUI interfaces, four to six experts will trap 80% to 90% of the problems (Nielsen & Phillips, 1993).

Regarding the Business Park example, the Business Park VR was not very natural in its representation or engagement as many building features were inoperable (Heuristic1: *score 3* or H1: *3*). The system was reasonably compatible with the user's task of exploration, and the domain reflected the expected topography of buildings (H2: *4*). The system failed Heuristic 3, as most actions were not natural (H3: *1*). This was partly a limitation of the interaction technology, a joystick, which did not support natural manipulations, for example, grasp, lift objects. Similarly, coordination of representation and action was poor (H4: *2*) as no self-presence was represented in the VE. This was also reflected in a poor rating for presence (H12: *2*). Feedback (H5: *4*) was partially realistic as many objects that were active gave reasonable feedback but many objects that might have been expected to be active were not. The user's viewpoint was reasonably faithful (H6: *3*) within the constraints of the technology, but there was a function that allowed the user to jump between locations inside and outside the building that violated Heuristics 2 and 6. Navigation and orientation support (H7: *2*) left room for improvement as several rooms were sparsely detailed, making recognition of location difficult; furthermore, the ability to "walk through walls" into enclosed spaces made disorientation probable. The entry and exit points to the VE were not marked (H8: *1*), and departures from natural action were neither consistent nor clearly marked (H9: *1*). There was limited support for learning in a partial guided tour (H10: *3*), but the system initiative was not clearly signaled (H11: *1*). Overall, the system scored poorly on the heuristic evaluation.

Walkthrough Evaluation

Walkthrough evaluation tests UIs that may be specifications, storyboards, and early prototypes. The method follows the cognitive walkthrough tradition (Wharton et al., 1994) of diagnostic questions linked to a cycle of interaction, in this case the extended Norman models introduced in chapter 3. In analytic mode, a walkthrough is performed by an expert, or users in conjunction with an expert. In this case, the questions are used during the walkthrough to try and spot potential problems as they arise. The evaluation may be carried out by non-HCI experts, although training in HCI improves the accuracy of the usability diagnosis.

The materials required are a description of the users' task(s) or exploration objectives; an outline profile of the expected users; system prototype, storyboard, or specification; and forms for recording results.

In the diagnosis mode, the user runs through a series of tasks or scenarios to evaluate the system. The walkthrough uses questions based on the GDPs described in chapter 3 in three groups reflecting the three cycles of interaction. In any one evaluation, the three checklists may have to be used as interaction may swap between the cycles.

Normal Task Action.   The evaluator steps through the scenario of use or task sequence, with the following questions:

1. *Can the user form or remember the task goal?*
   The answer to this question is yes unless the user has poor task knowledge. If this is the case, an aide-memoire may be provided by speech or as a bullet point list of task steps; otherwise, training should be provided.
2. *Can the user form an intention of what to do?*
   At this stage the user requires procedural memory of how to carry out the task with cues and affordances in the VE to suggest the best course of action. Affordances should be present, otherwise hints should be given about where the user might find them.
3. *Can the necessary objects be located?*
   The area of the environment necessary to carry out the task-action should be visible. Objects may be obscured or not visible although the user is sure that the appropriate part of the environment has been reached. The necessary object should be highlighted or made salient. Important objects should be rendered in more detail to help recognition. If highlighting offends naturalness criteria for the environment, speech cues may be used.
4. *Can the users approach and orient themselves so that the necessary action can be carried out?*
   Objects may be obscured, or rendered in 2D texture so depth perception is difficult. Objects should be modeled in 3D; alternatively the design of the "self" may need to be improved. Changing the user's viewpoint can help orientation; improving the direction con-

trols can facilitate orientation actions, via point and go-to-object controls (ray casting, snap-to).

5. *Can the user decide what action to take and how?*

The environment may not suggest the necessary cues or affordances for action. If the user cannot decide, then the problem may either be lack of detailed task knowledge or unclear design of the virtual objects. The representation of the object should be improved. If naturalness is not vital, the object can be animated to suggest actions to the user, otherwise speech or text instructions may be displayed.

6. *Can the user carry out the manipulation or action easily?*

If the action is difficult, it may be beyond the user's physical capabilities (i.e., manipulations are too precise or demand excessive perceptio–motor coordination); alternatively, the user may not have acquired the necessary physical skill. If naturalness is not vital, the size of the object (or the user's presence) may be scaled so that it is easier to manipulate; alternatively, the necessary action can be simplified or automated. Design of the self may need to be improved so that manipulations are easier for the user to control. If the user is using a virtual tool, this may need improving to make control more natural.

7. *Is the consequence of the user's action perceivable?*

Feedback may be either absent, ambiguous, or hidden (i.e., it happens but is in another part of the environment outside the user's immediate vision). The location of remote feedback should be signaled to the user. If feedback is not clear, the object may be highlighted to denote change. Change to objects should be faithful to the real world. Modalities are important here because, ideally, feedback should include haptic as well as audio and visual representations. If force feedback is not possible, cross-modal substitution may be used, for example, use audio tone or change in color to represent pressure.

8. *Can the user interpret the change?*

Unless the naturalness principle is offended, feedback should always be clear and unambiguous. The user should be able to interpret the effect in the light of his or her task or domain knowledge and the relation between the effect and the observable VE. If the effect of change is not clear, the feedback may need to be clarified or possibly explained to the user. Explanation agents may be necessary for complex effects; alternatively, the overall effect may be shown in slow motion to aid interpretation.

9. *Can the user decide what to do next?*

At this stage the pathway branches. If the user has completed a task procedure, then the next stage is to acquire the next goal, so repeat the analysis starting with number 1. Alternatively, if the user is within a procedure, the next step is to select the next action to perform. Failure at this step may be caused by memory failure or inadequate user task knowledge; however, failure may also be due to misleading or inappropriate cues in the VE. In this case, the environment needs to be redesigned to suggest actions that are compatible with the user's task. Note that this step may be related to iterations between questions 5 and 6 for closely coupled and continuous actions. When the user is skilled, deciding the next action is automatic.

Once the next action has been selected, the user may reenter the cycle at questions 2, 3, or 4, depending on where the necessary objects are located.

Goal-Directed Exploration.   In goal directed exploration, the user has a definite search target in mind, motivated either by the task or by the need to explore specific aspects of the environment. The walkthrough questions that follow are listed:

1. *Does the user know where to start looking for the search target?*
   If the user has poor knowledge of the VE or the environment gives no clues about where the search target may be located, then search will be by guesswork. Either familiarization of the virtual world should be provided by guided tours, or overview maps displayed to show an outline of the VE and its contents. In some applications with extensive virtual worlds, a search facility may be necessary so that the user can enter <find object x> and the system then takes the user to that point.

2. *Can the user determine a pathway toward the search target?*
   The environment should have a clear structure so pathways for movement are obvious. Other ways of remedying user problems are to give overview maps of the VE and indicate an appropriate path to a search target. Waymarks and salient landmarks can help memorization of paths and locations, and allowing the user to change the viewpoint can help provide a fresh perspective to find pathways.

3. *Can the user execute movement and navigation actions?*
   Poor design of the self-representation may cause problems at this step. For instance, if the user does not know the gestures for movement with a hand or dataglove presence, then training or an animated demonstration should be provided. Specification of power actions (e.g., flying metaphors, portals, magic carpets) should be explained to users. Speed and acceleration need to be controlled by natural movements and preferably separated from direction controls.

4. *Can the user recognize the search target?*
The search target may be obscured or not clear. The design should represent the desired objects in detail with a clear outline to enhance recognition or provide transparency see-through effects for occluded objects. If the user's search target is known, then it can be highlighted. When naturalness prevents highlighting, magnification facilities may be useful to help users identify small targets.

Once the user has found and recognized the search target, the walkthrough reenters the task action cycle at question 4.

Exploratory Browsing.   In this case, the user's aim is to explore the system either for curiosity or learning needs. Even if there is no specific goal, various objects may need to be investigated and remembered for future reference. The walkthrough questions follow an iteration of scan–navigate–interpret actions. The diagnostic guidelines are the same as goal-directed navigation steps 2 through 4, with the following additions:

1. *Can users interpret the identity, role, and behavior of objects?*
Interpretation depends on domain knowledge. User learning may be supported by making objects explain themselves when approached or on manipulation. Important objects should be represented in detail so interaction can take place.
2. *Can users remember important objects or locations?*
Memorization can be helped by designing important locations or objects in the environment to be salient, for example, use of color, movement, size, or shape. Important objects may be set apart from others, or key objects can be made to stand out as exceptions among a set. Other memory support facilities are waymarks that the user can place in the VE, a visit list so users can inspect where they have been, and replayable traces of previous explorations.

The outcome of exploratory browsing should be improved user knowledge of the VE and external memory tags to help future exploration and task action.

System Initiative.   There are two variants of system initiative. Either the system may take the complete initiative, in which case the user has little choice but to be passive, for example, in a guided tour; or agents within the system exhibit behavior. In the latter case, concurrent system and user actions are possible.
The walkthrough questions for the system initiative mode follow:

1. *Is it clear to the user that the system has taken control?*
   The onset of system initiative should be clearly signaled to the user, and appropriate conventions adopted in conversational applications, for example, gesture by mannequins when they wish to speak or act.
2. *Can the user resume control at any point and is the appropriate action clear?*
   In general, initiative should always reside with users so they are not frozen out of the application. The self should remain active when system agents are exhibiting behavior because the user may wish to ignore them.
3. *Are the effects of system actions recognizable?*
   Care should be taken that actions in a remote part of the VE are made visible or audible to the user or the presence of the active agent is cued. System actions should be easy to identify.
4. *Are system actions interpretable?*
   This depends on actions being known to the user. Actions and gestures carried out by agents should conform to the users' expectations. Actions should generally conform to the laws of physics unless such deviations are explicitly signaled.
5. *Is the end of system action clear?*
   The endpoint of system initiative should be clearly signaled so that the user knows when to resume command.

The same questions are used for both complete and partial system initiative, although in partial system initiative, signaling conventions may be more complex. For instance, it may be important to signal when concurrent activity is acceptable, or when the system agent has important information to convey. When system initiative involves other human-like agents, and assuming the user has noticed the signal from another agent, the evaluation questions as follows:

1. *Can the message be understood?*
   Problems might be caused by poor physical communication channels, for example, audio interference or poor image quality. Once these have been eliminated, suspect problems in the user's understanding of the language, for example, the gesture, icon, or visual symbols might be unknown or a foreign language has been used.
2. *Can the message be interpreted?*
   Interpretation depends on knowledge of the message content. Suspect user domain knowledge may be deficient, or the message has been expressed ambiguously.
3. *Is the message understood but inappropriate or not expected?*

Failure at the evaluation stage or pragmatic level of understanding points to content problems. The user either has no knowledge of the sender or his or her context, or the message doesn't relate to the current task or conversation. Providing background information about the sender, his or her location, and history may help. Correct messages are often delivered to the wrong person or at the wrong time, so the meaning should be checked with the sender.

4. *Does the user know how to respond?*
   Problems at this stage emanate from insufficient user knowledge of the sender, or the communication context, so response planning is inhibited. Providing more information about the other agent and any dialogue history can help.

5. *Is the user able to respond?*
   In some cases, the user is ready to respond but cannot because the appropriate communication channel is not available. Turn-taking problems may shut out the users, so an interrupt mechanism may be necessary; alternatively, the appropriate modality may not be present.

This completes the walkthrough evaluation. The problems encountered will be noted and design improvement made to features that appear to cause severe errors.

Business Park Example.   This section illustrates use of the walkthrough method covering all three cycles; however, space precludes an exhaustive description of the evaluation, so the method is illustrated with the representative task of finding out about equipment in the main building.

The first task implies goal directed exploration and task action for equipment operation, so questions from the task cycle are used. No problems were apparent for task or action walkthrough stages 1 to 3 (see Fig. 6.7) in finding out about the office equipment. Stage 4 gave problems, as it was difficult to approach and orient toward the draftsman's table, which was at a slight angle, as depicted in Fig. 6.7. Deciding what action to take (stage 5) was even worse as the object gave few cues about how it might be manipulated. A handle did suggest action and was active, but the board did not move until the handle had been pulled back. Note that this may offend the naturalness principle unless the concept of a handle lock is an important feature, as drawing boards are normally rotatable by pressing or lifting the surface. Stage 6 was blocked by the inability to find the correct cues. The effect of action was visible and interpretable as the drawing table changed orientation, but change was inconsistent with the degree of manipulation because of missing haptic feedback.

(a)   (b)

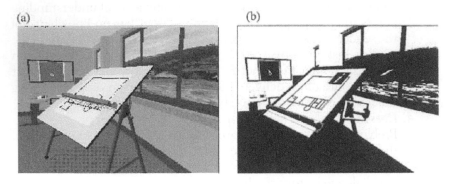

FIG. 6.7   View of office equipment in the Business Park premises, showing (a) original design, and (b) design after application of GDPs to make the action affordances clear. Images courtesy of VP Group.

Another example from task 1, illustrated in Fig. 6.8, was testing the electrical switchgear. Stages 1 to 4 gave no problems, but stages 7 and 8 were not supported because the feedback (a small red light) was not very visible and was difficult to interpret.

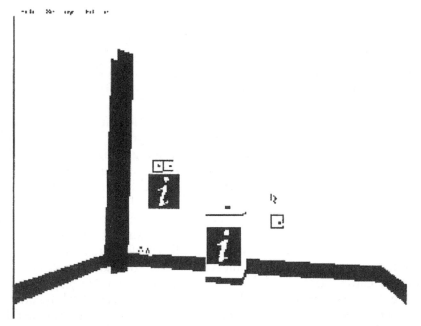

FIG. 6.8   View of electrical switchgear in the Business Park premises after application of the GDPs to cure the usability problem. Image courtesy of VP Group.

The walkthrough indicated that design changes were necessary to make the objects interact more faithfully according to the real-world model, and to provide better affordances and feedback. Improving the presence may also help alleviate manipulation problems.

The second task was goal-directed exploration of the building, including the layout of rooms and their function, and finding out whether the toilets were equipped for the disabled. Following the exploration cycle in Fig. 6.9, stages 1 and 2 presented some problems, as it was not clear where the toilets were located. To some extent this is a limitation of not knowing the environment. However, the real problems started with stages 3 and 4. The rooms, depicted in Fig. 6.9, are small and sparsely detailed. It was easy to become disoriented by an occluded view if the viewpoint was moved too close to a wall. Examining the facilities was difficult because the viewpoint could not be set sufficiently far away for an overview without going backwards through a wall. Furthermore, several objects were inactive (e.g., water taps in basin), so they did not provide affordances for action, thereby leading to misinformation about the real world that the VR was supposed to represent, that is, plumbing facilities in the building. This part of the design needed better details in the rooms and more functional objects. Also, an overview map of the building floor plan could help locate the toilets and improve the user's orientation.

The third task, exploring the general layout of the Business Park, the access roads, and its buildings, was partially helped by a system-initiated guided tour which started on entry to the VE as illustrated in Fig. 6.10. However, it was not apparent that the system had taken the initiative (stage 1). The user's view in the VE is automatically moved on the guided tour but no explanation was provided and there was no cue of the mode change. It was difficult to resume user control as the command implemented on a function

(a)

(b)

 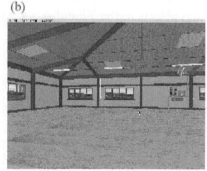

FIG. 6.9 Layout of a building in the Business Park premises (a) original design, and (b) after application of GDPs to improve visibility of significant objects. Images courtesy of VP Group.

FIG. 6.10   Two parts of the guided tour of the Business Park VE with the system taking the initiative, after application of GDP guidelines. The original design did not have an avatar to lead the user and no speech track was used. Images courtesy of VP Group.

key was not visible to the user (stage 2), and the effects of the system's actions were only partially recognizable and interpretable (stages 3 and 4). These problems were compounded if the user tried to operate the 3D mouse unaware of the system's initiative. Finally, the endpoint of the tour (stage 5) was cryptically signaled by the end of movement when the viewpoint was placed back at the starting point of the tour. The walkthrough suggests several design changes to make the initiative mode clear to the users and to allow resumption of user initiative at any moment.

In conclusion, the walkthrough uncovered several problems in the Business Park application, ranging from poor affordances for interaction to poor navigation support and inappropriate system initiative. The majority of problems related to poor affordances for action and inadequate feedback when objects in the VE didn't act as expected.

Diagnostic Evaluation

The procedure is similar to traditional, formative usability evaluations (e.g., Cooperative Evaluation; Monk & Wright, 1993) in which the user performs a set task, and the evaluator observes critical incidents (user difficulties) and breakdowns (severe problems when the user abandons the task or action).

In immersive environments, verbal commentary can be difficult because the user has to concentrate on the immediate (virtual) world while reporting problems in the real world. The first task is to categorize the observed problems and link them to missing requirements or inadequate design features. Missing requirements may reflect defects in the UI design; however, if the virtual prototypes are being tested, the defects may pertain to the (virtual) product. The key outcome is to link observed problems with the responsible design features and suggestions for improvement.

The following decision trees (see Fig. 6.11–6.16) help tracing observed problems to their potential cause. The decision trees are derived from the interaction models in chapter 3, so the analyst has to be able to classify the user's interaction in either exploring the VE, engaging in task action, or reacting to other agents and events.

Task Action Diagnosis.   The decision trees help to trace observable symptoms of user problems to their underlying causes. At the beginning of a task or subtask, if the user can't proceed or is puzzled, then suspect either missing functionality (requirement not implemented), hidden functionality error (can't find function or affordance), task fit error (missing functionality), or user error (poor task or domain knowledge).

The decision tree at this stage (see Fig. 6.11) traces problem causes in lack of user knowledge or vague intentions. If no explanation is found, then analysis proceeds to the next decision tree, Fig. 6.12.

The location analysis tree traces problem causes in finding affordances and commands. If the user has located the affordance/command but is still puzzled then the metaphor or VE feature does not support the action specification stage. If the user has found a target object/tool/VE feature but hesitates or can't proceed, then suspect cue/affordance/metaphor error. In these cases the problem may be an unpredictable action or reside in operation of the user's presence.

The action or manipulation tree (see Fig. 6.13) traces causes either to lack of integration with feedback, or to complex actions or poor devices that don't support precise motor control. Problems at this stage usually involve feedback causes as well (see Fig. 6.14). Inappropriate modality may also be responsible (e.g., action expected when speech commands are implied by the VE) or a virtual tool may have obscure controls. After a successful action, if the user can't proceed or is puzzled, then a goal formation problem is indicated, due either to missing or inadequate functionality or to task compatibility error. If the user has completed the action but is puzzled by an unexpected effect, then suspect that feedback is either inadequate or absent; otherwise, the user may be the victim of a mode error. In feedback, the tree traces causes back to problems in user knowledge and fit with their task; however, feedback problems often uncover hidden causes in modes or mismatches between the user's and system models.

Exploration or Navigation Diagnosis.   The decision tree for this mode differentiates the type of navigation, either following pathways, directions, or locating a target. The classic symptoms of navigation problems are

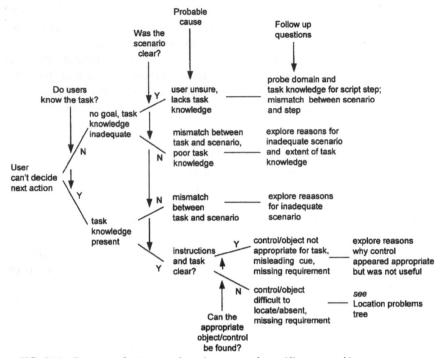

FIG. 6.11   Diagnostic decision tree for task action mode: goal/function problems.

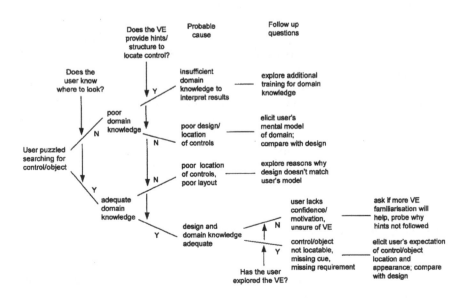

FIG. 6.12   Diagnostic decision tree for task action mode: location problems.

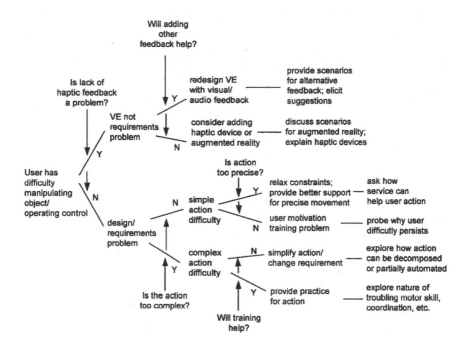

FIG. 6.13   Diagnostic decision tree for task action mode: action/manipulation problems.

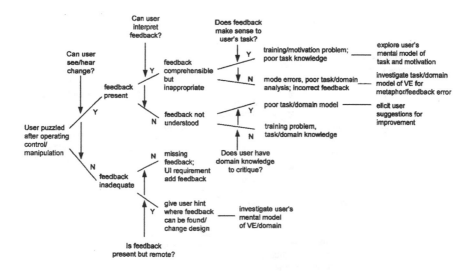

FIG. 6.14   Diagnostic decision tree for task action mode: feedback problems.

conceptual disorientation and random hunting for cues. The immediate causes may be perceptual confusion when users lose their reference point because they have moved too close to a surface or into an unfamiliar part of the VE. Beyond the perceptual problem, there are several wayfinding problems (see Fig. 6.15). If the users do not know where they are in the VE, then a spatial cue problem or lack of domain knowledge may be responsible. In sparse environments there may be insufficient cues; also, the user may have entered an unexpected area by a magic effect (see portals). An overview map will help the user search for the target to navigate to. If users have problems in orienting their viewpoint, then viewpoint controls or operation of the self-presence may be inadequate. When the user overshoots a target or has to take many corrective actions during navigation, inadequate presence movement and navigation controls may need to be tuned or redesigned. When the user cannot find an appropriate direction for travel, then the VE has insufficient cues, or too much clutter may obscure pathways, or the user may have insufficient information to plan his or her next move.

System Initiative Diagnosis.   Problems in this context will depend on whether the user has to recognize and respond to other agents in the environment, or interpret changes in system initiative. The decision tree depicted in Fig. 6.16 starts with symptoms of recognizing change and then

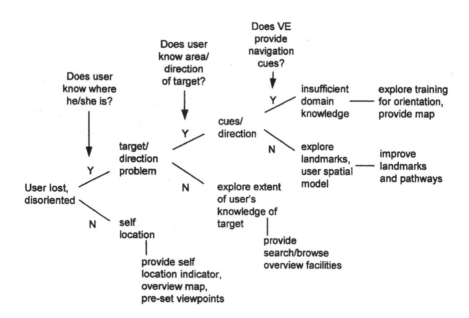

FIG. 6.15   Diagnostic decision tree for navigation problems.

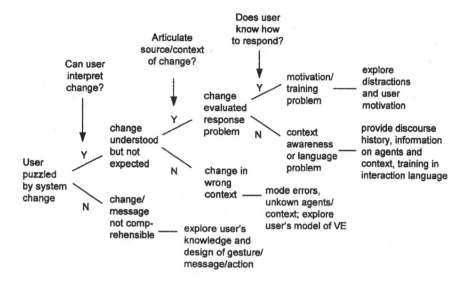

FIG. 6.16   Diagnostic decision tree for system initiative problems.

progresses to interpreting the change and planning a response. The user's symptoms may be caused by inappropriate actions when he or she has failed to recognize a change in initiative or another agent's actions, or being puzzled when unexpected change has occurred. If the user continues with previous actions that no longer have an appropriate effect, then it is likely the user has not noticed the initiative change. This may be caused by poor signaling by the system or other agent, or the event is not visible or audible in the user's current location. When the user perceives the change but cannot make sense of it, the message or event has not been signaled appropriately; alternatively, the user may not be able to interpret the event. Poor task or domain analysis may be to blame, or information in the event was not correct, or the user has inadequate domain knowledge. The user may not recognize the context of change, because the event does not make sense in relation to the objects or agents with which it is associated. If the user can interpret the event but cannot effect a response, then the appropriate tools or communication modalities may be missing.

In many cases, the source of usability problems is obvious, for example, an ambiguous affordance, poor tools, or incomprehensible feedback message; however, in other cases, the culpable design feature is not apparent. These errors are often caused by parameter settings or hidden or inadequate task models so that the system behaves in a manner that the user cannot comprehend; for instance controls with a hidden accelerator function make movement more rapid than the user expects.

SUMMARY

Three evaluation methods for multisensory UIs were described: expert evaluation that uses a checklist of heuristics to assess UIs, diagnostic evaluation of observed user problems, and cognitive walkthroughs. These methods are all established approaches for standard GUI evaluation; however, they needed to be extended for multimedia and VR. In multimedia, the important difference is to test users' memory for the content in tutorial and information-providing applications. Gaps in users' memory, when compared with a gold standard of the information content, point toward presentation problems. These problems can be diagnosed with walkthroughs or eye-tracking studies for detailed cases.

Usability problem causes are attributed using the taxonomy of information delivery and interaction errors, or requirements defects. In Internet applications and multimedia, assessing usability is not sufficient. The attractiveness and appeal of a user's interface is important. Heursitics for assessing the appeal of multimedia interfaces are organized within a model of Web site operation. First, the attractiveness of the interfaces is evaluated using general heuristics for aesthetic qualities, followed by a content-related set for motivation. The assessment of attractiveness, choice of content to motivate users, navigation, and general usability was illustrated by a case study of three Web sites that showed the contributions made by aesthetic attractiveness, content-related attraction, and standard usability.

Three approaches to VR evaluation were described. First is expert evaluation that starts by assessing the requirements for naturalness, and then uses heuristics to assess design quality and problems encountered with a VE. Second, walkthrough evaluation uses interaction models in combination with question checklists to discover potential usability problems. Finally, the diagnostic approach also follows the cooperative evaluation procedure for data collection and analysis with decision trees that trace observed symptoms of user problems to their underlying causes in usability defects. The decision trees are based on the interaction models described in chapter 3; hence, they are structured as a set of questions to ask according to the type of interaction (task, exploratory, responsive) and interaction stage (goal formation, location, action, interpreting feedback).

7

Applications, Architectures, and Advances

In this final chapter, two application areas for multimedia and VR are investigated in more depth, then the future of multisensory interaction will be reviewed to discuss how technology may make interaction more useful, ubiquitous, and universal. Ubiquitous computing envisages software in devices spread throughout our environment (Weiser, 1991). Interaction may be through explicit UIs, but in many cases we will be interacting with computers via everyday products and furniture, for example, displays in desks, mobile phones, on glasses, ear pieces and so on. Education and training are key markets for multimedia, and increasingly for VR; however, the contribution from advanced technology to successful learning outcomes is not clear. Connections between the design guidance given in earlier chapters and construction of educational applications are discussed. The second area is design and requirements analysis. Simulation and interactive microworlds are an important contribution of both VR and multimedia. VR in particular has become important for virtual prototyping and refining designs by simulation. Current research in progress in the ISRE project is described and guidance given on VE-driven requirements analysis.

EDUCATIONAL APPLICATIONS

This short section provides some background guidance on the dialogue design issues for Computer-Aided Learning and Computer-Based Training (CAL and CBT) with multimedia and VR. First, some words of caution. I firmly believe that 90% of the design effort and corresponding reasons for successful learning products does not reside in the UI, multisensory or oth-

241

erwise. Multimedia, and to a lesser extent VR, has been the subject of a large amount of unjustified hype. The evidence that multisensory interaction on its own actually improves learning is remarkably hard to find although many believe that it does. Indeed, there is evidence that current products have poor learning outcomes (Rogers & Scaife, 1998). The objectives of this chapter are not to repeat a tutorial on design of educational software; this would require another book, and there are already plenty on the market (e.g., Boyle, 1997; Elsom-Cook, 2000; Laurillard, 1993). Instead, I concentrate on the intersection of interaction and presentation design for effective learning outcomes. It is difficult to talk about learning outcomes without some view on pedagogical design, so I start with a brief review of the design problem before the UI.

Learning Environments

The education world has been debating the merits of instructionist versus constructionist approaches to learning for several decades. Instuctionism is learning by telling and emphasizes delivery of content; in contrast, constructionist approaches emphasize learning by doing. The latter tradition (Papert, 1980) is generally accepted to be the superior approach. Constructivism advocates tuition in which the student learns by trying out problems, constructing things, and interacting with the world. This makes sense in terms of basic psychology because learning and problem solving are closely linked; the more we think about the subject matter, the deeper the encoding of a memory schema. However, not all learning may need a constructionist approach. Training and more in-depth education have differing objectives:

- *Training* aims to impart knowledge to usually motivated individuals. The knowledge in training is frequently procedural or task-based explanations, and skilled operation is the expected outcome. Instructionist approaches can be appropriate for training.
- *Education* aims to create a deeper understanding of a domain than does training. The knowledge that the learners should acquire will be multifaceted, for example, concepts, causation, and more complex knowledge. Education also aims to teach students about the learning process itself: learning how to learn, and the ability to reflect on experience. Constructionist approaches and their relative, guided discovery learning, (Elsom-Cook, 2000) are more appropriate.

Design of software for training is easier because the learning ambition is lower; however, the boundary between the two is not clear-cut. Many training applications need to impart deeper knowledge, considering the growth of knowledge–worker economy and distance learning.

Learning is a complex business. To lay out the dimensions of the problem, three layers need to be considered: technology, where interactive system design and other artifacts may influence the outcome; cognitive; and social. These levels are examined to illustrate the potential and limitations of multisensory technology.

Individual-Level Learning

At this level the focus is primarily on the individual, although in most contexts the social and cognitive levels are integrated. Motivation is a major cognitive factor influencing learning. Better-motivated students learn more effectively, but the process of motivating people for learning is not well understood. Motivation may be influenced by high level societal values, such as one's career aims; more immediate incentives to do well in an exam or test; or interest in the content itself. Finally, entertainment and fun can motivate learning. Multisensory UIs can help the motivation problem by representing personalities, by choice of engaging media, stimulating dialogues and, in the short term, by the novelty of technology.

Content and delivery may be linked to the students' cognitive style. Unfortunately, this property is difficult to analyze. Briefly, cognitive style comes in many variants, but they all tend to boil down to difference in people's ability for abstract thought. Some individuals like to reason with the specific facts and construct ideas "bottom-up." These field dependent students find abstraction more difficult. Other field independent people reason top-down and more abstractly. If these differences could be detected reliably, then field dependent individuals should benefit more from being given abstract structures and analogies, whereas field independent individuals should benefit from scenarios and concrete examples, (i.e. microworlds, virtual environments) to encourage testing ideas (Cairncross, 2001). As abstract thought is a trained aspect of human cognition, whether cognitive style exists is a contentious matter. Cognitive style in visualize–verbalize individual differences is probably one of the most dependable design indicators for multimedia.

Social-Level Learning

Learning frequently occurs in groups. When we are puzzled or don't understand something, the most natural course of action is to ask another person to help. Conversations help learning at three levels:

- When engaged in the *primary learning task,* dialogues with others help to share insights, express problems, and build on each other's suggestions. Dialogues between experts and novices support learning by explanations, critiques, mentoring, and challenging under-standing.

- Materials that are not the direct subject matter but help the learner, such as exercises, examples, back-up explanations, illustrative scenarios, and so forth, are referred to as *secondary material*. Conversations while trying out exercises and discussions of examples help to develop insight into primary material.
- Conversations about the process of learning and material generated during the process, such as comments on difficult concepts, new analogies, counter examples, and learning related to one's own experience, are examples of *tertiary learning material*. In this case, the conversation itself becomes useful for learning not only when it happens but also as a recorded artifact that can be shared with others. These learning conversations often produce new insights that the instructor may miss (Laurillard, 1993; Lee & Owens, 2000).

Social learning can be supported by groupware multisensory systems, also referred to as Computer Mediated Communication (CMC). Some systems are in everyday use such as e-mail and chat, but these share experiences by the impoverished medium of text. Adding multimedia in video conferencing-style interaction provides speech and image but there are several problems in designing CMC systems for effective interaction.

First, there is turn-taking in multiparty conversations. Judging when to speak in groups is complex enough in face-to-face interaction. People use small gaps in spoken discourse, overt invitations to take turns, and a variety of nonverbal cues in body language and facial expression. In spite of the sophistication of natural conversation management, interruptions and shutouts occur. In large groups (more than 5 or 6 individuals), turn-taking can become a problem and moderator roles are used to impose order. Turn-taking can be made more complex in distributed applications when delays in speech transmission make detecting conversation gaps very difficult. Turn-taking is related to the second problem of group-wide views. In natural conversations, we can scan most members in a group of up to roughly 10 to 12 people. In video mediated communication, the view limitations of camera technology mean that either a few participants are shown in sufficient detail to see nonverbal communication or the whole group is visible, but detail of facial expressions and gesture is poor. Of course, two images may be shown, one in foreground detail and the other in background, but then the user has to scan both images to extract the necessary information. Showing a mosaic of many individuals in close-up just makes the scanning problem worse. In short, video conferencing has the television producer's problem: what to show in close-up when it is difficult to predict where the focus of debate will go within a group.

One alternative is to converse in VEs. Avatars replace real-life images. The design question in VEs is how to communicate nonverbal discourse. Groupware VEs have simple facial expressions such as smiles, frowns, and surprise (Benford et al., 1995). This has led to more realistic presences with the ability to direct gaze, more facial expressions, and other gestures such as head nods and shoulder shrugs (André & Rist, 2000; Cassell et al., 1999).

When artificial agents are implemented, behaviors can be scripted, but for computer-mediated communication, the problem becomes one of user control. We normally perform gestures and facial expressions unconsciously. Giving people controls to make an avatar frown, laugh, (facial expressions), agree (head nod), or show indifference (shoulder shrug) just gives users a cognitive overload. Trying to plan nonverbal communication concurrently with speaking causes competing processes in the implication level running both visual and morphological subsystems (see ICS model in chap. 3). New high-level controls are needed so users can express emotional reactions (e.g., surprise, disappointment, joy) in CVEs, as well as mechanisms for turn-taking. In spite of these limitations, multiparty VE conversations do work even with very limited (text or chat) multisensory interfaces in the inhabited worlds of the World Wide Web. In these cases, users have adopted conventions to direct conversation by addressing remarks to individuals in speech and turning their avatars to face the personae being addressed (see Fig. 7.1). Alternatively, more formal controls for turn-taking can be provided.

An interesting side effect of media choice in CMC is communication of identity. In video, identity is accessible assuming that the other person is known; however, in e-mail and chat, identity can be hidden by aliases. Some reports suggested that antisocial behavior, for example, being offensive or flaming in e-mail, may be more common when identity is masked. More comprehensive research has shown this not to be the case, and group behavior, negotiation, and building consensus is remarkably similar with or without explicit identity. People circumvent absence of identity by dialogue, asking questions and looking for cues. Design of identity is still a concern, especially for privacy and political reasons. Text media can mask the origin of the individual, organization, and location by eliminating header or address information; speech requires voice modulation; and video images are made anonymous by pixel area blurring. Such techniques are common in television reporting.

The aforementioned discussion has assumed that communication is synchronous; however, multisensory systems can also support learning conversations in asynchronous systems. The traditional CSCW cube, recapitulated for learning conversations, is illustrated in Fig. 7.2.

In asynchronous communication for both same and different places, multisensory interfaces can help to distribute secondary and tertiary learning materials. Text media are useful because of their persistence: comments can

(a)   (b)

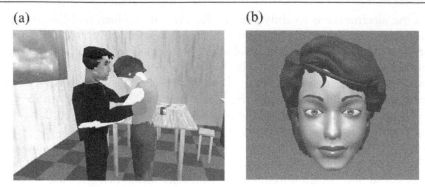

FIG. 7.1   VE of system with more complex presences with facial expressions. Reprinted with permission by Mel Slater (a) and Catherine Pelachaud (b).

Place

	Same	Different
Same	Virtual workbenches Shared AR systems	Video conferencing Chat rooms Text messaging Phone conversations
Different	Multimedia notes annotations video messages design versions of art i facts	Multimedia notes annotations video messages design versions of art i facts

Time is the left-axis label between Same and Different rows.

FIG. 7.2   CSCW cube model: same/different, place/time.

be annotated on learning conversations developed over weeks or months. Speech and video clips motivate learners by making the communication more personal; also, judicious use of image and personalities can have persuasive effects, as described in chapter 4 (Reeves & Nass, 1996). In synchronous, same-place conversations, the main need is to distribute a lecture to large groups that cannot all fit within the constrained space. Video transmission of lectures is a partial solution. More difficult is giving large groups access to shared demonstrations and simulations. This point is taken up in the following section. Finally, in the same time, different place cell, both multimedia video conferencing and VE communication may be used. Sharing tertiary material usually implies use of text and speech, because this is the usual medium of origin. However, comments and annotations may be made on media that represent primary and secondary learning materials, so groupware environments need to support attachment of voice notes, and drawings and doodles on top of primary learning media, as well as text annotations.

EDUCATION SOFTWARE TECHNOLOGY

The previous section reviewed dimensions of the design problem. We now progress to design implications for multisensory UIs. From the constructivist tradition, several general design principles can be drawn. Interaction is desirable as it encourages exploration and user-directed learning. Active engagement helps to promote active learning because the user has to solve problems via an interactive dialogue. Interactive microworlds and simulations have a long heritage going back to Steamer for interactive simulations (Hollan et al., 1984) and the ARK (Alternative Reality Kit; Smith, 1987). The ARK environment provides a game-like world for teaching Newtonian physics, in which students could roll balls down a slide and observe how far the ball flew before hitting the ground. Controls allowed the mass of the ball, angle of the slide, and the strength of gravity to be changed so that different trajectories can be interpreted according to Newton's laws. However, interactive microworlds may not be suitable for all learning domains, so for training, instructionist approaches may be appropriate. In order of increasing complexity, the different styles of tutorial dialogue, with their implications for multisensory UIs, are described in the following section.

Scripted Presentations and Hypermedia

The simplest form of dialogue is a hypermedia model of links. Some interaction is possible so that learners have limited control over content delivery. The user views a presentation that may have several options to explore, presented as menus or different hypermedia hotspots. The dialogue may have differing degrees of branching from a major path with side paths where users are encouraged to follow up on more detail; for example, in a tutorial on animal ecology, the major path explains the food chain from primary producers (plants) through to animals up the food chain. Side links give more details of the types of plants and animals at each level.

More complex navigation can be provided as a multipath network where the student is free to follow many different paths through the learning material. However, to counteract the possibility of getting lost, it is advisable to provide a "guided tour" which takes the student through the preferred path; once having traversed it, students are free to explore on their own.

Depending on the level of guidance desired in the learning, hypermedia can converge with scripted presentations; for example, see the following:

- *No predetermined pathway*—This implies hypermedia in which the user is free to follow any links provided by the designer.
- A *preferred pathway* is specified but the application also supports exploratory browsing of the material. Recommended pathways may be provided as hints on an overview map, or as guided tours.
- The pedagogical design specifies a *predetermined* pathway as a scripted presentation.

Although hypermedia is an effective means of promoting user exploration, it is still a fairly passive mode of interaction, and the user is not learning by doing.

Once the user has viewed the material, an interactive quiz can be provided, with multiple-choice questions for machine-based assessment. The user is given a score and rewarded with congratulations if he or she gets the answer right, or the opportunity to retry the quiz question if he or she gets it wrong (see Fig. 7.3). Although quizzes are popular, they are still only assessing the student's learning after viewing the material.

Design issues include how to link components in hypermedia models; and within components, how to integrate multimedia. Learning goals frequently require students to compare information from different sources or viewpoints. Concurrent multimedia help comparisons and cross-referencing because the student can view all the relevant information at once, whereas sequential presentation, enforced by hypermedia, can make this task more difficult. The following principles reiterate the design advice given in chapter 4 but place it within a learning context:

- When several pieces of information are necessary to achieve a learning goal, display the information concurrently as far as possible, and integrate the content with contact points. Concurrent presentation allows the student to scan all the content without having to burden working memory.
- Place key information in static media, augmented by summaries using text, diagrams, and images. Dynamic media have a stimulating effect and are attractive, but effective information transfer is limited to the gist or high-level concepts. Dynamic media, however, have a role to play in integrating information (see procedure patterns in chap. 4).

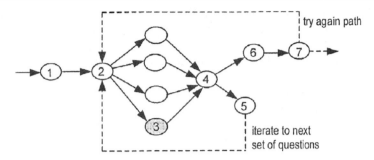

1. Tutorial sequence
2. Quiz menu: choose answer from list
3. Student's response
4. Assessment step
5. Correct answer
6. Incorrect answer
7. Explain possible reasons; offer choice: try again or quit

FIG. 7.3   Dialogue pattern for quiz test with multiple-choice questions.

- Integrate information by use of contact point sequences. Revealing elements of a story in a sequence attracts attention and builds up the necessary knowledge toward the learning goal. For instance, explaining the causation of the El Nino weather effect starts by showing ocean temperatures followed by a slide show presentation of the heat build-up reversing flow of currents, transfer of warm water from west to east, increased evaporation near South America, and more rain. Contact point captions point out key items in the image sequence.
- Use video showing people with speech to motivate and attract students. Judicious use of video showing an instructor can attract attention by personalizing the presentation.
- Make the presentation as interactive as possible. Interaction is dealt with in more depth in the next section; however, even within a limited ambition, multimedia interaction can be encouraged. Contact point cues can be embedded in material to encourage exploration of supplementary information. Active cursor techniques with pop-up text can reveal contact points. Questions and miniquizzes can be triggered by exploring items within presentations.

A typical multimedia application with contact point links is shown in Fig. 7.4 (based on the Pondworld of Rogers & Scaife, 1998).

Interactive Microworlds and Active Engagement

This approach is motivated by constructivist learning. The system becomes a multisensory simulation of the domain, which makes the development more expensive, but the payback should be more effective learning. Users interact by direct manipulation in a VE or simulated world, or by changing parameters and observing the effects of different simulation runs; see Fig. 7.5. For example, in teaching the ecology of food chains, a graphical image of a pond is shown containing plants, herbivores (tadpoles, mayflies, snails), and carnivores (fish, birds, otters, etc.). Realistic images can be combined with diagrams to show the food chain relations among animals. The user can interact with the simulation by running animations that show plants being eaten by animals progressively higher in the food chain, or by setting parameters to change the numbers of animals and plants at each level and then running the simulation to see the effect of different numbers. The system uses graphs to show the effect on herbivore, carnivore, and plant populations and the image is edited to show

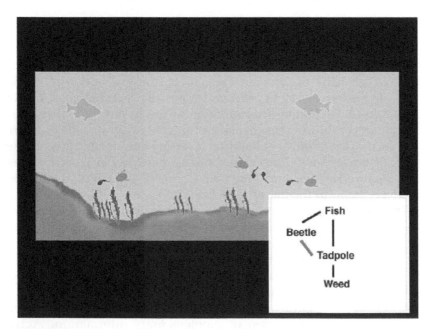

FIG. 7.4   Tutorial multimedia application Pondworld; the contact point can be activated dynamically by pointing to nodes or arcs on the diagram which causes the appropriate animals to highlight in the picture. Reprinted with permission by Yvonne Rogers.

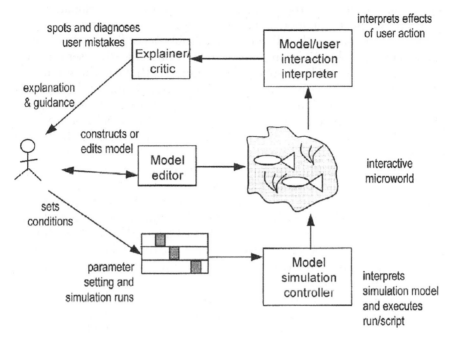

FIG. 7.5   Conceptual architecture for multisensory systems with interactive microworlds.

fewer or more animals and plants. Alternatively, users can drag and drop various pollutants from different sources (bucket icons); then the simulation runs to show the effect of pollutants being concentrated up the food chain leading to death of animals at the top of the food chain.

This form of interaction allows users more freedom to explore the simulation as an interactive microworld and engages them in active learning by experimentation. In VE implementations, the student interacts with the world by becoming one of the actors immersed in the environment. Concepts from drama theory, well understood by games designers, can be employed to improve student motivation, for instance, by planning surprise where exploration triggers agents to appear, which challenge the learner. As the environment is explored, the level of difficulty increases so material is gradually assimilated. This follows the minimalist concept of learning (Carroll, 1997), in which the student is only exposed to the bare essentials at the onset of learning, then the content is gradually exposed with increasing levels of complexity. Linking experience to abstraction is the most difficult part of the design. Students may interact with microworlds but only at the level of observing surface effects, so they may fail to abstract the causal explanation. Use of critique agents to question and challenge students is one answer.

Design of microworlds will vary considerably according to the domain and pedagogical objectives. In simulation environments, the user interacts with a designed world by changing the parameters that run the simulation and observing effects. An example is the interactive Pondworld (Rogers & Scaife, 1998) where pollutant and population parameters can be set to explore the effects on animal and plant populations. In virtual worlds inhabited by the user or a surrogate persona, the simulation may be similar but immersion encourages learning by an enhanced sense of engagement. An example is exploring a dangerous environment to plan crime prevention; the user walks through dark and threatening streets to experience the sense of menace. Environments in which the students can design the solution for themselves are true constructive learning environments in which the learners become designers. They are given the basic building blocks for a solution, hints about how to proceed, and then left to solve the problem by construction. The act of problem solving by doing encourages depth of encoding and learning. An example is the augmented reality system for urban planning where the student can move houses, streetlights, and so forth, to design a new street and then run the simulation to observe the effect on crime statistics, and reaction of the inhabitants (Fischer et al., 1995) The SimCity® system is a popular example of the genre.

The essence of microworld-based tutorials is an embedded model of the domain that contains laws governing reactions of objects and agents. The user is provided with those objects and agents as building blocks, and an outline environment in which to design. The system interprets the user's design, so that when it is run, the domain laws can be invoked to predict a probable outcome. The essentials of microworld architecture are summarized in Fig. 7.5.

The architecture consists of a model editor that provides the users with components and a means of constructing their solution. The model simulation-controller interprets the solution and runs it against the domain laws. The consequent effects are displayed to the student within the microworlds with additional summaries where necessary. The pedagogical aspect of the dialogue is implemented by system agents that take initiative to actively tutor the student or help when they have made mistakes, as explainers and critics.

Multisensory User Interface Issues.   Many of the multisensory design issues for microworld-based systems are shared with their less ambitious scripted cousins. However, microworlds imply agent roles as explainers, critics, or student representations, and this raises issues of multimodal communication. Ideally, speech is the preferred form of communication; however, the limitations of natural language processing and artificial intelligence will keep human tutors in business for a long time to come. Software tutoring systems may be a useful addition to the battery of teaching aids but they are no substitute for a flesh-and-blood tutor.

In spite of these limitations, advances have been made in automated question answering systems. Restricted natural language and use of question type taxonomies help the system interpret formatted questions from the student. Planning techniques based on Rhetorical Structure Theory (Mann & Thompson, 1988) enable the system to automatically compose the answers from knowledge (and media) fragments in the content database (see André & Rist, 2000; Maybury, 1999). Speech will play an increasingly important role in the future.

The link between speech generation and projection of personality by artificial agents is an opportunity for future research. Personality can be mimicked by fairly crude visual representations, especially when integrated with speech. The guidelines provided in chapter 4 can be employed, although current research is only starting to explore the implications of designing pedagogical agent interfaces (Cassell et al., 1999; Oviatt & Cohen, 2000).

Once agents have been designed, the next issue is the choice between augmented and virtual reality. If the user is exploring the world by navigation, then VR is sufficient. An example is NASA's Mars explorer in which the student can learn about the effects of climate and geology by flying through a virtual Martian landscape. Little haptic interaction is required. In true constructive environments, haptic interaction is often necessary. In these applications, augmented reality is superior because the student can pick and place components more easily. The system still has to detect where components have been placed so the simulation model can be run, and feedback is projected on top of the augmented reality. Tangible domains such as engineering, architecture, and urban planning are good candidates for augmented reality (Fjeld et al., 1998). In contrast, interaction in more abstract domains can be kept in the virtual world, a good example being the agentsheets construction environment (Repenning, 1993), which can be specialized to create many different simulations; Fig. 7.6 illustrates an interactive simulation for scheduling applications developed using agentsheets.

The final issue is how to represent the user's presence and whether to provide virtual tools in the VE. The student's viewpoint can be set as egocentric, in which case the world is experienced with full immersion. The sense of presence and engagement is greater, which may motivate learning, but the disadvantage is the inability to see the overview. Conversely, an exocentric view allows learners to see their own presence within the VE, and hence, get a better feel for the context of their interaction. There is little research to suggest which view will have better learning outcomes, so the best advice is to consider providing both views, to enable the student to be immersed in the experience and then swap to overview mode to see the wider context.

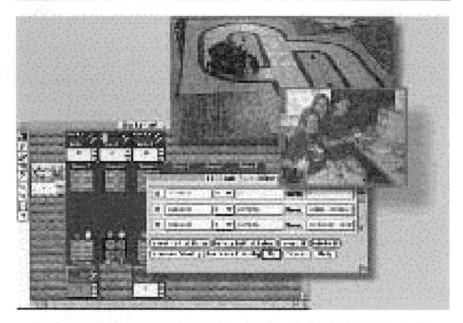

FIG. 7.6   Interactive simulation for scheduling applications developed using agentsheets. The control panel in the foreground scripts the behavior of agents that are placed in the simulation design in the background.   When the simulation is run it controls the movement of cars on a racetrack in the upper right image. Reprinted with permission by Alex Repenning.

This concludes the brief review of multisensory UI design for educational and tutorial applications. Much research needs to be done both at the level of pedagogical theory and how to translate theoretical motivations into effective interaction. In the next section, the second application area of design and requirements analysis is reviewed.

VIRTUAL PROTOTYPING

Multisensory interfaces have a great potential for supporting design. Indeed, one of the significant markets for VR is in design exploration and requirements validation, often called virtual prototyping.

VEs help designers debug products that have not been built. The appeal of VE design support is saving the cost of physical mock-ups and prototypes. However, the usability requirements for virtual prototypes can be quite demanding. In operational testing, fidelity with the real life design is important. In these applications, the user–tester needs to experience as close an approximation to the reality of operating the design as possible. Furthermore, in design applications, close coupling with specifications and Computer Aided Design (CAD) is important. This was the significant advance in Boeing's use of VR for design of the 777 aircraft. Close coupling of the CAD system with VR simulation enabled designers to visualize the layout of wiring controls and a myriad of other physical design components. They could reason spatially using the VR and then transfer their conclusions to the accurate CAD model that formed the basis for manufacture. Although virtual prototyping has become established practice, there is little understanding of the usability issues involved.

Requirements Analysis With Virtual Environments

Requirements engineering with VEs introduces some interesting parallels with usability evaluation. The VE representation of a design is being investigated, so in some sense a design is being evaluated. The important issue for designers of the VE (rather than the product) is to make sure usability issues do not interfere with assessment of the product. A virtual prototyping environment is depicted in Fig. 7.7.

Having gone to the expense of creating a virtual prototype, it is important to capitalize on the investment. The VE can be used in slightly different versions to gain feedback on several different aspects of design; for example, see the following:

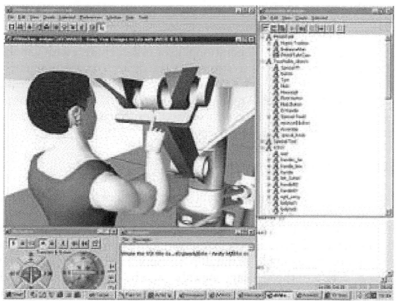

FIG. 7.7 Virtual prototyping environment showing the virtual world with the user's presence therein. Image courtesy of VP Group.

- *Physical and spatial fit*—This is achieved by realistic modeling to check that components can fit into the spaces specified, that movement and composition of objects is physically possible, and that people can move in constrained spaces, reach switches, and so forth. Close coupling of spatial specifications in CAD models is necessary.
- *Human operations and tasks are feasible and effective.* This set of requirements needs a realistic design including operational controls. Scenarios are walked through to check that the user can find and understand the necessary information portrayed in the design. Limitations of VE come into play here if operations involve haptic feedback. When haptic feedback is important, augmented reality should be considered.
- *Operation can take place under a variety of environmental conditions.* This is where virtual prototyping really starts to pay off. The VR design can run under a variety of simulation conditions, for example, degrees of lighting, visibility, noise, and so forth. The scenario simulation environment that surrounds the basic design can be changed for different test runs.
- *Operation will be effective with different user roles.* This is the most complex part of prototyping, with immersed actors playing different user roles, or automated agents are scripted to respond with different degrees of skill.

Scenarios that describe the user tasks are acted out in the VE. The prototype is run against a series of operational user task scenarios with variations of environmental conditions to stress-test the design. As requirements are captured in the form of design critiques, these are recorded in the requirements specification or CAD model and subsequently become design improvements. The cycle of scenario-based testing is repeated until an effective and usable solution is produced.

Designing Virtual Prototypes

A virtual prototype of a command and control system is shown in Fig. 7.8. The virtual design provides the general layout of the environment, the ship's guns, and details of equipment. The extent of the viewable, external environment will depend on the operational scenario and environmental specializations. For example, in the ship gunnery training system, illustrated in Fig. 7.8, details of the seascape viewable can be changed for fog, clouds, high seas, etc. The operators are immersed or represented as mannequins that they can control for limited movement.

FIG. 7.8   Navy gunnery system mock up with exogenous viewpoint. Image courtesy of VP Group.

The design components and interactions in the VE should be represented as accurately and completely as possible within resource constraints. Realistic detail always costs more development effort, so it should be concentrated on areas to be investigated in the scenarios, rather than background and contextual detail. Inaccurate representation can bias results and lead to inaccurate analysis and results. For example, a radar screen is depicted in detail so that tracks can be seen, but the sonar equipment is only represented in outline. Multisensory feedback through the use of visual, audio, and haptic channels improves realism and sense of engagement. Haptic is desirable for complex manipulations of objects, although cross-modal substitution may be necessary if it is available. For example, audio is added for background noise of equipment and spoken communication. Sounds or color changes represent contact and pressure to substitute for haptic feedback.

For operational scenarios, all users will need to be represented as virtual actors in the VE. The mannequins should support the range of actions involved in the scenarios; for example, leaning forward or bending down for testing ergonomic requirements and gesticulation for communication. Ideally, users and operators should be able to move their mannequin to mirror their own body movements. When avatars are represented, ideally, full body suit sensors are necessary to map movement of the real operator's limbs and body to the mannequin. This is expensive and difficult to resource so scripted interaction of mannequins or limited single limb movement are more usual. Anthropometrically precise mannequin tools are available for ergonomics testing of human movements. Devices should be chosen according to the type of interactions involved in the scenarios, so a 3D mouse may suffice for simple interactions but a glove (hand presence) will be necessary for complex object manipulations.

Two approaches are possible for running scenarios. First is scripting operational scenarios so mannequins carry out actions that the analyst can observe; basic ergonomic action scenarios can be preprogrammed and run automatically in the VE. Second, immersed actors can carry out operational tasks. Ideally, these should be potential users of the future system; alternatively, operational scenarios are run with trained operators role-playing scenario scripts. Running scenarios with operators controlling their own presence is more complex.

Immersive (Head Mounted Display or HMD) viewing for close examination and manipulation of objects provides extra realism and sense of presence where needed. CAVE or large projection screens facilitate multiuser viewing and peripheral views including the wider context. This option is useful for complex scenarios involving collaboration between people. Desktop viewing may be chosen for solo tasks not requiring direct interaction or close object examination, and for longer scenarios when immersive interaction is not necessary.

The analyst may be immersed in the VE to observe users directly and experience interaction from their viewpoint, or have an external viewpoint to see interaction in a wider context. An analyst immersed with the users or operators will have a better sense of the shared experience, but the ability to gain an overview is lost. Moreover, no two users' viewpoints will be the same. In shared VEs, one user has to be the dominant actor whose movement controls changing the viewpoint. Other users receive the dominant user's viewpoint, which is less than 100% natural. Another consideration is that audio in the VE or the use of immersive displays may obstruct users' verbal reports.

The trade-off for the analyst's viewpoint is how closely the analyst needs to mirror the user's experience so usability problems can be interpreted. One compromise is for the analyst to observe the immersed users first and note problem areas, then follow up with solo immersed walkthroughs to inspect specific problems. Controls for changing the analyst's viewpoint on the VE are desirable, so that user interaction can be observed from different angles. In complex VEs, map-like displays of the environment showing the current position of users may be helpful in tracking their progress and location in the VE. In group scenarios, if one user is controlling the view, then the analyst's view, should to be tied to this. Otherwise, switching between the overall and individual viewpoints to obtain more detail can help.

Having covered the design of virtual prototypes, the next step is to review the process for requirements analysis with VE designs.

Scenario-Based Requirements Analysis

Requirements analysis with virtual prototypes shares many techniques with usability evaluation of VEs. Indeed, the two processes are similar and share the same objective of design improvement. In usability evaluation, the focus of attention is on improving the usability of the VE itself, whereas virtual prototyping concerns design refinement prior to building a real product. Virtual prototyping with scenario analysis can be carried out using one of two different approaches:

- *Design walkthroughs*—This approach involves the analyst walking through the design using himself or herself as a surrogate user, and asking questions at set points in the operational scenario. The walkthrough produces a checklist audit of design faults and recommendations for improvements. Walkthroughs are quick and cheap to do, but may suffer from the analyst's lack of domain knowledge.
- *Observation of user problems*—In this approach, human operators follow scripts and act out tasks in the VE. The requirements analyst observes the operators and asks them to think out aloud. Problems are detected by observing difficulties in operating equipment, by failure to achieve operational performance targets, or by misunderstanding and difficulties reported by users during interaction or in debriefing interviews. Analysis is diagnostic in nature, that is, when the user experiences some difficulty, the analyst has to trace the problem back to either a fault in the design or a problem in the operating procedure or possibly a false assumption about what is humanly possible.

In walkthroughs, the participants follow the scenario scripts to the best of their ability, role-playing the actions as closely as possible to real life. The analyst follows their interactions, making notes of any difficulties. The user is encouraged to provide a running commentary of what he or she is doing and his or her perceptions. Unexpected behavior and the user's comments on the system are noted, especially critical incidents or breakpoints indicating difficulty in interaction or understanding. The point in the scenario script when the incident occurs is noted, as well as any design features implicated in the problem.

After the walkthrough, debriefing interviews follow up on observed issues. Comments and positive or negative views are gathered to help understand the design and validate requirements.

Observed problems need to be attributed to design features or the testing environment. Problems are categorized (using diagnostic decision trees, illustrated in chap. 6) into the following sets:

- *User training problems*—Users do not understand or follow the scenario script; these problems are caused by poor user domain knowledge or training, or misunderstanding of the scenario script.
- *Usability problems*—Users experience difficulty with VE features that do not directly represent the design solution, such as the navigation method or additional controls. For example, problems in controlling movement, navigation, or conceptual disorientation, limited realism or haptic feedback, mean that manipulations appear to be more difficult than they would be in reality.
- *Design problems*—These involve users having difficulty with an aspect of the VE that directly represents the prototype design. These problems point to requirements issues and design refinements.

The output of this approach is a set of observed problems cross-referenced to the scenario context in which they occurred and the design feature involved.

The final section of this chapter returns to the introductory theme of multisensory interaction and reviews some prospects for the future.

FUTURE TRENDS

In this volume I have concentrated on UIs that are currently grouped under the headings of multimedia and VR. In writing about multisensory UIs I have tried to show that there is really little difference between multimedia and VR: both are just part of a trend toward richer forms of human–computer interaction. This trend has been with us since the transition from text and command line UIs into direction manipulation and GUIs. No doubt sensory enrichment of human–computer interaction will continue, but it will probably take two quite different paths. In the final part of this chapter, I look at the prospects for multisensory UIs: first, along the path of increased intelligence in communication, the natural language route; and second, convergence with topics so far only mentioned in passing, ubiquitous and mobile computing. In the quest to make computers useful, usable, and universal, we can try to make the computer smarter, enhance its ability to communicate with us in a variety of ways, and integrate it into our everyday environment so that communication is not a conscious act and interaction becomes part of our experience.

Intelligent Multisensory User Interfaces

Adapting to the user, anticipating needs and automating more complex tasks have been quests of intelligent user interface (IUI) research for a number of years. I will not review the user modeling and adaptable UI debate; if the reader is interested in such subjects, there are plenty of papers in the IUI conference series and the journal *User Modeling and Adaptable Interfaces*. Instead, my focus is on the prospects for developing intelligence for enhanced communication. There are several prospects on this path.

First and most predictable is *natural language processing*. Speech recognition systems are already approaching reliabilities in the order of 98% accuracy in speaker-dependent word recognition, but correcting two errors in every hundred is still an annoying burden. Ironically, in human–human communication, we put up with similar or higher error rates in speech, and hardly notice the error correction problem. Machine-based systems have yet to achieve a similar vertical integration from speech recognition through semantic analysis and parsing, to pragmatic resolution of ambiguity. Once this is achieved, speech recognition systems will not need to improve their basic accuracy. Higher order processing will automatically correct errors, just as people do.

Natural language interaction, however, still has to solve the problem of the knowledge acquisition bottleneck. General-purpose natural language understanding with common sense reasoning will probably take some time to solve, but limited-domain language processing is already possible. Whereas we use around 8,000 words in our everyday vocabulary, when we converse about technical subjects, sublanguages restrict the scope of reasoning and communication to a narrow domain. Examples are legal arguments, air traffic control dialogues, and the communication of foreign exchange dealers. Small vocabularies, restricted syntax, and constrained knowledge for pragmatic interpretation characterize sublanguages. This simplifies natural language processing by reducing the complexity of the domain knowledge base required for efficient processing.

Alternatively, software systems can extend their own vocabulary by being taught or asking the user to explain the meaning of words. Systems with extendable vocabularies work well initially, but as the user extends the system lexicon (by adding new words to existing categories then adding new subcategories), the system knowledge becomes inconsistent. Learning systems with better knowledge acquisition dialogues may be able to cure this problem.

Natural language will also become more pervasive as an output or generated form of communication. One limitation to date has been the complexities of planning utterances in the context of what has been said by the human party. Understanding and generation are closely linked; however, natural language planners can now create sophisticated dialogues that integrate gesture, nonverbal communication, speech, and the content being communicated (André et al., 1998). Intelligent agents with multisensory interfaces will become increasingly capable of holding complex dialogues that integrate communication on different modalities. Where understanding breaks down, improved dialogue repair planning will enable the conversation to continue even when there is misunderstanding, as happens in natural human–human dialogues. The second limitation is the naturalness of synthetic speech where the technical difficulties of generating natural voice intonations are being solved. Soon synthetic speech will no longer sound artificial and intelligent agents will be able to express emotion, surprise, and so forth, in a natural sounding voice.

Intelligent agents will become a common feature of multisensory UIs. Developing rules that govern natural conversations with intelligent agents will require dialogue planners based on discourse theory, and agent representations that behave with appropriate personalities and emotional responses according to the user's dialogue, task, and context. conversational agents are already with us that can talk while communicating with appropriate facial expressions and gaze (e.g., Rea; Cassell et al., 1999). Other social agents can be given characters and react with simple models of emotion to show surprise and disappointment (André et al., 2000). The frontiers are making automated virtual agents more believable and realistic with more sophisticated models of motivation and emotion while increasing the sophistication of facial expressions, gaze control, and expression of emotional response by blushing, and so on. Another challenge is design controls so users can inhabit virtual agents and control them with appropriate facial expressions, movement, and gaze. Robotics will converge with UI design for complex virtual presences. Encapsulating knowledge from social psychology and linguistics within interaction planners for agents will be a considerable challenge.

The vision of intelligent multisensory UIs revisits the debate on system initiative between advocates of passive representation of system facilities and active system support (by Shneiderman, 1998, amongst others). The role of representation will remain important because people will want to remain in control in many domains. However, the inexorable drive to embed software intelligence in products from cars to homes will mean that intelligent multisensory interfaces are inevitable. Because intelligent agents will always make mistakes, we can only hope their designers make them humble enough to admit it, and have users in control.

Frontiers for Multisensory Interaction

In this volume, there has been a tacit assumption that multisensory interaction is dominated by visual and audio modalities. Haptics got a look in occasionally; olfaction and gustation only appeared in the introduction. In the future, that balance will change.

Olfaction and gustation will use standardized rendering and detecting devices in multisensory workstations (if workstations still exist). We will be able to send complete sensory experiences to each other. The 3D immersive video of our holiday will include the sound of the seaside, the smell of the forest, and the taste of exotic food. This will require considerable advances in generative technologies, but the principles of generation of aerosols for smell and solutions for taste are known. Smell and taste can already be generated at resolutions way beyond human capabilities, so with the development of standardized coding schemes for chemical smells and tastes, full multisensory communication will be a reality.

The future of haptic and proprioceptive interaction is less sure. One view is that there is a law of diminishing returns in building ever more complex haptic feedback devices. Most haptic devices are currently point pressure systems, working on one fingertip at a time. Engineering whole-hand haptic feedback devices is very complex given the variety of potential movements that the human hand can make and the sensitivity of touch. Exoskeletons have tackled proprioceptive feedback for limbs where the freedom of movement is more restricted. No doubt these devices will become more sophisticated, but there is a question about whether users will want to wear these cumbersome, heavy, and intrusive devices. Future advances will probably come from electro-sensitive materials, transforming haptic feedback into a wearable computer. The material deforms to express pressure and resistance for force feedback, and thixotropic properties change to mimic touch. The other alternative is to accept that VR may not always be the best solution. When touch and physical interaction are important, augmented devices may be superior.

Finally, visual interfaces still have a considerable potential for advances. VR currently uses projected displays. Laser-generated holographic images will be exploited in the future. Virtual environments will develop from the current CAVE technologies so that everyday rooms will become immersive 3D environments with holographic images of agents. Shared 3D environments for teleconferencing and many other tasks will become ordinary. We will share our real augmented reality desks with others in virtual teleworking environments. Immersive 360-degree audio is already impressive, and this too will develop so that long-range soundscapes can be projected. The boundaries between virtual and real reality are already beginning to disappear. In an innovative theatrical application, Steve Benford and his colleagues have created a VE that allows actors to move between the virtual and real worlds, as illustrated in Fig. 7.9 (Benford et al., 2000). The virtual world is projected onto a fine water spray curtain so the user can interact as in an immersive VE; however, the user can then walk through the virtual

FIG. 7.9   Virtual reality theater application which allows actors to move between real and virtual reality. In the first image the user is viewing the VE, in the second the user is in part of the real world stage, while the third shows the rain curtain on which the VE is projected and through which the user can walk to reach the real world. Reprinted with permission by Steve Benford.

world projected on the spray curtain into reality, enjoying a seamless virtual–real experience, albeit at the expense of getting wet. This technology has been used in collaborative theater where actors play out scripts partially in the VE world and then reenter reality (Craven et al., 2001).

The long-range vision for multisensory environments is to eliminate the interface completely. First, the technology will become invisible as it is engineered into the walls and furniture of our everyday environment. Then, the technology will become wearable and part of us. We owe the vision of ubiquitous computing to Weiser (1991), who conceived a world in which computers become pervasive and embedded in our everyday world. No longer will we interact with a PC; instead, computers in our cars, desks, furniture, and floors will respond to speech, touch, and gaze. Interface technology may go even further and become part of us, as implants. The idea of direct implants into our brains for computer-mediated communication tends to make us squirm. However, surgery for the biotechnology interface is already with us. Electrodes are being implanted to give the blind a crude sense of vision. In the near future, multisensory technology will allow the blind to see and the deaf to hear via biosoftware interfaces. The biotechnology interface in the future may not require any invasive surgery. Use of radio, ultrawaves, and manipulation of electric circuits in the brain from wearable devices may allow multisensory experience to be directly transmissible from one person's perception to another person's memory. This raises interesting questions of how such experiences are sent and perceived. The fact that we see and hear the world via memory will not change, so sending a multisensory experience from artificial devices directly into a person's mind will create different experiences according to the preprocessing provided by the designer. Also, swapping sensory experience from our memories may create weird effects of how we experience the event (a wedding) compared with the receiver's view (the bride's). We may indeed be finally able to see into each other's minds. No doubt younger readers of this volume will be around to experience some of these conundrums. I now turn to how multisensory interfaces may merge into the environment, in the growth of ubiquitous computing.

Ubiquitous Multisensory Experience

Computers and their interfaces are starting to blend into the everyday world. Mobile phones become computers with Internet access; interactive televisions are computers; software and microchips are embedded in our homes, offices, and cars. We can even wear computers as fashion accessories, intelligent garments, and augmented reality devices (Barfield & Caudell, 2001). The days of the computer as a standalone PC are numbered. In the future, we will use a variety of software-augmented appliances (Norman, 1999). As computers merge into the world, the classic UI of keyboard, VDU, and mouse will vanish. The interface will become our environment. Augmented reality will come of age in a new sense of software driven interfaces within everyday artifacts from refrigerators to cars and phones. We will still need information, and text will still play a role with diagrams and graphics. However, delivery of information will be where we want it, mobile, and with us, on demand via projected displays on our glasses, useful for the ageing population who wear them, or in displays in our mobile phones, watches, office furniture, walls, and ceilings of our homes. Tasks will still drive interaction, but many cognitive tasks such as decision making, planning, and judgment will be carried out with the support of mobile and unobtrusive interfaces.

Ubiquitous computing has been with us since Weiser (1991) developed the vision of pervasive, unobstrusive technology (see Abowd & Mynatt, 2000, for a review). Ubiquitous systems extend the view of the user's context in the following "five-Ws" framework:

1. Who?—The system needs to be aware of the individual user. This is manifest in the growing trend for customization and personalization of the interface; the problem for the machine is knowing who it is interacting with if it hasn't been told (i.e., by the person logged on). Future systems will be enhanced by perceptual mechanisms such as image recognition and identification from eye iris or fingerprint patterns.
2. What?—This involves guessing what the user is doing. It is a longstanding ambition of intelligent UIs to acquire a model of the user's

behavior. This is still a difficult research problem of understanding activity from low-level data. Future systems might have improved input from model-based scene recognition; image-understanding systems with a semantic model that enables them to interpret what they see.

3. Where?—This is a quintessential ubiquitous mobile property, but even with Global Positioning Systems (GPS), it isn't as easy to detect. GPS is only accurate out of doors and even then accuracy is limited to 10 m. Improvements may come with local wireless communications such as BlueTooth networks that may be able to track receivers more accurately. "Where" also raises the interpretation problem. The system not only needs a model of the user (who, what) but also a map.

4. When?—Time is an important thread of interaction. Many of our interactions are long-running and intermittent. We start a task then pick it up later and elsewhere. Mobile devices need to keep track of our time line, so we can be advised of meetings wherever we happen to be. Time also has an interpretation problem when linked to activity; for example, just how long does looking at something indicate real interest as opposed to absent-minded gaze?

5. Why?—This is the most difficult question because it revisits the user modeling problem. To infer just what a human user intends and why requires intelligence bordering on the human. It also needs some understanding of human emotional responses, currently being studied in affective computing (Picard, 1997).

One consequence of mobile and ubiquitous interfaces is that they will become context and location aware. Multisensory interfaces should adapt to suit the user and his or her task, but mobility adds another layer of complexity. Adaptation to the environment is the first level of customizing multisensory interfaces. For instance, the system turns the sound up in a noisy environment, improves contrast and adjusts color balance in bright sunlight, or chooses the appropriate modality according to the context. Thus, my mobile phone selects text and low frequency sound communication when I take it diving, and speech and graphical GPS sensitive compass and map when I am driving.

All this requires more awareness by the device of where it is and the context. This makes multisensory input a key factor in the next generation of devices. Unless the system can perceive its environment it will not be able to adapt to it. Simple solutions such as embedded transmitters in the environment to tell mobile devices their location are a stopgap solution. Transmitters have to be designed to broadcast information to a heterogeneous population of mobile devices, and their (users') needs will be difficult to predict. Furthermore, instrumenting the environment is an enormous task, which is likely to be unacceptable on economic and environmental grounds. Nobody will want microtransmitters in every tree and street corner. Consequently, systems themselves are going to have to sense the world. UIs will converge with image recognition and speech understanding systems, to say nothing of chemo-sensing and gravity perception. Image interpretation has been a challenge in computer vision and robotics for many years, and current systems have reasonably reliable abilities to recognize simple worlds. However, machine vision is no different from human vision—what you see is what you know—so the need to interpret sensory input still has to overcome the domain knowledge acquisition bottleneck. In spite of this problem, the ability to integrate information from different modalities will help machines understand their environment. In mobile applications, the challenge is to synthesize information from motion sensors (accelerometers, gyros for position) with external sources of location (GPS and wireless triangulation techniques), with interpretation of visual and audio input. The system will require a world model to interpret even simple aspects of the world, such as awareness of being indoors or outdoors. These problems, of course, have concerned robot designers for many years. Robots have to make sense of the world because they are mobile. The lessons from robotics are that learning about the world is a difficult task. Humans do it in the early years, as babies crawling around experimenting with everything in their environment. Intelligent multisensory systems will have to do the same. Advances in neural computing promise that development of autonomous learning machines should be possible in the midterm future.

So, will multisensory systems be robots, agents that bring artificial reality to life? Will virtual agents live on in artificial worlds? No doubt both. The interface of the future will become part of our reality. We will interact by manipulating objects in our environment. Feedback and output will come from a variety of devices; some will be recognizable displays, others may be robots embedded in the environment. VR and telesensory experience will become accepted as part of our communication infrastructure, which will be ubiquitous and personalized. Thus, if this vision becomes true, UI design and human–computer interaction will have achieved the ultimate success of solving the problem of interaction, because we will no longer see the problem. The computer, as Norman predicted (1999), will have become invisible.

SUMMARY

This final chapter has reviewed the application of multisensory interfaces to learning systems and for requirements analysis with design prototyping. In computer-aided learning, it is a mistake to focus on the multisensory interaction alone. Most of the problem lies in pedagogical design; nevertheless, multimedia and VR can enhance the design of learning environments by providing rich interactive microworlds for problem-oriented learning. Multisensory UIs can also facilitate social learning by computer-mediated communication; however, several difficult problems still await solution to improve this technology; for instance, the video conferencing and the viewpoint problems.

In design and virtual prototyping, VR gives us the ability to experience our designs before we have to create tangible artifacts. Furthermore, VR allows us to simulate a variety of different scenarios so the design can be tested in a range of operational conditions. Virtual prototyping needs a systematic approach to select the necessary scenarios for testing, and evaluation by immersion poses new problems of interpretation when the problems arise from usability or are design faults in the virtual application.

In the future of multisensory interaction, natural language and intelligent UIs will increase the expressive power in inhabited spaces where the identity of the human and the artificial will become increasingly blurred. Sensory communication will become enhanced by new ways of 3D visual realism, augmented reality with haptics, natural language, as well as olfactory and gustatory communication. Furthermore, machines will have to sense and interpret the world as much as they provide a rich and natural way of communicating with humans. As computers become universal, ubiquitous and wearable, the convergence of multisensory interaction and intelligent agents will lead to a real world inhabited by ourselves communicating with varieties of software entities. Some will be simple devices embedded within our environment, some will be things we wear, others will be agents with personas that assist us in real or artificial worlds; ultimately, some will be artificial life forms in our world.

This leads me to my epilogue. Most of what I have written, I hope, will be useful as design guidance for multisensory interfaces as well as providing some theoretical background for the design process. Design support tools have received little attention, primarily because there are few such tools, although Kaur (1998) and Faraday and Sutcliffe (1998b) are some exceptions. In the future, designing multisensory UIs may itself be a redundant activity. No doubt we will still design computerized agents, but the environment in which they interact will become part of our infrastructure and the agents will learn to adapt to our need. Asimov's laws of robotics and Kubrick's HAL will have joined our world.

Appendix A

Multimedia Design Guidelines From ISO 14915, Part 3— General Guidelines for Media Selection and Combination

This appendix contains general guidelines for media selection and combination that map information types to appropriate media types for effective delivery. Two or more media are considered combined if their presentation is concurrent or contiguous when the media are explicitly grouped in a display in adjacent windows.

Combining media can have advantages for the user. First, interfaces can be created that present information in a way similar to the real world. Depending on the context of use, this can make users' tasks easier, or more natural, especially where features of the information match the users' experiences of the real world. For example, a picture of a beach presented together with the sound of waves provides a better evocation of the subject than the picture or the sound alone. Combining media can also help accommodate user preferences for information in a particular format. For example, presenting text as well as pictures can accommodate users with a preference for either.

SUPPORTING USER TASKS

Media should be selected and combined to support the users' tasks.

Example   To compare two views, an architect's drawings with corresponding photographs showing the side and front elevation of a building are placed side by side.

Note   Some tasks benefit more from combination than others. If the task
              involves learning, or drawing attention to specific information, then
              the users can benefit from media combination that presents infor-
              mation redundantly. If, however, the task is focused predominantly
              on one medium, for example visual inspection of diagrams, then
              there can be considerably less benefit from combination. The char-
              acteristics of the user's task can also influence the sequence or
              concurrency of presentation; for instance, if comparison is required,
              two images can be presented concurrently.

SUPPORTING COMMUNICATION GOALS

Media should be selected to achieve the communication goal in the application.

Example   In a safety critical application, the communication goal is to warn
              the users and protect them from danger. In an aircraft emergency
              evacuation demonstration, speech is used for the instructions, with
              a diagram to show the evacuation route.

ENSURING COMPATIBILITY
WITH THE USERS' UNDERSTANDING

Media should be selected to convey the content in a manner compatible
with the users' existing knowledge.

Example   A radiation symbol is used to convey danger to users who have the
              appropriate knowledge. An architectural diagram is used to convey
              the structural layout of a building to architects and design engineers.
Note   The user's ability to understand the message conveyed by a particu-
              lar medium should influence selection. This is particularly impor-
              tant for nonrealistic image media (diagrams, graphs) when
              interpretation is dependent on the user's knowledge and culture.

SELECTING MEDIA APPROPRIATE FOR USERS'
CHARACTERISTICS

The characteristics of the user population should be considered when selecting media.

Example   Text is substituted by speech for blind users. Large point size text is
              accompanied by spoken representation of the text for older users.

Note   Users can be categorized as visualizers or verbalizers using psycho-
               logically-based questionnaires. This information can be used to aid
               selection of image or language-based media.

SUPPORTING USERS' PREFERENCES

If appropriate to the task, users should be provided with alternative media
from which they can select a preferred medium or suppress certain media.

Example   The user chooses to display text captions on a picture rather than a
               speech commentary, or suppresses an audio dialogue in a noisy envi-
               ronment. A blind user selects speech rather than text.
Note   Some users can prefer to interact with systems using a particular me-
               dium. The abilities of the users and properties of the users' machines
               are important, therefore users may be given the option of low- or
               high-resolution graphics displays.

CONSIDERING THE CONTEXT OF USE

Selection and combination of media should be appropriate in the context of use.

Example   An inappropriate combination is the presentation of auditory as
               well as visual display of bank account details that could compromise
               the user's privacy. A training video depicting an action accompa-
               nied by spoken "This is not correct," could be missed if the speech is
               inaudible in a noisy environment.
Note   Certain environments can impede accurate perception of infor-
               mation presented in a specific medium; for example, a visual
               warning might not be seen if presented in an environment with
               strong ambient light.

USING REDUNDANCY FOR CRITICAL INFORMATION

If important information is to be presented, then the same subject matter
should be presented in two or more media.

Example   An alarm clock displays functions visually as well as aurally. In a lan-
               guage learning application, words are spoken and displayed in text.
Note   Effective redundant combinations present similar but not identical
               content on different media. Redundant representation is useful for
               training and educational applications.

AVOIDING CONFLICTING PERCEPTUAL CHANNELS

The same perceptual channel (e.g., hearing or vision) should not be used in concurrently presented dynamic media if the user needs to extract information from both media.

Example	Playing two or more videos with unrelated content is avoided because these will interfere with each other and distract attention.
Note	Concurrent presentation of two or more dynamic media makes it difficult for the user to perceive information from each individual source unless the information is easy to integrate. Exceptions to this guideline occur in entertainment applications when conveying information is not important, such as playing two unrelated videos in popular music promotions.

AVOIDING SEMANTIC CONFLICTS

Presentation of conflicting information in any combination of media should be avoided.

Example	Avoid aural presentation of the words "press the blue button" while the visual display shows a black and white image.
Note	Users cannot comprehend or gain an integrated understanding of conflicting information from different media, especially in concurrent presentations.

DESIGNING FOR SIMPLICITY

Minimal combination of media should be used to convey the information necessary for the user's task.

Example	In a musical tutorial, the sound of music is combined with textual representation of the musical score. Adding a video of a concert performance gives little extra information and distracts the user.
Note	As the number of media used increases, the user's effort required to attend to and process each medium also increases, as does the effort in cross-referencing media. The trade-off between simplicity and more complex combinations will depend on the user and task.

COMBINING MEDIA FOR DIFFERENT VIEWPOINTS

Wherever appropriate to the task, different views on the same subject matter should be provided by media combination.

Example	Musical notation in a diagram gives the composer's structural view of a symphony, speech commentary gives the musician's view of the structure, and music on the sound channel provides the aesthetic view. Two movies are played in separate windows to show different viewpoints on the same scene, one showing a long shot context of a football game, the other a close-up of a foul between two players in the long shot.
Note	Presenting different views can help the user to assimilate information that is related to the same topic or theme.

CHOOSING MEDIA COMBINATIONS TO ELABORATE INFORMATION

Whenever appropriate to the task, media combinations should be selected to extend the information content.

Example	Showing a diagram of planets revolving around the sun with speech explaining forces of gravity and momentum.
Note	Media combination is used to add information to an existing topic, whereas combining media for different viewpoints presents different aspects of the same topic.

GUARDING AGAINST DEGRADATION

Technical constraints should be considered when selecting media delivery to avoid degraded quality or unacceptable response times.

Example	To avoid delay in downloading a web page, moving images are segmented into storyboard stills and displayed as a slide show. The display area of a moving image is reduced rather than slowing the frame rate. Simple images with lower bandwidth requirements are used rather than photographic quality images. Users are warned of transmission delays.
Note	Visual media, especially moving images, are more prone to degradation if there are bandwidth or network constraints in distributed multimedia. Degradation can result in poor image quality, slower than acceptable frame rates for moving image, and poor audio quality.

PREVIEWING MEDIA SELECTIONS

If appropriate for the task, the media available for selection should be viewable by the user in a preview facility.

Example   A Web link to video allows the user to view miniature samples of the
               video before it is downloaded.
Note   When control over media selection is given to the user, previewing
               can be combined with controls to choose the way media are down-
               loaded in high or low resolution.

USING STATIC MEDIA FOR IMPORTANT MESSAGES

Still image and text should be used for important information other than
time critical warnings.

Example   Key points in an engine assembly task are shown with still images
               and bullet points in text.
Note   Little detail is remembered from video and speech. Dynamic media
               can be used to alert users and direct their attention to important
               messages that are conveyed in static media.

Appendix B

Generalized Design Properties

First, general Generalized Design Properties (GDPs) are described for multimedia applications and virtual worlds. GDPs for the task-action, navigation, and system initiative cycles follow. GDPs specify the usability requirements for design features that may be implemented as graphics, controls, and services in the VE, or information and explanation facilities. Each set of GDPs for the three cycles is followed by the correspondence rules for the appropriate model stages. The expert user rules are stated first, followed by the novice rules, which may inherit some of the expert's GDPs. The novice rules add interaction support features that compensate for lack of well-developed task, domain, and device knowledge.

Correspondence rules link GDPs with specific stages in the interaction models; however, subsequent stages frequently benefit from GDPs advised for earlier stages; hence, the design advice in the rules suggest when the GDP (or its more specific realization) should be present, but leave the question of when to remove the design effect to the designer's discretion. Generally, goal formation GDPs will also prove useful for location and action specification stages; action execution stage GDPs are more restricted in their scope. GDPs in the first side of the cycle (e.g., goal formation to action execution in the task-action model) will be replaced with the feedback family for the second half of the cycle.

Many GDPs recommend design effects that could be intrusive, so the design advice has to be moderated by the naturalness principle in VR, and further rules propose constraints on GDPs that can be deployed if naturalness has to be obeyed.

GENERAL MULTIMEDIA GDPs

Multimedia GDPs are subdivided into navigation and control, which link to the intention–action side of the interaction cycle; and feedback and presentation, which are linked to the recognize–interpret–evaluate part of the cycle. The presentation and feedback GDPs are essentially plans that describe how information should be delivered in multimedia, whereas control GDPs help find the desired information. The associations between cycle stages and GDPs are provided in chapter 3, Fig. 3.1, and Table 3.1, so they will not be duplicated by stating correspondence rules in this appendix.

Navigation and control

Navigation and control (NC) GDPs follow:

NC1   *Information* is provided that is appropriate to the user's task.

NC2   *Feature hints*, lists of commands, or functions relevant to the user's task are displayed.

NC3   *Conceptual maps* of information structure, use of metaphors to provide conceptual models of the information, for example, houses, rooms metaphor are used.

NC4   *Clear prompts* and cues for navigation commands and controls are provided.

NC5   *Information scent* comprises cues for categories and pathways to targets that may interest the user.

NC6   Lists, structures and thesauri, organizing, and *classifying information* help users locate promising search directions.

NC7   Navigation *pathways and waymarks* on maps help the user decide on areas to browse or hypermedia links to follow.

NC8   Operational *affordances* and metaphors suggest manipulations and actions, for example, active sliders allow users to constrain value ranges in a search; video controls are provided for dynamic image media.

NC9   *Clear controls* and commands, for example, buttons, icons, and hypermedia links, provide clear prompts for functions or destinations.

NC10 Operation of commands and controls is *within human motor and perceptual abilities*, for example, selectable areas on an image are sufficiently large so the user can place the cursor on the target without difficulty.

NC11 *Task modality mapping*—Choose a navigation metaphor appropriate to the distance and precision of the user's need;

for long-distance travel, fast paths, accelerators, or portals are advisable.

Feedback and Presentation

Feedback and presentation (FP) GDPs follow:

FP1   Information is presented so the user can *see or hear it easily*, for example, image brightness is adjusted for ambient light.

FP2   Information is presented in an *appropriate modality* and location, for example, if the user is expecting visual feedback, it is presented in the currently visible window or a new window is popped up.

FP3   Attention is directed to *key information*, for example, overloading on a diagram of a power distribution network is highlighted in red.

FP4   *Direct contact points*—Use of a highlighting technique in both source and destination medium when linking message components is vital.

FP5   *Indirect contact points*—Use of a salience technique in the source medium to indicate content in a second if integration of message components is more general.

FP6   *Appropriate media* for the message, for example, change in location, is displayed on a map or diagram.

FP7   *Congruent messages* in integrated media—The subject matter in different media fits together, for example, picture of a whale and audio of a whale song.

FP8   *Thematic integration*—The operation of a human heart is shown as a step-by-step animation of each phase of contraction.

FP9   Reinforcing messages and viewpoints—A motor vehicle engine is shown using a photograph and as a diagram illustrating its components.

FP10 *Augmented viewpoints*—Additional information that the user may require for their task is presented.

FP11 *Changes* are presented so they match the user's expectation and task model.

FP12 Information is presented so it *matches the user's level* of task and domain knowledge.

GENERAL VIRTUAL WORLD GDPs

General virtual world (GV) GDPs follow:

GV1   *Stereo display* is preferred when the user's task involves continuous motion, complex spatial coordination, depth of field interpretation, and egocentric views.

GV2   *Shared virtual worlds* (CAVEs) are superior for multiuser interaction.

GV3   *Immersive single user interaction* (HMDs) is preferred when sense of presence and exploration are important task requirements.

GV4   *Fishtank* VR or immersive workbenches are preferred when the task requirements are for collaboration or manipulation of objects in a restricted space.

GV5   *Feature hints*—The presence of system services and facilities are signaled during the entry phase of the interface, for example, top-level menus, overview maps, and speech explanation when entering a VE.

GV6   Organizational and operational *metaphors* map to the user's mental model, thereby suggesting appropriate action.

GV7   *Presence matching to task*—The user is provided with a representation that enables the movement and manipulations implied by the task, so for high precision, a complex hand and arm presence is needed with haptic feedback.

GV8   *Consistent modality*—The important choice is between speech interaction and manipulation. If speech commands are used for action, then this mode should be consistent throughout the application.

GV9   *Multimodality*—Providing multimodal feedback and/or speech plus action modalities increases naturalness, reduces the user's learning burden, and improves task performance.

GV10   *Appropriate agents*—The presence of agents and their behavior is determined by the user's preferences and task requirements. The choice of scripted versus intelligent interactive agents depends on the sophistication of behavior demanded by the task.

TASK-ACTION CYCLE

Intention and Action Specification
    Intention and action specification (IAS) GDPs follow:

IAS1   *Appropriate system services* or virtual tools are present to support the user's task: this should result from a thorough task and requirements analysis; for example, in a virtual architect's design studio, the user can resize windows and adjust the lighting.

IAS2   *Appropriate information* is presented for decision making or supporting the user's task—Task information modeling specifies the necessary information groups and types; progress indicators remind users of the current task goal.

IAS3   Appropriate choice of communication *modality for the task* is necessary, for example, a drawing task uses a graphic tablet and stylus.

IAS4   Guided *tours and tutorials*—An active explanation of system operation to support task and device knowledge integration is provided.

IAS5   Clear indication of the user's *location and state* within the task sequence—A list of task steps or a goal tree is displayed with the current step highlighted. Maps represent goal sequences in the task model.

IAS6   Clear *spatial layout* of the environment to facilitate location of tools and affordances for action is necessary.

IAS7   Tools and interactive features are located to correspond with the *user's mental model,* for example, drawing instruments are placed next to a virtual paper surface.

IAS8   *Search facilities* to find tools and controls in complex environments are provided.

IAS9   *Clear affordances* for controls, and virtual tools that are appropriate for the user's tasks are necessary.

IAS10   *Clear indication* of objects and controls that are active in the virtual environment and UI are necessary.

IAS11   *Requisite detail*—Interactive objects and their surroundings are rendered in more detail than backgrounds to virtual worlds, and active objects are marked with labels.

IAS12   Appropriate *representation of user presence* is necessary; for example, a task requiring precise manipulation, such as threading a needle, has user presence with sensors on each finger joint.

IAS 13 Object *selection and manipulation points* should be clearly marked.

IAS14   *Explanatory agents*—Virtual tools or active objects are animated to demonstrate their potential actions.

Intention and Action Specification Correspondence Rules

IAS correspondence rules follow:

Expert

Form Intention Stage

> IF Task Knowledge is complete THEN GDPs IAS1 (services), IAS2 (information), and IAS3 (modalities) should be present ELSE functionality mismatch error.

Novice

> IF Task Knowledge is minimal THEN GDPs IAS4 (tutorial) and IAS5 (task maps) should be present ELSE goal formation error.

Locate Feature Stage (Expert–Novice subheadings omitted)

> IF Domain and Task Knowledge is complete THEN GDPs IAS6 (layout) and IAS7 (expected location) should be present ELSE hidden functionality error.

> IF Domain and Task Knowledge is minimal THEN GDP IAS8 (feature search) should be present ELSE goal formation error.

> IF Naturalness requirement is important THEN avoid GDPs IAS4 (guided tours), IAS5 (task maps), and IAS8 (feature search facilities).

Specify Action Stage

> IF Domain and Task Knowledge is complete THEN GDPs IAS9 (affordances), IAS10 (active objects), IAS11 (requisite detail), IAS12 (user presence), and IAS13 (manipulation points) should be present ELSE unable to proceed or specify action.

> IF Domain and Task Knowledge is minimal THEN GDP IAS14 (animate agents) should be present ELSE unable to proceed or specify action.

> IF Naturalness requirement is important THEN avoid GDPs IAS14 (explanation agents).

Manipulation and Action

Manipulation and action (MA) GDPs follow:

MA1   *Object inspection*—Support object inspection for complex or large objects by controls such as flip and rotate or by rotation manipulations using object handles. Alternative user views such as a gravity mode switch can be provided so the user can spin free-floating objects.

MA2 Controls allow *change of the user's viewpoints* and scale of presence, for example, the user can change to a side view and reduce his or her virtual size and hence, viewpoint, to access small spaces.

MA3 Clear *space surrounding objects* and controls to enable access and easy manipulation—The environment is not cluttered with unnecessary objects that might hinder user action.

MA4 *Flexible presence*—User presence enables movement into a position for action, for example, to manipulate an object in a small confined space, the user's hand has wrist rotation and ability to flex all digits.

MA5 Make *layers transparent* to facilitate access to occluded objects.

MA6 *Simplify access*—Design the VE with a clear access path to interactive objects.

MA7 *Consistent controls*—The controls for an action are the same wherever the user is located in the VE.

MA8 Controls, tools, and operable features must be *within normal human bounds* of motor precision.

MA9 *Minimize feedback response time*—When manipulating objects, the response time delay between user movement and visual feedback should be < 50 msec.

MA10 *Precise control* of the user presence and viewpoint—The user's presence, such as a virtual hand, enables movements with a precision appropriate to the task and maps to the sensor devices.

MA11 Render *control surfaces and features in detail*, for example, active objects and areas of the VE that are manipulated are portrayed in detail, whereas other areas are rendered in less detail.

MA12 *Undo and reversible action*—If appropriate for the domain, actions should be reversible and where they lead to state changes it should be possible to undo them.

MA13 *Scalable power* effects for difficult actions are necessary; for example, flying movement for long distance navigation.

MA14 *Active object identity*—Objects display hover text when approached. Proximity indicators—Visual indications of surrounding aura signal approach to an active object, and collision detection is signaled when approaching an object.

MA15 Support is given to selection and manipulation by *signaling interactive state*.

MA16 *Multiple selection support* is enabled by bounding box, lasso, or rubber band.

MA17 Support should be provided for object selection by a *consistent metaphor*, for example, pinch, grasp, snap-to, point, and select command.

MA18   Support is needed for object selection in complex worlds with occluded objects by *transparency*, movement planes, and layer-filter controls.

MA19   Support can be provided for *small object selection* by ray casting and snap-to functions.

MA20   *Distant object selection support*—This is done by ray casting and cone-spotlights.

MA21   Provide *haptic feedback* for force-related actions; for example, grip, squeeze, push, pull.

MA22   *Power effects* substitute for lack of haptic feedback is necessary; for example, user's presence automatically grasps active objects when they are approached.

MA23   *Gain control*—Allow users to customize the correspondence between physical and virtual actions.

MA24   *Automate or semiautomate* complex actions so the user only has to initiate the sequence.

Manipulation and Action Correspondence Rules

MA correspondence rules follow:

Preparatory Action Stage

IF Domain and Task Knowledge is complete THEN GDPs MA1 (inspect), MA2 (views), MA3 (clear space), and MA4 (flexible presence) ELSE approach difficulty error.

IF Domain and Task Knowledge is minimal THEN GDP MA5 (transparency) and MA6 (simplified access) ELSE approach difficulty error.

IF Naturalness requirement is important THEN avoid GDPs MA2 (views), MA5 (translucent), and MA6 (simple access).

Execute Action Stage

IF Domain and Task Knowledge is complete THEN GDPs MA7 (consistency), MA8 (motor precision), MA9 (quick feedback), MA10 (presence control), MA11 (control detail) MA12 (reversible), and MA14 (active identity) ELSE action slip or execution error.

IF Domain and Task Knowledge is complete and Action is complex THEN GDP MA13 (power effects)
ELSE action execution error.

IF Domain and Task Knowledge is complete and Action requires selection THEN GDPs MA15 (interactive state), MA16 (multiple select), and MA17 (metaphor)ELSE object selection error.

IF Domain and Task Knowledge is complete and Action requires selection and Objects are small, distant, and complex THEN GDPs MA18 (transparent layers), MA19 (snap-to), and MA20 (ray-cast) ELSE object selection error.

IF Domain and Task Knowledge is complete and Action requires pressure THEN GDPs MA21 (haptic) or MA22 (substitute haptics) ELSE action execution error.

IF Domain and Task Knowledge is minimal THEN GDP MA23 (gain controls) ELSE action execution/precision error.

IF Domain and Task Knowledge is minimal THEN GDP MA24 (semiautomate) ELSE learning difficulty or action execution error.

IF Naturalness requirement is important THEN avoid GDPs MA13 (power effects), MA14 (active identity), MA15 (interactive state), MA18 (layers), MA19 (snap-to), MA20 (ray cast), MA22 (substitute haptics), MA23 (gain controls), and MA24 (semiautomate).

Feedback Interpretation

Feedback interpretation (FI) GDPs follow:

FI1   Feedback that is *available and locatable*—Selecting an object is signaled by a temporary change in color; change is signaled visually in the user's field of view.

FI2   *Appropriate modality*—Feedback is given in the expected modality, speech in conversation, image for action.

FI3   *Active notification of invisible changes*—Feedback on objects outside the user's current view is signaled by an indicator in peripheral vision or a pop-up menu in central vision.

FI4   *Discriminable events*—Feedback is given within the normal range of human perception, for example, sound within 300 to 20000 Hz; image contrast is sufficient for the user to see an object.

FI5   *Modal substitution for lack of haptic feedback*, for example, audio tone is used to signal pressure of a grip and deformation of an object.

FI6   *Clear warnings and error messages*, for example, warn the user that flying through solid objects is prevented by the system.

FI7   *Accurate reflection of state change*—Feedback helps interpretation of the effects of action, for example, a manipulation that deformed an object causing material failure is shown as a fracture.

FI8   *Continuous effects of change*—Incremental feedback to show the effect of action is necessary, for example, as the user turns a virtual screwdriver, the virtual screw turns in tandem.

FI9   *Semantic match to user language*—If a message contains semantic information, it is provided in a form known to the user; for example, natural language, known gestures, and symbols.

FI10   *Simplify complex messages* so the user can interpret them.

FI11   *Explain complex state changes* or messages with helper agents or by using a complementary modality, for example, speech explanation of complex action.

FI12   *Objects that can be interrogated* for further information—Objects explain their role or function by speech or text while visually signaling their response.

FI13   *Changes and messages match the user's task and domain knowledge*; for example, dissecting a body in a virtual surgery simulation is displayed with the correct anatomical detail as exposed by the user's dissecting actions.

FI14   Indication of *limits of future action*—Feedback should be cooperative and indicate only options available for future action according to the state of the system and the user task; for example, navigation controls follow the real world so the move through and down control is inactive when the user is on a solid surface.

FI15   Message *matches* level of user's domain and task knowledge; for example, a natural language utterance is linked to the user's pragmatic knowledge for understanding; or, ensure the user is given domain knowledge to understand the dangerous implications of an unsafe action.

FI16   *Explain any mode setting* and effects on system action and responses, for example, rapid transit mode uses a magic carpet metaphor.

FI17   Provide facilities for *comparing before and after* states.

FI18   Supplementary *context*—Provide information on history, causality, and background to help user understand implications.

Feedback Interpretation Correspondence Rules

FI correspondence rules follow:

Recognize Feedback Stage

IF Domain and Task Knowledge is complete THEN GDPs FI1 (available feedback), FII2 (expected modality), FI3 (notify), and FI4 (discriminable) ELSE feedback not perceived problem.

IF Domain and Task Knowledge is complete and Action involves grip or pressure THEN GDP FI5 (modal substitution) ELSE feedback not perceived problem.

IF Naturalness requirement is important THEN avoid GDPs FI3 (notify) and FI5 (modal substitution).

Interpret Feedback Stage

IF Domain and Task Knowledge is complete THEN GDPs FI6 (simple message), FI7 (accurate reflection), FI8 (incremental), and FI9 (semantic match) ELSE user will be unable to interpret event or message.

IF Domain and Task Knowledge is minimal THEN GDP FI10 (simplify message), FI11 (explanation), and FI12 (interrogate objects) ELSE user will be unable to interpret event or message.

IF Naturalness requirement is important THEN avoid GDPs FI10 (simplify message), FI11 (explanation), and FI12 (interrogate objects).

Evaluate Feedback Stage

IF Domain and Task Knowledge is complete THEN GDPs FI3 (task context), FI4 (future limits), and FI5 (knowledge match) ELSE user will be unable to evaluate the implications of the event or message.

IF Domain and Task Knowledge is minimal THEN GDP FI16 (explain modes and status), FI17 (compare contexts), and FI18 (add context) ELSE user will be unable to evaluate the implications of the event or message.

IF Naturalness requirement is important THEN avoid GDPs FI16 (explain modes and status), FI17 (compare contexts), and FI18 (add context).

NAVIGATION AND EXPLORATION CYCLE

GDPs for navigation divide into *cues* for wayfinding designed into the VE, and *controls* to help navigation and movement by the user's presence. In navigation, the stages tend to be more concurrent than task-action, so users will be selecting cues, deciding direction, and specifying navigation movements at the same time. The correspondence rules attach the GDPs to the more appropriate stage of the cycle; however, some GDPs will contribute to several stages. Many of the feedback stage GDPs from the task-action cycle also apply to the navigation cycle so they are not repeated. The navigation feedback GDPs suggest facilities to help users when feedback fails (i.e., when they become lost), as well as design for presenting feedback.

Navigation Planning–Action Stages

Navigation and planning–action (NV) GDPs follow:

NV1   *Popularity indicators*—Search is supported by indicating where other users have been in a VE; the social popularity of a location is indicated in the VE by a "top ten" list.

NV2   *Metaphors* that map to the underlying system structure or content, for example, city blocks, streets, buildings, floors, and rooms are used to organize hierarchically classified information.

NV3   *Reusable searches*—Users can pick previous queries from a reusable library or select previous journeys through a VE.

NV4   Highlight *targets* that the user may be interested in on a minimap of the VE.

NV5   *Explain navigation facilities* and environments by animated guided tours.

NV6   *Perceivable environment*—Cues in the VE are visible and audible within the normal human perceptual range.

NV7   *Faithful presentation* of real world—The virtual world is rendered in detail to help wayfinding.

NV8   *Landmarks* and salient features to help navigation—Odd shapes are designed in the VE; objects such as exclamation marks can be added, or VE features altered (change color, size) to help memorization.

NV9   *Target scent*—Portals and pathways provide hints about where they lead.

NV10 *Clear system structure* that indicates navigation pathways is necessary; for example, virtual roads guide the user to important locations.

NV11 Clear *representation* of user's location in overall system and content space—The user's presence is always visible or accessible even if it is has become occluded.

NV12 *Bird's-eye view* of the overall navigable space—Zoom-out controls show the whole environment; or a minimap of VE is provided, oriented from the current viewpoint.

NV13 Mark *pathways* toward the user's target if it is known.

NV14 In *sparse environments* with few landmarks, provide a direction-finding function, for example, compass bearing to target location.

NV15 Support user navigation by providing *maps of the virtual world*, orient maps in user's direction of travel, show user's location on the map, and supply grid lines in the VE for orientation.

NV16 Controls based on *navigation metaphors* reduce learning or effort, for example, flying by hand gesture, helicopter-like controls, magic carpets, and portals that teleport users into new virtual worlds.

NV17 *Match navigation controls* to task requirements—This is necessary when the task demands manipulation use of head and body movement, treadmills, or gaze, switch, and movement controls; for hands-free tasks, use presence and gesture-flying controls.

NV18 *Simplify controls* for ease of navigation, for example, combine velocity and height for overviews (helicopter metaphor).

NV19 Controls of *user representation* (presence) afford easy orientation and movement in appropriate directions (6 degrees of freedom in virtual environments).

NV20 Controls for rapid but *flexible motion* allow the user to move quickly while preserving the ability to change the speed of movement; for example, motion and velocity are interpreted by rate of change in hand movement away from the user's body.

NV21 *Adaptable velocity*—Navigation controls should allow users to move fast for long-distance travel with slower precise movement for approaching targets. The gain setting between physical and virtual movement needs to be under user control.

NV22 *Search facilities* to find and go to specific locations—The user can teleport to certain points in the VE and search by queries for the desired location, x, y coordinates, or relative location "within 3 m of object (x)."

Navigation Planning-Action Stages Correspondence Rules

NV correspondence rules follow:

Form Navigation strategy stage

IF Domain and Task Knowledge is complete THEN GDPs NV1 (social indicators) and NV2 (world metaphors) ELSE user will be unable to decide on a strategy.

IF Domain and Task Knowledge is incomplete THEN GDPs NV3 (reusable searches), NV4 (interesting target), and NV5 (guided tours) ELSE user will be unable to decide on a strategy.

Scan Environment stage
>IF Domain Knowledge is complete THEN GDP NV6 (visible, audible world) ELSE user will become disoriented.

>IF Domain Knowledge is incomplete THEN GDP NV8 (landmarks) ELSE user will become disoriented.

Select Cues Stage
>IF Domain and Task Knowledge is complete THEN GDPs NV7 (representation) and NV8 (landmarks) ELSE user unable to find directional cues.

>IF Domain and Task Knowledge is incomplete THEN GDPs NV9 (target scent) ELSE user unable to find directional cues.

Decide Direction Stage
>IF Domain and Task Knowledge is complete THEN GDPs NV10 (environmental structure), NV11 (self location), and NV12 (overview) ELSE user unable to decide the direction of travel.

>IF Domain and Task Knowledge is incomplete THEN GDPs NV13 (pathways) and NV14 (bearing) ELSE user unable to decide the direction of travel.

Specify Navigation Action Stage
>IF Domain and Task Knowledge is complete THEN GDPs NV15 (maps), NV16 (power metaphors), and NV17 (task match) ELSE user unable to specify navigation movement.

>IF Domain and Task Knowledge is incomplete THEN GDP NV18 (simplify controls) ELSE user unable to specify navigation movement.

Execute Navigation Action Stage
>IF Domain and Task Knowledge is complete THEN GDPs NV19 (easy movement), NV20 (flexible motion), and NV21 (adaptable velocity) ELSE user may have difficulty in moving effectively.

>IF Domain and Device Knowledge is incomplete THEN GDP NV22 (go to) ELSE user may have difficulty in moving effectively.

Most navigation planning action GDPs provide user support by offending the naturalness principle, so if naturalness is necessary, choice is severely restricted; for example, see the following:

IF Naturalness requirement is important THEN avoid all GDPs apart from NV6 (visible–audible world), NV7 (clear representation), NV10 (environmental structure), NV17 (task match), and NV19 (easy movement)

Navigation feedback stages

Navigation feedback (NF) GDPs follow:

NF1   Provide *orientation feedback*: current location, viewpoint.

NF2   *Preserve context* when moving over long distances or through complex spaces (e.g., local maps show trace of journey).

NF3   *Position overview*—For novice users, provide location of self on minimap cross-referenced to user's current view of the VE.

NF4   *Progress cues*—Place waymarks on the user's route so progress toward the target can be assessed.

NF5   *Progress tracks*—Provide trails so users can see from where they have come.

NF6   *Contextual explanation*—Provide explanation facilities so if the user is lost, he or she can determine his or her location and see current locus on an overview map.

NF7   *Backtracking to reorient*—To help disoriented users, provide backtracking facilities so they can return to areas in the VE with known landmarks.

NF8   *Waymarks* for revisiting favorite locations—Provide bookmarks in information spaces and personalized annotation (virtual graffiti) to mark locations.

Navigation Feedback Correspondence Rules

NF correspondence rules follow:

Recognize and Interpret Location stage
IF Domain Knowledge is complete THEN GDP NF1 (orientation) and NF2 (context) ELSE users will be unable to understand where they are. IF Domain Knowledge is incomplete THEN GDP NF3 (overview) ELSE users will be unable to understand where they are.

Evaluate Progress and Location Stage
IF Domain Knowledge is complete THEN GDPs NF4 (progress cues) and NF5 (tracks) ELSE users will be unable to evaluate where they are.

IF Domain Knowledge is incomplete THEN GDP NF6 (explain locus) ELSE users will be unable to evaluate where they are. IF user is lost then GDP NF7 (backtracking).

Record Location Stage
IF Domain and Task requires repeat visits THEN GDP NF8 (place landmarks).

In navigation feedback, all GDPs offend the naturalness principle to some degree.

RESPONSIVE ACTION CYCLE

GDPs for this cycle depend on the context. The user may be responding to an event in the VE or to the system taking initiative (*responding to events or system initiative*). Alternatively, conversation involves interaction with other people or intelligent agents that will be treated as people (*conversation response*). If the user is responding to an event, the cycle concerns analyzing the event and planning a response; however, if the system has taken the initiative, then this change needs to be explained to the user with opportunities to reassert control. Hence, in the system initiative cycle, two different views on users' response are possible, one in response to an external event, the other in reaction to system initiated action.

Conversation Response

Conversation response (CV) GDPs follow:

CV1   *Location of interactive agents*—The agent presence is visible within the user's normal field of view.

CV2   *Perceivable message*—Natural speech should be captured with good fidelity and conveyed to the receiving agent. If speech cannot be supported, text-typing facilities are second best.

CV3   For complex messages or multiparty conversations, *simplify spoken language*, adopt slow speech rates, and control turn-taking.

CV4   If users don't understand the agent's communication, *explain complex terms* and symbols, or use nonverbal communication (gestures, signs).

CV5   Indicate the *role and status of communicating agents*; for example, the visual image of an army officer is indicated by a mannequin in military uniform with the appropriate rank.

CV6   *History of conversations* or interactions—The agent or other system facilities can be queried to replay previous actions or conversations.

CV7   Indication of *agent's mood*—Avatars should use body posture, gesture, and facial expression to convey the agent's internal emotion when appropriate; for example, communicate excitement, indifference, pleasure, displeasure, or anger.

CV8   When users are unfamiliar with the other agent, explain its *role and background*.

CV9   Indication of *agent's intentions*—The agent signals its intentions by speech, facial expression, or movement; for example, turn head and look away signals a break in conversation.

CV10   *Synthesizing reply*—If the user's speech and image cannot be captured directly and transmitted verbatim, then a means of planning discourse is necessary. This may be implemented by scripts for natural language generation, accompanied by nonverbal speech acts; for example, show pleasure for polite reply, or controls for facial expressions at the logical level (fear, surprise, displeasure, etc.), and gestures (head nod for agreement, head shake for disagreement).

CV11   If the subject matter is complex or the user is not familiar with it, provide *dialogue templates* for structuring the conversation.

CV12   Provide *preplanned responses* for regular, structured conversations.

CV13   *Augmenting replies*—If natural communication is difficult, a means for helping the user to reply should be provided. This may be by scripts or composition tools using a thesaurus and syntax- and usage-directed tools that try to "guess-ahead" and complete the sequence being composed.

CV14   *Nonverbal communication*—Simple controls for nonverbal communication should be provided so the user can operate his or her avatar by high-level commands for smile, frown, surprise, and so forth.

CV15   *Automated response*—When users are unfamiliar with the domain or communication language, provide automatic generation of replies from high-level scripts.

CV16   Means of conveying speech, nonverbal communication, and acting in the world should not exceed *human abilities to integrate* communication and action.

Conversation Response Correspondence Rules

CV correspondence rules follow:

Recognize and Interpret Message Stage

IF Domain Knowledge is complete THEN GDPs CV1 (location) and CV2 (natural speech) ELSE the user will not understand the other agent's message.

IF Domain Knowledge is incomplete THEN GDPs CV3 (simplify speech) and CV4 (explain language) ELSE the user will not understand the other agent's message.

IF Naturalness requirement is important THEN avoid GDPs CV3 (simplify speech) and CV4 (explain language)

Evaluate Message Stage

IF Domain Knowledge is complete THEN GDPs CV5 (agent status) and CV7 (agent's mood) ELSE the user will not evaluate the other agent's message.

IF Domain Knowledge is incomplete THEN GDPs CV6 (dialogue history) and CV8 (agent background) ELSE the user will not evaluate the other agent's message.

Decide and Plan Response Stage

IF Domain Knowledge is complete THEN GDPs CV9 (agent intentions) and CV10 (synthesized reply) ELSE the user will not be able to plan his or her reply.

IF Domain Knowledge is incomplete THEN GDPs CV11 (dialogue templates) and CV12 (pre-planned replies) ELSE the user will not able to formulate a reply.

IF Naturalness requirement is important THEN avoid GDPs CV11 (templates) and CV12 (preplanned replies).

Locate and Specify Reply Mechanism Stage

IF Domain Knowledge is complete THEN GDPs CV13 (compose reply) and CV14 (nonverbal) ELSE the user will not be able to carry out his or her planned reply.

IF Domain Knowledge is incomplete THEN GDP CV15 (automated response) ELSE the user will not be able to carry out his or her planned reply.

Execute Response Stage
IF Domain Knowledge is complete THEN GDP CV16 (feasible
integration) ELSE the user will not be able to carry out his or her
planned reply.

Responding to Events and System Initiative

Responding to events and system initiative (SI) GDPs follow:

SI1   *Clear signal*—The user's attention is drawn to events requiring his or her attention, or change to system action is notified to the user; for example, speech is used to warn the user of system initiative in a teleporting activity.

SI2   *Explanation of system initiative* (events triggered by a system agent or another user)—For example, the system explains that it is giving a guided tour.

SI3   *Automatic response to hazardous event*—The system takes initiative in responding to dangerous events when there is insufficient time for the user to respond. The user is given the opportunity to review and change automatic responses.

SI4   *Continuous feedback*—If the system's actions are not directly visible, feedback on progress should be provided.

SI5   *Feedback on initiative duration*—For example, a timer is displayed to show the remaining duration of the guided tour.

SI6   *User override of system initiative*—A command is available for the user to regain control.

SI7   The system should indicate *when initiative changing* is possible and invite the user to regain control at set points.

SI8   Provide analysis of the *consequence of dangerous events* with recommendations for safe action.

SI9   Provide *preplanned responses* to known events.

SI10   Indicate appropriate *controls and commands for response*.

SI11   Controllable *pace of interaction*, allowing time for response—If a user response is expected, the system does not have a short timeout before continuing with its actions.

SI12   Sufficient *time* should be allowed for the user's response.

Responding to Events and System Initiative
Correspondence Rules

SI correspondence rules follow:

Recognize and Interpret Change Stage
IF Domain Knowledge is complete THEN GDPs SI1 (signal) and
SI2 (clarify initiative) ELSE the user will not understand the system's
mode change.

IF Domain Knowledge is incomplete THEN GDP SI3 (automated
response) ELSE the user may be placed in a dangerous situation.

Evaluate Change Stage
IF Domain Knowledge is complete THEN GDPs SI4 (visible
feedback) and SI5 (initiative duration) ELSE the user will not be
able to evaluate what the system is doing.

Decide and Plan Response Stage
IF Domain Knowledge is complete THEN GDPs SI6 (interrupt points),
SI7 (invite control), and SI8 (diagnose hazard), ELSE the user will
not be able to plan his or her response.
IF Domain Knowledge is incomplete THEN GDP SI9 (preplanned
responses) ELSE the user will not be able to plan his or her response.

Locate and Specify Reply Mechanism stage
IF Domain Knowledge is complete THEN GDP SI11 (paced action)
ELSE the user will not be able to regain control.

IF Domain Knowledge is incomplete THEN GDP SI10 (suggest control)
ELSE the user will not be able to execute his or her response.

Execute Response Stage
IF Domain Knowledge is complete THEN GDP SI12 (action time) ELSE
the user will not be able to carry out his or her planned response.

Most of the system initiative GDPs offend the naturalness principle because they advise on support for system control or safety critical response to
hazardous events.

REFERENCES

Abowd, G. D., & Mynatt, E. D. (2000). Charting past, present and future research in ubiquitous computing. ACM *Transactions on Computer–Human Interaction*, 7, 29–58.

Ahlberg, C., & Shneiderman, B. (1994). Visual information seeking: Tight coupling of dynamic query filters with starfield displays. In B. Adelson, S. Dumais, & J. Olson (Eds.), *Human Factors in Computing Systems: CHI 94 Conference Proceedings* (pp. 313–317). New York: ACM Press.

Alty, J. L. (1991). Multimedia: What is it and how do we exploit it? In D. Diaper & N. V. Hammond (Eds.), *People and Computers VI: Proceedings of the HCI 91 Conference* (pp. 31–41). Cambridge, England: Cambridge University Press.

Alty, J. L. (1997). Multimedia. In A. B. Tucker (Ed.), *Computer science and engineering handbook* (pp. 1551–1570). New York: CRC Press.

Anderson, J. R. (1985). *Cognitive psychology and its implications*. New York: Freeman.

Anderson, J. R., & Lebiere, C. (1998). *Representing cognitive activity in complex tasks*. Mahwah, NJ: Lawrence Erlbaum Associates, Inc.

André, E., & Rist, T. (1993). The design of illustrated documents as a planning task. In M. T. Maybury (Ed.), *Intelligent multimedia interfaces* (pp. 94–116). Cambridge, MA: AAAI/MIT Press.

André, E., & Rist, T. (2000). Presenting through performing: On the use of multiple lifelike characters in knowledge-based presentation systems. *Proceedings: Second International Conference on Intelligent User Interfaces: IUI 2000* (pp. 1–8). New York: ACM Press.

André, E., Rist, T., & Müller, J. (1998). WebPersona: A life-like presentation agent for the World-Wide Web. *Knowledge-Based Systems*, 11, 25–36.

Annett, J. (1996). Recent developments in hierarchical task analysis. In S. A. Robertson (Ed.), *Contemporary ergonomics 1996*. London: Taylor & Francis.

Arens, Y., Hovy, E., & Van Mulken, S. (1993). Structure and rules in automated multimedia presentation planning. *Proceedings: IJCAI–93: Thirteenth International Joint Conference on Artificial Intelligence*.

Baddeley, A. D. (1986). *Working memory*. Oxford, England: Oxford University Press.

Baggett, P. (1989). Understanding visual and verbal messages. In H. Mandl & J. R. Levin (Eds.), *Knowledge acquisition from text and pictures* (pp. 101–124). Amsterdam: Elsevier.

Barfield, W., & Caudell, T. (Eds.), (2001). *Fundamentals of wearable computers and augmented reality*. Mahwah, NJ: Lawrence Erlbaum Associates, Inc.

Barfield, W., Zeltzer, D., Sheridan, T., & Slater, M. (1995). Presence and performance within virtual environments. In W. Barfield & T. A. Furness (Eds.), *Virtual environments and advanced interface design* (pp. 473–513). New York: Oxford University Press.

Barnard, P. (1987). *Mental models and industrial process operation*. London: Academic.

Barnard, P. (1991). Bridging between basic theories and the artefacts of human computer interaction. In J. M. Carroll (Ed.), *Designing interaction: Psychology at the human computer interface*. New York: Cambridge University Press.

Barnard, P., & May, J. (1999). Representing cognitive activity in complex tasks. *Human–Computer Interaction, 14*, 93–158.

Barnard, P., May, J., Duke D., & Duce, D. (2000). Systems, interactions and macrotheory. *ACM Transactions on Computer–Human Interaction, 7*, 222–262.

Bates, M. J. (1989). The design of browsing and berrypicking techniques for the on-line interface. *On-line Review, 13*, 407–424.

Bellotti, V. (1993). Integrating theoreticians' and practitioners' perspectives with design rationale. In S. Ashlund, K. Mullet, A. Henderson, E. Hollnagel, & T. White (Eds.), *Human Factors in Computing Systems: INTERCHI 93 Conference Proceedings* (pp. 101–114). New York: ACM Press.

Bellotti, V., Buckingham Shum, S., MacLean, A., & Hammond, N. (1995). Multidisciplinary modelling in HCI design: Theory and practice. In I. R. Katz, R. Mack, L. Marks, M. B. Rosson, & J. Nielsen (Eds.), *Human Factors in Computing Systems: CHI 95 Conference Proceedings* (pp. 146–153). New York: ACM Press.

Benford, S., Greenhalgh, C., Bowers, J., Snowdon, D., & Fahlen, L. E. (1995). User embodiment in collaborative virtual environments. In I. R. Katz, R. Mack, L. Marks, M. B. Rosson, & J. Nielsen (Eds.), *Human Factors in Computing Systems: CHI 95 Conference Proceedings* (pp. 242–249). New York: ACM Press.

Benford, S., Greenhalgh, C., Craven, M., Walker, G., Regan, T., Morphett, J., et al. (2000). Inhabited television: Broadcasting interaction from within collaborative virtual environments. *ACM Transactions on Computer–Human Interaction, 7*, 510–547.

Bernsen, N. O. (1994). Foundations of multimodal representations: A taxonomy of representational modalities. *Interacting with Computers, 6*, 347–371.

Bertin, J. (1983). *Semiology of graphics*. Madison: University of Wisconsin Press.

Beyer, H., & Holtzblatt, K. (1998). *Contextual design: Defining customer-centered systems*. San Francisco: Kaufmann.

Bieger, G. R., & Glock, M. D. (1984). The information content of picture–text instructions. *Journal of Experimental Education, 53*, 68–76.

Bolas, M. (1994). Designing virtual environments. In C. G. Loeffler & T. Anderson (Eds.), *The virtual reality casebook*. New York: Van Nostrand.

Booher, H. R. (1975). Relative comprehensibility of pictorial information and printed word in proceduralized instructions. *Human Factors, 17*, 266–277.

Borchers, J. (2001). *A pattern approach to interaction design*. Chichester, England: Wiley.

Bowman, D. A., Koller, D., & Hodges, L. F. (1997). Travel in immersive virtual environments: An evaluation of viewpoint motion control techniques. *Proceedings: IEEE 1997 Virtual Reality Annual International Symposium* (pp. 45–52). Los Alamitos, CA: IEEE Computer Society Press.

Boyle, T. (1997). *Design for multimedia learning*. Upper Saddle River, NJ: Prentice Hall.

Brewster, S. (1994). *Providing a structured method for integrating non-speech audio into human-computer interfaces*. Unpublished doctoral dissertation, University of York, England.

British Airways. (2001). *Home page*. Retrieved March 22, 2001, from http://www.britishairways.com

Brown, P., & Levinson, S. C. (1987). *Politeness: Some universals in language usage.* Cambridge, England: Cambridge University Press.

Buxton, W. (1995). Touch, gesture and marking. In R. M. Baecker, J. Grudin, W. Buxton, & S. Greenberg (Eds.), *Readings in human computer interaction: Towards the year 2000* (2nd ed.). San Francisco: Kaufmann.

Cairncross, S. (2001). *Interactive multimedia and learning: Realizing the benefits.* Unpublished doctoral dissertation, School of Computing, Napier University, Edinburgh, Scotland.

Card, S. K., Mackinlay, J. D., & Shneiderman, B. (1999). Information visualization. In S. K. Card, J. D. Mackinlay, & B. Shneiderman (Eds.), *Readings in information visualization: Using vision to think* (pp. 1–34). San Francisco: Kaufmann.

Card, S. K., Moran, T. P., & Newell, A. (1983). *The psychology of human computer interaction.* Hillsdale, NJ: Lawrence Erlbaum Associates, Inc.

Carroll, J. M. (Ed.). (1995). *Scenario-based design: Envisioning work and technology in system development.* New York: Wiley.

Carroll, J. M. (1997). Reconstructing minimalism. *Proceedings. SIGDOC '97: 15th Annual International Conference on Computer Documentation* (pp. 27–34). New York: ACM Press.

Carroll, J. M., & Rosson, M. B. (1992). Getting around the task–artifact framework: How to make claims and design by scenario. *ACM Transactions on Information Systems, 10,* 181–212.

Cassel, J., Bickmore, T., Billinghurst, M., Campbell, L., Chang, K., Vilhjalmsson, H., et al. (1999). Embodiment in conversational interfaces: Rea. In M. G. Williams, M. W. Altom, K. Erhlich, & K. Newman, (Eds.), *Proceedings of CHI'99: Human Factors in Computing Systems, Pittsburgh PA* (pp. 520–527). New York: ACM Press.

Clark, H. H. (1996). *Using language.* Cambridge, England: Cambridge University Press.

Cockton, G., & Lavery, D. (1999). A framework for usability problem extraction. In A. Sasse & C. Johnson (Eds.). *Proceedings: INTERACT 99* (pp. 347–355). London: IOS Press.

Costabile, M. F. (1999). Usable multimedia applications. *Proceedings of ICMCS99, Vol. 1: IEEE International Conference on Multimedia Systems 99* (pp. 124–127). Los Alamitos, CA: IEEE Computer Society Press.

Craven, M., Taylor, I., Drozd, A., Purbick, J., Greenhalgh. C., Bebford, C., et al. (2001). Exploiting interactivity, influence, space and time to explore non-linear drama in virtual worlds. In J. A. Jacko, A. Sears, M. Beaudouin-Lafon, & R. J. K. Jacob (Eds.), *CHI 2001 Conference Proceedings: Conference on Human Factors in Computing Systems* (pp. 30–37). New York: ACM Press.

Crowcroft, J. (1997). *Internetworking multimedia.* London: Taylor & Francis.

Crozat, S., Hu, O., & Trigano, P. (1999). A method for evaluating multimedia software. *Proceedings of ICMCS 99, Vol.1: IEEE International Conference on Multimedia Systems 99* (pp. 714–719). Los Alamitos, CA: IEEE Computer Society Press.

Darken, R. P., & Sibert, J. L. (1996). Wayfinding strategies and behaviours in large virtual worlds. In M. Tauber, V. Bellotti, R. Jeffries, J. D. Mackinlay, & J. Nielsen, (Eds.), *Human Factors in Computing Systems: CHI 96 Conference Proceedings* (pp. 142–149). New York: ACM Press.

Dimitrova, M. T., & Sutcliffe, A. G. (1999). Designing instructional multimedia applications: Key practices and design patterns. In B. Collins & R. Oliver, (Eds.), *Proceedings: Ed–Media 99* (pp. 358–363). Seattle, WA: Association for the Advancement of Computing in Education.

Duke, D. J., Barnard, P. J., Duce, D. A., & May, J. (1998). Syndetic modelling. *Human–Computer Interaction, 13,* 337–393.

EasyJet Airline Company Ltd. (2001). *Home page.* Retrieved March 22, 2001, from http://www.easyjet.com/en/

Eden, C. (1988). Cognitive mapping. *European Journal of Operational Research, 36,* 1–13.

Elsom-Cook, M. (2000). *Principles of interactive multimedia.* London: McGraw-Hill.

Faraday, P. (1998). *Theory-based design and evaluation of multimedia presentation interfaces.* Unpublished doctoral dissertation. Centre for HCI Design, School of Informatics, City University, Lomdon.

Faraday, P., & Sutcliffe, A. G. (1996). An empirical study of attending and comprehending multimedia presentations. *Proceedings ACM Multimedia 96: 4th Multimedia Conference* (pp. 265–275). New York: ACM Press.

Faraday, P., & Sutcliffe, A. G. (1997a). Designing effective multimedia presentations. In S. Pemberton (Eds.), *Human Factors in Computing Systems: CHI 97 Conference Proceedings* (pp. 272–279). New York: ACM Press.

Faraday, P., & Sutcliffe, A. G. (1997b). Evaluating multimedia presentations. *New Review of Hypermedia & Multimedia, Applications & Research, 3,* 7–38.

Faraday, P., & Sutcliffe, A. G. (1998a). Making contact points between text and images. *Proceedings ACM Multimedia 98: 6th ACM International Multimedia Conference* (pp. 29–37). New York: ACM Press.

Faraday, P., & Sutcliffe, A. G. (1998b). Providing advice for multimedia designers. In C. M. Karat, A. Lund, J. Coutaz, & J. Karat (Eds.), *Human Factors in Computing Systems: CHI 98 Conference Proceedings* (pp. 124–131). New York: ACM Press.

Faraday, P., & Sutcliffe, A. G. (1999). Authoring animated Web pages using contact points. In M. G. Williams, M. W. Altom, K. Erhlich, & K. Newman (Eds.), *Human Factors in Computing Systems: CHI 99 Conference Proceedings* (pp. 458–465). New York: ACM Press.

Fischer, G., Lindstaedt, S., Ostwald, J., Stolze, M., Sumner, T., & Zimmermann, B. (1995). From domain modeling to collaborative domain construction. In G. M. Olson & S. Schuon (Eds.), *Conference proceedings: DIS '95 Symposium on Designing Interactive Systems: Processes, Practices, Methods and Techniques* (pp. 75–85). New York: ACM Press.

Fisher, S. (1994). *Multimedia authoring: Building and developing documents.* Cambridge, MA: AP Professional.

Field, M., Lauche, K., Dierssen, S., Nichel, M., & Rauterberg, M. (1998). BUILD-IT: A brick based integral solution supporting multidisciplinary design tasks. In A. G. Sutcliffe, J. Zeigler, & P. Johnson (Eds.), *Designing effective and usable multimedia systems: Proceedings of IFIP working group 13.2* (pp. 131–142). Boston: Kluwer.

Fogg, B. J. (1998). Persuasive computer: Perspectives and research directions. *Human Factors in Computing Systems: CHI 98 Conference Proceedings* (pp. 225–232). New York: ACM Press.

Frécon, E., & Stenius, M. (1998). DIVE: A scaleable network architecture for distributed virtual environments. *Distributed Systems Engineering Journal, 5,* 91–100.

Fukumoto, M., Mase, K., & Suenaga, Y. (1995, May). *Finger-pointer: A glove free interface.* Poster Session presented at Human Factors in Computing Systems: CHI 95 Conference Proceedings, New York.

Furnas, G. W. (1997). Effective view navigation. In S. Pemberton (Ed.), *Human Factors in Computing Systems: CHI 97 Conference Proceedings* (pp. 367–374). New York: ACM Press.

Gabbard, J. L., & Hix, D. (1997). *A taxonomy of usability characteristics in virtual environments: Deliverable to Office of Naval Research* (Grant no. N00014-96-1-0385). Blacksburg, VA: Virginia Polytechnic Institute, Department of Computer Science.

Gabbard, J. L., Hix, D., & Swan, J. E. (1999). User-centered design and evaluation of virtual environments. *IEEE Computer Graphics and Applications, 19,* 51–59.

Gentner, D., & Stevens, A. L. (1983). *Mental models.* Hillsdale, NJ: Lawrence Erlbaum Associates, Inc.

Gibson, J. J. (1986). *The ecological approach to visual perception.* Hillsdale, NJ: Lawrence Erlbaum Associates, Inc.

Gobert, M. A., Orth, M., & Ishii, H. (1998). Triangles: Tangible interfaces for manipulation and exploration of digital information topography. In C. M. Karat, A. Lund, J. Coutaz, & J.

Karat (Eds.), *Human Factors in Computing Systems: CHI 98 Conference Proceedings* (pp. 49–56). New York: ACM Press.

Graham, L. (1998). *Principles of interactive design*. Albany, NY: Delmar.

Grice, H. P. (1975). Logic and conversation. *Syntax and Semantics, 3*.

Hammond, N., & Allinson, L. (1989). Extending hypertext for learning: An investigation of access and guidance tools. In A. G. Sutcliffe & L. Macaulay (Eds.), *Proceedings of HCI 89: People and Computers V* (pp. 293–304). Cambridge, England: Cambridge University Press.

Harrison, M. D., & Barnard, P. J. (1993). On defining the requirements for interaction. In S. Fickas & A. C. W. Finklestein (Eds.), *Proceedings: 1st International Symposium on Requirements Engineering–RE'93* (pp. 50–55). Los Alamitos, CA: IEEE Computer Society Press.

Hart, S. G., & Staveland, L. E. (1988). Development of a NASA–TLX (Task Load Index): Results of empirical and theoretical research. In P. S. Hancock & N. Meshkati (Eds.), *Human mental workload* (pp. 139–183). Amsterdam: Elsevier.

Hegarty, M., & Just, M. A. (1993). Constructing mental models of text and diagrams. *Journal of Memory and Language, 32*, 717–742.

Heller, R. S., & Martin, C. (1995). A media taxonomy. *IEEE Multimedia, 2*, 36–45.

Hix, D., Swan, J. E., Gabbard, J. L., McGee, M., Durbin, J., & King, T. (1999). User-centered design and evaluation of a real-time battlefield visualization virtual environment. In L. Rosenblum, P. Astheimer, & D. Teichmann, (Eds.), *Proceedings: IEEE Virtual Reality 99* (pp. 96–103). Los Alamitos, CA: IEEE Computer Society Press.

Hochberg, J. (1986). Presentation of motion and space in video and cinematic displays. In K. R. Boff, L. Kaufman, & J. P. Thomas (Eds.), *Handbook of perception and human performance, 1: Sensory processes and perception*. New York: Wiley.

Hollan, J. D., Hutchins, E. L., & Weitzman, L. (1984). Steamer: An interactive inspectable simulation-based training system. *AI Magazine, 5*(2), 15–27.

Hollnagel, E. (1998). *Cognitive reliability and error analysis method: CREAM*. Oxford, England: Elsevier.

Höök, K., & Dahlback, N. (1992, December). Can cognitive science contribute to the design of VR applications? *5th MultiG Workshop, Stockholm* Available: ftp://ftp.kth.se/pub/MultiG/conferences/MultiG5.

Hubbold, R., Cook, J., Keates, M., Gibson, S., Howard, T., Murta, A., et al. (1999). GNU/MAVERIK: A micro-kernel for large-scale virtual environments. *Proceedings: VRST 99, ACM Symposium on Virtual Reality Software and Technology*. New York: ACM Press.

IBM. (2000). *Ease of use: Design principles*. Retrieved November 20, 2000, from http://www.ibm.com/ibm/easy/eou ext.nsf/Publish/6

Ibster, C., Nakanishi, H., Ishida, T., & Nass, C. (2000). Helper agent: Designing an assistant for human–human interaction in a virtual meeting space. In T. Turner, G. Szwillus, M. Czerwinski, & F. Paterno (Eds.), *CHI 2000 Conference Proceedings: Conference on Human Factors in Computing Systems* (pp. 57–64). New York: ACM Press.

Ishii, H., Mazalek, A., & Lee, J. (2001). Bottles as a minimal interface to access digital information. In J. A. Jacko, A. Sears, M. Beaudouin-Lafon, & R. J. K. Jacob (Eds.), *CHI 2001 Extended Abstracts: Conference on Human Factors in Computing Systems* (pp. 187–188). New York: ACM Press.

Ishii, H., & Ullmer, B. (1997). Tangible bits: Towards seamless interfaces between people, bits and atoms. In S. Pemberton (Ed.), *Human Factors in Computing Systems: CHI 97 Conference Proceedings,* (pp. 235–241). New York: ACM Press.

ISO (International Organization for Standardization). (1997). *ISO 9241: Ergonomic requirements for office systems with visual display terminals (VDTs)*: Author.

ISO (International Organization for Standardization). (1998). *ISO 14915 Multimedia user interface design software ergonomic requirements, Part 1: Introduction and framework; Part 3: Media combination and selection*: Author

ISO (International Organization for Standardization). (2000). *ISO 14915–3: Software ergonomics for multimedia user interfaces. Part 3: Media selection and combination. Draft international standard*: Author

Jacobson, I., Christerson, M., Jonsson, P., & Overgaard, G. (1992). *Object-oriented software engineering: A use-case driven approach*. Reading, MA: Addison-Wesley.

John, B. E., & Kieras, R. E. (1995). The GOMS family of user interface analysis techniques: Comparison and contrast. *ACM Transactions on Computer–Human Interaction, 3*, 320–351.

Johnson, C. (1998). On the problems of validating desktop VR. *People and Computers XIII. Proceedings: HCI 98* (pp. 327–338). Berlin, Germany: Springer-Verlag.

Johnson, P. (1992). *Human computer interaction: Psychology, task analysis and software engineering*. London: McGraw-Hill.

Johnson, P., & Nemetz, F. (1998). Towards principles for the design and evaluation of multimedia systems. In H. Johnson, L. Nigay, & C. Roast (Eds.), *Proceedings of HCI 98: People and Computers XIII* (pp. 255–272). Berlin, Germany: Springer-Verlag.

Johnson-Laird, P. N., & Wason, P. C. (1983). *Thinking: Readings in cognitive science*. Cambridge, England: Cambridge University Press.

Kalawsky, R. S. (1998). New methodologies and techniques for evaluating user performance in advanced 3D virtual interfaces. *Digest 98/437: IEE Colloquium on 3D Interface for the Information Worker* (pp. 5/1–8). London: IEE.

Kalawsky, R. S. (1999). VRUSE: A computerised diagnositc tool: For usability evaluation of virtual/synthetic environment systems. *Applied Ergonomics, 30*, 11–25.

Kaur, K. (1998). *Designing virtual environments for usability*. Unpublished doctoral dissertation. London: Centre for HCI Design, School of Informatics, City University, London.

Kaur, K., Maiden, N. A. M., & Sutcliffe, A. G. (1996). Design practice and usability problems with virtual environments. *Proceedings: Virtual Reality World 96, Stuttgart* [Informal proceedings].

Kaur, K., Maiden, N. A. M., & Sutcliffe, A. G. (1999). Interacting with virtual environments: An evaluation of a model of interaction. *Interacting with Computers, 11*, 403–426.

Kaur, K., Sutcliffe, A. G., & Maiden, N. A. M. (1998). Improving interaction with virtual environments. *Proceedings: IEE Colloquium on 3D Interface for the Information Worker* (pp. 4/1–4). London: IEE.

Kaur, K., Sutcliffe, A. G., & Maiden, N. A. M. (1999). Towards a better understanding of usability problems with virtual environments. In A. Sasse & C. Johnson, (Eds.), *Proceedings of INTERACT 99: IFIP TC.13 Conference on Human Computer Interaction* (pp. 527–535). Amsterdam: IFIP/IOS Press.

Keenan S.L. (1996). *Product usability and process improvement based on usability problem classification*. Unpublished doctoral dissertation. Virginia Tech, Department of Computer Science, Blacksburg VA.

Kieras, D. E., & Meyer, D. E. (1997). An overview of the EPIC architecture for cognition and performance with application to human computer interaction. *Human–Computer Interaction, 12*, 391–438.

Kitajima, M., & Polson, P. G. (1997). A comprehension-based model of exploration. *Human–Computer Interaction, 12*, 345–390.

Kolb, D. (1984). *Experiential learning: Experiences as the source of learning and development*. Englewood Cliffs, NJ: Prentice Hall.

Kollok, P. (1999). The production of trust in online markets. In E. J. Lawler, M. Macy, S. Thyne, & H. A. Walker (Eds.), *Advances in group processes, vol. 16*. Greenwich, CT: JAI.

Kosslyn, S. M. (1980). *Image and mind*. Cambridge, MA: Harvard University Press.

Kristof, R., & Satran, A. (1995). *Interactivity by design: Creating and communicating with new media*. Mountain View, CA: Adobe Press.

Laurillard, D. (1993). *Rethinking university teaching: A framework for the effective use of educational technology*. London: Routledge & Kegan Paul.

Lee, W. W., & Owens, D. L. (2000). *Multimedia-based instructional design: Computer-based training, Web-based training and distance learning*. San Francisco, Jossey-Bass.

Leplatre, G., & Brewster, S. (1998). An investigation of using music to provide navigation clues. *Proceedings: Conference of International Community for Auditory Display* [Informal proceedings].

Levie, W. H., & Lentz, R. (1982). Effects of text illustrations: A review of research. *Educational Computing and Technology Journal, 30*, 159–232.

Lohse, G. L. (2000). Usability and profits in the digital economy. In S. McDonald, Y. Waern, & G. Cockton, (Eds.), *People and Computers XIV: Usability or Else; Proceedings: BCS–HCI Conference* (pp. 3–16). Berlin, Germany: Springer.

Lowe, D., & Hall, W. (1998). *Hypermedia and the web*. Chichester, England: Wiley.

Mackinlay, J. D., Rao, R., & Card, S. K. (1995). Organic user interface for searching citation links. In I. R. Katz, R. Mack, L. Marks, M. B. Rosson, & J. Nielsen (Eds.), *Human Factors in Computing Systems: CHI 95 Conference Proceedings* (pp. 67–73). New York: ACM Press.

Mann, W. C., & Thompson, S. A. (1988). Rhetorical Structure Theory: Toward a functional theory of text organisation. *Text, 8*, 243–281.

Marr, D. (1982). *Vision*. New York: Freeman.

Maslow, A. H., Frager, R., McReynolds, C., Cox, R., & Fadiman, J. (1987). *Motivation and personality* (3rd ed.). New York: Addison-Wesley.

May, J., & Barnard, P. (1995). Cinematography and interface design. In K. Nordbyn, P. H. Helmersen, D. J. Gilmore, & S. A. Arnesen (Eds.), *Proceedings: Fifth IFIP TC 13 International Conference on Human–Computer Interaction* (pp. 26–31). London: Chapman & Hall.

Maybury, M. T. (1999). Putting usable intelligence into multimedia applications. *Proceedings of ICMCS99, Vol.1: IEEE International Conference on Multimedia Systems 99* (pp. 107–110). Los Alamitos, CA: IEEE Computer Society Press.

Miller, L. D. (1994). *A usability evaluation of the Rolls-Royce virtual reality for aero engine maintenance system*. Unpublished Master's thesis, University College London.

Mills, S., & Noyes, J. (1999). Virtual reality: An overview of user-related design issues. *Interacting with Computers, 11*, 375–386.

Monk, A. G., & Wright, P. (1993). *Improving your human–computer interface: A practical technique*. London: Prentice Hall.

Morris, T. (2000). *Multimedia systems: Delivering, generating and interacting with multimedia*. London: Springer-Verlag.

Muller, M. J., Hanswanter, J. H., & Dayton, T. (1997). Participatory practice in the software lifecycle. In M. G. Helander, T. K. Landauer, & P. V. Prabhu (Eds.), *Handbook of human computer interaction*. Amsterdam: Elsevier.

Mullet, K., & Sano, D. (1995). *Designing visual interfaces: Communication oriented techniques*. Englewood Cliffs, NJ: SunSoft Press.

Narayanan, N. H., & Hegarty, M. (1998). On designing comprehensible interactive hypermedia manuals. *International Journal of Human–Computer Studies, 48*, 267–301.

Nass, C., & Gong, L. (2000). Speech interfaces from an evolutionary perspective. *Communications of the ACM, 43*(9), 37–43.

Nielsen, J. (1993). *Usability engineering*. New York: Academic.

Nielsen, J. (1995). *Multimedia and hypertext: The Internet and beyond*. Boston: AP Professional.

Nielsen, J. (1999). *Designing web usability: The practice of simplicity*. New Riders Publishing.

Nielsen, J., & Phillips, V. L. (1993). Estimating the relative usability of two interfaces: Heuristic, formal and empirical methods compared. *Human Factors in Computing Systems: INTERCHI 93 Conference Proceedings* (pp. 214–221). New York: ACM Press.

Norman, D. A. (1986). Cognitive engineering. In D. A. Norman & S. W. Draper (Eds.), *User-centered system design: New perspectives on human–computer interaction*. Hillsdale, NJ: Lawrence Erlbaum Associates, Inc.

Norman, D. A. (1988). *The psychology of everyday things*. New York: Basic Books.

Norman, D. A. (1999). *The invisible computer: Why good products can fail, the personal computer is so complex, and information appliances are the solution*. Cambridge, MA: MIT Press.

Ortony, A., Clore, G. L., & Collins, A. (1988). *The cognitive structure of emotions*. Cambridge, England: Cambridge University Press.

Oviatt, S., & Cohen, P. (2000). Multimodal interfaces that process what comes naturally. *Communication of the ACM, 43*(3), 45–53.

Papert, S. (1980). *Mindstorms: Children, computers, and powerful ideas*. New York: Basic Books.

Park, I., & Hannafin, M. J. (1993). Empirically-based guidelines for the design of interactive multimedia. *Educational Technology Research and Development, 41*, 63–85.

Parlangeli, O., Marchigiani, E., & Bagnara, S. (1999). Multimedia systems in distance education: Effects of usability on learning. *Interacting with Computers 12,* (1), 37–49.

Payne, S. J., & Green, T. R. G. (1989). The structure of command languages: An experiment on task–action grammar. *International Journal of Man–Machine Studies, 30*, 213–234.

Peters, R. G., Covello, V. T., & McCallum. (1997). The determinants of trust and credibility in environmental risk communication: An empirical study. *Risk Analysis, 17*, 43–54.

Pezdek, K., & Maki, R. (1988). Picture memory: Recognizing added and deleted details. *Journal of Experimental Psychology: Learning, Memory and Cognition, 14*, 468–476.

Picard, R. W. (1997). *Affective computing*. Cambridge, MA: MIT Press.

Pirolli, P., & Card, S. (1999). Information foraging. *Psychological Review, 106*(4), 643–675.

Poggi, I., & Pelachaud, C. (2000). Performative facial expressions in animated faces. In J. Cassel, S. Sullivan, S. Prevost, & E. Churchill (Eds.), *Embodied conversational agents* (pp. 155–188). Cambridge, MA: MIT Press.

Portigal, S. (1994). *Auralization of document structure*. Unpublished Master's thesis. University of Guelph, Ontario, Canada.

Poupyrev, I., & Ichikawa, T. (1999). Manipulating objects in virtual worlds: Categorization and empirical evaluation of interaction techniques. *Journal of Visual Languages and Computing, 10*, 19–35.

Rasmussen, J. (1986). *Information processing in human computer interaction: An approach to cognitive engineering*. Amsterdam: North-Holland.

Rational Corporation. (1999). *UML: Unified Modelling Language method*. Retrieved 1999, from http://www.rational.com

Reason, J. (1990). *Human error*. Cambridge, England: Cambridge University Press.

Reeves, B., & Nass, C. (1996). *The media equation: How people treat computers, television and new media like real people and places*. Stanford, CA/Cambridge, England: CLSI/Cambridge University Press.

Reiman, J., Young, R. M., & Howes, A. (1996). A dual space model of iteratively deepening exploratory learning. *International Journal of Human–Computer Studies, 44*, 743–775.

Repenning, A. (1993). *Agentsheets: A tool for building domain oriented-dynamic visual environments*. (Tech. Rep. No. CU/CS/693/93). Boulder: University of Colorado, Department of Computer Science.

Richardson, A. (1977). Visualisers–verbalisers: A cognitive style dimension. *Journal of Mental Imagery, 1,* 109–125.

Riding, R., & Rayner, S. G. (1998). *Cognitive styles and learning strategies.* David Fulton.

Rogers, Y., & Scaife, M. (1998). How can interactive multimedia facilitate learning? In J. Lee (Ed.), *Intelligence and multimodality in multimedia interfaces: Research and applications.* Menlo Park, CA: AAAI Press.

Rosch, E. (1985). Prototype classification and logical classification: The two systems. In E. K. Scholnick (Ed.), *New trends in conceptual representation: Challenges to Piaget's Theory.* Hillsdale, NJ: Lawrence Erlbaum Associates, Inc.

Russel, J. A., & Fernandez-Dols, J. M. (1997). *The psychology of facial expression.* Cambridge, England: Cambridge University Press.

Scaife, M., Rogers, Y., Aldrich, F., & Davies, M. (1997). Designing for or designing with? Informant design for interactive learning environments. In S. Pemberton (Ed.), *Human Factors in Computing Systems: CHI 97 Conference Proceedings* (pp. 343–350). New York: ACM Press.

Schank, R. C. (1982). *Dynamic memory: A theory of reminding and learning in computers and people.* Cambridge, England: Cambridge University Press.

Schiano, D. J., Ehrlich, S. M., Rahrjardja, K., & Sheridan, K. (2000). Face to interface: Facial affect in (hu)man and machine interaction. In T. Turner, G. Szwillus, M. Czerwinski, & F. Paterno (Eds.), *CHI 2000 Conference Proceedings: Conference on Human Factors in Computer Systems* (pp. 193–200). New York: ACM Press.

Shneiderman, B. (1998). *Designing the user interface: Strategies for effective human–computer interaction* (3rd ed.). New York: Addison-Wesley.

Simon, H. A. (1973). The structure of ill-structured problems. *Artificial Intelligence, 4,* 181–201.

Slater, M., Usoh, M., & Steed, A. (1995). Taking steps: The influence of a walking technique on presence in virtual reality. *ACM Transactions on Computer–Human Interaction, 2,* 201–219.

Smith, I. A., & Cohen, P. R. (1996). Toward a semantics for an agent communications language based on speech-acts. *Thirteenth National Conference on Artificial Intelligence and the Eighth Innovative Applications of Artificial Intelligence Conference, Portland, OR,* pp. 24–31.

Smith, R. B. (1987). The Alternate Reality Kit: An example of the tension between literalism and magic. In J. M. Carroll & P. P. Tanner (Eds.), *Human Factors in Computing Systems and Graphical Interfaces: CHI + GI 87 Conference Proceedings.* New York: ACM Press.

Sowa, J. F. (2000). *Knowledge representation: Logical, philosophical and computational foundations.* Pacific Grove, CA: Brooks/Cole.

Spool, J. M., Scanlon, T., Snyder, C., Schroeder, W., & De Angelo, T. (1999). *Web site usability: A designer's guide.* San Francisco: Kaufmann.

Springett, M. V. (1995). *User modelling for evaluation of direct manipulation interfaces.* Unpublished doctoral dissertation, Centre for HCI Design, School of Informatics, City University, London.

Suchman, L. A. (1987). *Plans and situated actions: The problem of human–machine communication.* Cambridge, England: Cambridge University Press.

Sutcliffe, A. G. (1995a). *Human computer interface design* (2nd ed.). London: Macmillan.

Sutcliffe, A. G. (1995b). Requirements rationales: Integrating approaches to requirements analysis. In G. M. Olson & S. Schuon (Eds.), *Designing Interactive Systems: DIS 95 Conference Proceedings* (pp. 33–42). New York: ACM Press.

Sutcliffe, A. G. (1997). Task-related information analysis. *International Journal of Human–Computer Studies, 47,* 223–257.

Sutcliffe, A. G. (1998). Scenario-based requirements analysis. *Requirements Engineering Journal, 3,* 48–65.

Sutcliffe, A. G. (1999a). A design method for effective information delivery in multimedia presentations. *New Review of Hypermedia & Multimedia*, 5, 29–58.

Sutcliffe, A. G. (1999b). User-centered design for multimedia applications. *Proceedings ICMCS 99, Vol. 1: IEEE Conference on Multimedia Computing and Systems* (pp. 116–123). Los Alamitos, CA: IEEE Computer Society Press.

Sutcliffe, A. G. (2000). On the effective use and reuse of HCI knowledge. *ACM Transactions on Computer–Human Interaction*, 7, 197–221.

Sutcliffe, A. G. (2001). Heuristic evaluation of website attractiveness and usability. *Proceedings: 8th Workshop on Design, Specification and Verification of Interactive Systems* (pp. 188–199). Glasgow, Scotland: University of Glasgow, Department of Computer Science.

Sutcliffe, A. G. (2002a). Assessing the reliability of heuristic evaluation for website attractiveness and usability. *Proceedings HICSS–35: Hawaii International Conference on System Science*. Honolulu: University of Hawaii.

Sutcliffe, A. G. (2002b). *The Domain Theory: Patterns for knowledge and software reuse*. Mahwah, NJ: Lawrence Erlbaum Associates, Inc.

Sutcliffe, A. G. (2002c). *User-centered requirements engineering*. London: Springer-Verlag.

Sutcliffe, A. G., & Carroll, J. M. (1999). Designing claims for reuse in interactive systems design. *International Journal of Human–Computer Studies*, 50, 213–241.

Sutcliffe, A. G., & Faraday, P. (1994). Designing presentation in multimedia interfaces. In B. Adelson, S. Dumais, & J. Olson (Eds.), *Human Factors in Computing Systems: CHI 94 Conference Proceedings* (pp. 92–98). New York: ACM Press.

Sutcliffe, A. G., & Kaur, K. D. (2000). Evaluating the usability of virtual reality user interfaces. *Behaviour and Information Technology*, 19, 415–426.

Sutcliffe, A. G., & Maiden, N. A. M. (1992). Analogical software reuse: Empirical investigations of analogy-based reuse and software engineering practices. In G. C. V. Veer, S. Bagnara, & G. A. M. Kempen (Eds.), *Cognitive ergonomics: Contributions from experimental psychology*. Amsterdam: Elsevier/North-Holland.

Sutcliffe, A. G., & Patel, U. (1996). 3D or not 3D: Is it nobler in the mind? In M. A. Sasse, R. J. Cunningham, & R. L. Winder (Eds.), *People and Computers XI. Proceedings: HCI–96* (pp. 79–94). London: Springer-Verlag.

Sutcliffe, A. G., Ryan, M., Doubleday, A., & Springett, M. V. (2000). Model mismatch analysis: Towards a deeper explanation of users' usability problems. *Behaviour and Information Technology*, 19, 43–55.

Sutcliffe, A. G., & Springett, M. V. (1992). From users' problems to design errors: Linking evaluation to improving design practice. In A. Monk, D. Diaper, & M. D. Harrison (Eds.), *People and computers VII* (pp. 117–134). Cambridge, England: Cambridge University Press.

Sutherland, I. E. (1963). Sketchpad: A man–machine graphical communication system. *Proceedings: Spring Joint Computer Conference* (pp. 329–346). Montvale, NJ: AFIPS Press.

Tan, D. S., Robertson, G. R., & Czerwinski, M. (2001). Exploring 3D navigation: Combining speed coupled flying with orbiting. In J. A. Jacko, A. Sears, M. Beaudouin-Lafon, & R. J. K. Jacob (Eds.), *CHI 2001 Conference Proceedings: Conference on Human Factors in Computing Systems* (pp. 418–425). New York: ACM Press.

Teasdale, J. D., & Barnard, P. (1993). *Affect, cognition and change: Re-modelling depressive thought*. Hillsdale, NJ: Lawrence Erlbaum Associates, Inc.

Treisman, A. (1988). Features and objects: Fourteenth Bartlett memorial lecture. *Quarterly Journal of Experimental Psychology*, 40A, 201–237.

Tromp, J., Sandos, A., Steed, A., & Thie, S. (1998). COVEN (*Collaborative Virtual Environments*), D3.5: *Usage Evaluation of the Online Applications* (Public Deliverable Report of ACTS Project No. AC040).

Tufte, E. R. (1997). *Visual explanations: Images and quantities, evidence and narrative.* Cheshire, CT: Graphics Press.

Tullis, T. (1988). Screen design. In M. Helander (Ed.), *Handbook of human–computer interaction* (pp. 337–341). Amsterdam: North-Holland.

Vetere, F., Howard, S., & Leung, Y. (1997). A multimedia interaction space. In S. Howard, J. Hammond, & G. Lingaard, (Eds.), *Proceedings: INTERACT '97* (pp. 205–211) London: Chapman & Hall.

Vicente, K. J. (2000). HCI in the global knowledge-based economy: Designing to support worker adaptation. ACM *Transactions on Computer–Human Interaction, 7,* 263–280.

Virgin Atlantic Airways. (2000). *Home page.* Retrieved October 2000, from httto://www.virgin- atlantic.com/main.asp?page=0.1

Virgin Atlantic Airways. (2001). *Home page.* Retrieved March 22, 2001, from httto://www.virgin-atlantic.com/main.asp?page=0.1

W3C. (2000). *World Wide Web Consortium: user interface domain, synchronised multimedia [SMIL].* Retrieved November 1, 2000, from http://www.w3c.org/AudioVideo/

W3C. (2001). *Synchronised Multimedia Integration Language (SMIL 2.0): Working draft 01 March 2001.* Retrieved April 18, 2001, from http://www.w3c.org/TR/smil20/

Wann, J., & Mon-Williams, M. (1996). What does virtual reality NEED? Human factors issues in the design of three-dimensional computer environments. *International Journal of Human–Computer Studies, 44,* 829–847.

Ware, C. (2000). *Information visualization: Perception for design.* San Francisco: Kaufmann.

Warren, R. M., & Warren, R. P. (1970). Auditory illusions and confusions. *Scientific American, 223,* 30–36.

Watson, A., & Sasse, M. A. (1998). Evaluating audio and video quality in low cost multimedia conferencing systems. *Interacting with Computers, 8,* 255–275.

Weiser, M. (1991). The computer for the 21st century. *Scientific American, 265,* 94–104.

Weizenbaum, J. (1983). ELIZA: A computer program for the study of natural language communication between man and machine. *Communication of the ACM, 26*(1), 23–28.

Wharton, C., Reiman, J., Lewis, C., & Polson, P. (1994). The cognitive walkthrough method: A practitioner's guide. In J. Nielsen & R. L. Mack (Eds.), *Usability inspection methods* (pp. 105–140). New York: Wiley.

Wickens, C. D., & Baker, P. (1995). Cognitive issues in virtual reality. In W. Barfield & T. A. Furness (Eds.), *Virtual environments and advanced interface design* (pp. 514–541). New York: Oxford University Press.

Wilson, S., Bekker, M., Johnson, P., & Johnson, H. (1997). Helping and hindering user involvement: A tale of everyday design. In S. Pemberton (Ed.), *Human Factors in Computing Systems: CHI 97 Conference Proceedings* (pp. 178–185). New York: ACM Press.

Author Index

Subject Index

A

Action/manipulation
    effective action, 5
    modality characteristics, 16t
    modality defined, 15
    motor coordination, 15, 36
ACT-R/PM model, 66
Aesthetics
    multimedia design, 134—138
    multimedia evaluation, 210—212
    problem solving, 56
    usability evaluation, 2—3
Affective computing
    emotion, 58—59
    technology future, 266
Affordances, 49—50
Agents, *see* Intelligent agents
Algorithms
    JPEG files, 17
    lossless algorithms, 18
    lossy algorithms, 18
    media storage, 17, 18
    MPEG files, 17
Alternative Reality Kit (ARK), 247
Ambient optical array, 36—37
Amplitude, 32
Analogical memory defined, 47—49
Analogue media, 6, 8
Application, *see also* Education application;
    Prototype
    application; Training application
    banking, 162
    e-commerce, 213
    entertainment, 12—14, 161

    geography, 167
    Internet, 141—142, 144—145, 213
    marketing, 114, 161, 162
    psychology, 12, 14
    surgery, 178, 179
    teleoperation, 161, 263, 267
    theater, 118—119, 122t, 131, 134f, 139f,
        142, 263—264
    virtual libraries, 167, 169—170, 194
    virtual reality (VR) design, 160,
        161—162, 167, 169—170, 178,
        179, 185, 194
Architectures
    augmented reality, 12
    multimedia, 6—9
    overview, 6
    tangible user interface (TUI), 12—14
    virtual reality (VR), 9—12
Arousal, 55—58
Articulatory subsystem (ICS), 40—42
Artistic design, 109, 210—211
ASCII files
    media defined, 19
    media storage, 17
Asynchronous communication, 245—246
Asynchronous multimodality, 15
Attention
    design implications, 29, 30—31
    multimedia design, 132, 149—158
    multimedia evaluation, 206, 209—210,
        212, 213
    preattentive processing, 29—30
    problem solving, 53—55, 56, 57f
    selective, 38, 53, 71, 109
    vision perception, 29—31

About the Author

Alistair Sutcliffe is Professor of Systems Engineering at the Department of Computation, UMIST (University of Manchester Institute of Science and Technology) and Director of the Centre for Human Computer Interface Design. He is principal investigator on current EPSRC projects SIMP, CORK and ISRE, and on several completed European Union and UK projects on multimedia user interfaces, requirements engineering, safety critical systems and cognitive modelling. He researches in Human Computer Interaction and Software Engineering, takes a leading role in organizing INTERACT and SIG-CHI conferences, and is on the editorial boards of *International Journal of Human-Computer Studies*, *Requirements Engineering* and *Journal of Automated Software Engineering*. Alistair Sutcliffe is founder and chair of IFIP TC-13 Working Group 13.2 *Methodology for User Centred Design*, and is editor of the forthcoming ISO standard 14915, on *Multimedia user interface design*. He has over 150 publications including four textbooks and several edited volumes of papers. Among the former is *The Domain Theory: Patterns for Knowledge and Software Reuse*, published by Lawrence Erlbaum Associates in 2002.

Printed and bound by CPI Group (UK) Ltd, Croydon, CR0 4YY

01/11/2024

01782626-0014